trout SENSE

troutSENSE

A FLY FISHER'S GUIDE TO WHAT TROUT SEE, HEAR, & SMELL

Jason Randall

HEADWATER BOOKS

STACKPOLE BOOKS

Published by
STACKPOLE BOOKS
5067 Ritter Road
Mechanicsburg, PA 17055
www.stackpolebooks.com

Printed in the United States of America

First Edition

Photos by the author except where noted
Illustrations by Thomas Barnett

Library of Congress Cataloging-in-Publication Data

Randall, Jason.
Trout sense : a fly fisher's guide to what trout see, hear, and smell / Jason Randall. — First edition.
pages cm
Includes bibliographical references.
ISBN 978-0-8117-1331-3
1. Trout—Sense organs. 2. Trout fishing. 3. Fly fishing. I. Title.
QL638.S2R36 2014
597.5'714—dc23

2014005469

dedication

To Erin and Evan;
a dad could not ask for
two better fishing partners

contents

acknowledgments

A work of this size and breadth draws from more scientific fields, disciplines and areas of angling expertise than can be found in any one individual, and requires the collaborative effort of many different people. I would like to acknowledge and thank the many experts who were gracious with their time and knowledge and without whose contribution this work would be incomplete.

Trout Sense: A Fly Fisher's Guide to What Trout See, Hear and Smell, as the third book in the Fly Fisher's Guide trilogy, marks its completion. I would like to thank Jay Nichols for taking a chance, three books ago, on a small-time author with a big-time idea. *Trout Sense*, in fact, was his suggestion as the third book and I'm grateful for his sense of timing and intuitive feel for what is relevant and needed in the world of angling literature. It is an honor to work him again, as well as with Tim Gahr, Stackpole Books and Headwater books.

I will always be indebted to Lefty Kreh, whose friendship and mentorship have had a profound influence on me. He is wholly committed to the sport of fly fishing, generously and enthusiastically sharing his passion with other anglers. All those who know him would surely agree. To those who have not yet had the pleasure of meeting him, any good and kind thing you may have heard about him is probably an understatement.

Many scientific experts have contributed their time and talent to this book, especially Dr. Iñigo Novales Flamarique, Department of Biology at Simon Fraser University in B.C., Canada. As a leading researcher and expert on trout vision, his input was extremely helpful as was his review of the manuscript for accuracy. Dr. Aaron Adams, PhD in marine biology and fellow fly fishing author, and Dr. Steven Cooke both shared their expertise in olfaction and alarm cues. Thank you all.

It is a joy to work with Tom Barnett again, benefiting from his artistic talent. Watching him transform my scribbled notes and stick figure sketches into illustrative works of art is metamorphic magic.

When I count my blessings, I always start with my family—my wife Jo, our daughter Erin and our son, Evan. Watching your children grow up to find their passions in life is one of the rewards of parenting. I am lucky they share my love for the outdoors in general and fly fishing in particular. The love and support of our entire family is a joy in the life of each.

Most importantly, I thank God for the beautiful places trout live and every opportunity He gives me to step into a river, especially to find the occasionally rising trout.

introduction

No other sport I've encountered offers as many challenges on as many different levels as fly fishing. The sport's physical aspects are the most evident to the novice angler and are usually addressed as the initial rung on the hierarchal ladder of angling skills. Even at this level we fall short of mastery; by eventually reaching a comfortable acceptance of its absence, we are able to deliver the fly to the fish with a credible cast, control line well enough to achieve a decent presentation, and tie most fishing knots. Reaching for the next rung, we then apply ourselves to a new challenge, and so forth—each time with the goal of becoming a better angler.

"Fly-fishing is a unique avocation," Vince Marinaro wrote in his classic 1976 book *In the Ring of the Rise*. "It is intellectually stimulating and emotionally satisfying. Its many thousands of devotees have the choice of occupying various levels of dedication or indulgence and remaining there, or they can climb to new heights according to the depth and width of their personal involvement."

I'm all about new heights and challenges. My personal angling journey bears a marked similarity to the "evolution of man" poster, which shows a hunched-over ape on one end, evolving in stages until it emerges as an upright and fully developed man on the other end. I usually envision my fly-fishing self as somewhere in the middle of that progression. The occasions when I see myself approaching the higher end of the evolutionary scale usually coincide with some embarrassing situation that reminds me of my shortcomings.

This illustrates another aspect of fly fishing: no other sport I've encountered, with the possible exception of golf and its slice-prone balls, can be as frustrating. On windy days, with the fly line wrapped around your neck and the hook embedded in the back of your shirt, even golf looks like a more attractive alternative to fly fishing. Perhaps it is the combination of angling's multidimensional aspect and the impossibility of perfection that captivates us for a lifetime.

Fly fishing is also an intellectual pursuit. The mental aspects of the sport kind of sneak up on us anglers, often as we are still focused on honing the foundational skills. Latin seeps into our vernacular and our shelves become cluttered with fly-fishing books. It seems that one challenge cannot be met before the next declares itself. A quest for knowledge within our sport drives us ever higher.

"The peak of the fly-fisherman's ascent in terms of knowledge and appreciation is not yet in sight nor will it ever be," Marinaro wrote in his analysis of angling and anglers. "There are those whose zeal and curiosity will lead them further and further afield in an effort to penetrate the murky gloom that obscures many aspects of fly fishing, to dredge up bits of knowledge and to pry loose a few of the delicious secrets reluctantly yielded by a grudging nature."

It's rather nice to know that things now are not much different than they were in Marinaro's day. What was true then is still true today: anglers still seek knowledge to make them better anglers. Our intellectual pursuit of angling nirvana eventually takes us to the fish themselves; after all, they are the objects of our desire. The better we understand trout, the better our chances of catching them, right?

We merely have to look at the world of competitive sports to find a relevant analogy. Coaches, as a part of their pregame preparation, scout the other team to improve their squad's chances of winning. I once read a scouting report prepared by an assistant coach for a college basketball team. It broke down the other team player by player, listing each one's strengths and weaknesses. I was amazed by the detail. It was a compilation of stats, figures, and endless hours of watching game film.

We need to bring the same approach to angling—let's scout the other team. See what makes them tick. That way, we won't enter the contest unprepared. We can stack the deck in our favor.

Two ingredients make us better anglers: experience and knowledge. Nothing replaces time on the water. If I had a choice between reading about fly fishing and spending time on the river with a rod in my hand, I would put the book down and pick up the rod. But the beauty of fly fishing is that we can improve between our visits to the river—we can pick up that book and return to the river as a better angler.

chapter one

The Skeptical Consumer

Joe Humphreys recently told me a good joke about a salesman while we were presenting at an East Coast fly-fishing show. The joke stuck with me, probably since I frequently equate angling to salesmanship. It goes like this:

> A traveling salesman knocks at a door.
>
> A young boy, about twelve years old, answers the door wearing nothing but his boxers. In one hand is a bottle of beer, in the other a cigar. Under his arm is a *Playboy* magazine.
>
> Puzzled, the salesman finally asks, "Is your mother home?"
>
> "What do you think?" the boy asks sarcastically.

Although we don't sell door to door, anglers are also salesmen or saleswomen. And if we want to find someone home when we knock, we'd better be prepared.

We are marketing our wares to a skeptical consumer, one that is often not quite convinced it wants what we are selling. To help us make the sale, we need the equivalent of market analysis. A good salesman considers two things: the target audience and how the product appeals to the target audience.

The first basic truth of salesmanship is to know your target audience; in other words, know what motivates your consumers. Knowing their needs and wants is important, as is knowing what reassures them, what frightens them, and what it takes to seal the deal. We'll need to know the information and the criteria our consumers will use in making their decision about our product. What makes it irresistible? Imagine if a salesman wanted to convince you to buy something about which *you* were skeptical. He would need to understand you. He would need to see things from your perspective.

The second truth of salesmanship is to know your product. Does it satisfy the needs of the consumers? Is it what they are looking for? Will they buy it? If needed, we can modify our product to make sure it fits the bill. It has to be convincing, or it'll be "no sale."

THE DECISION-MAKING PROCESS

To catch a trout, we have to get him to eat our fly, which is designed to imitate the food the fish eats. Trout are predatory; their diet comprises multiple prey species including immature insects, crustaceans, smaller fish, and other tempting morsels. A few streamer strikes are territory-defense responses directed at competitive incursions by other fish, meaning not *every* fish caught is a beguiled trout looking for an easy meal. But the overwhelming majority of strikes are mistaken assumptions on the part of the trout—they mistake our fly for food. The question then becomes, how do we entice more of these mistaken assumptions?

As humans, we rely heavily on past experience to decide what to eat. We know what we like, although we still like to read the menu just in case something new strikes our fancy. Trout are similar in that they already know the river's menu of available food, they know the daily special, and they also know what they like. The positive reinforcement of successful prey encounters has ingrained patterns of feeding and prey selection in the trout. The trout's memory is imprinted with the standard criteria of previous successes, against which they measure all future feeding opportunities, whether it is the prey's appearance, sound, smell, or taste. They assess the validity of each new prey encounter by comparing it with previous prey encounters; their template has been reinforced through multiple repetitions. Although the trout may not use a mental checklist, any future food item must pass the comparison test. Nature has taught trout to be careful, and so they scrutinize everything.

People also use information provided by our senses when we decide what to eat. We can identify most foods using only one sense, such as the pleasing aroma of freshly baked bread, but all of our senses are usually involved. Aroma memory is a strong determinant in food selection for humans. Smells are deeply imprinted, and certain ones are often associated with pleasant memories or experiences.

For example, I associate the smell of bacon with Sunday mornings. Usually the first in the house to wake, I would quietly sneak downstairs, have a cup of coffee, and enjoy the morning paper. A while later, I would start some bacon in the frying pan and the aroma would fill the house. Drawn by the scent of bacon, the kids would stumble downstairs, but sometimes only after I called up the stairs a few times. By the time they heard the pop and sizzle of the bacon or saw the plate of pancakes, their mouths were already watering. They were hungry and they knew they wanted pancakes and bacon long before they tasted them.

Ironically, we use almost every sense—smell, hearing, sight, and even touch—long before the sense of taste kicks in. By the time taste becomes a factor, we have already decided to eat the food item, or at least to put it in our mouth. Based on the final perception of taste, we continue to eat the food if it has met our expectations; if it doesn't, we might spit it out were such a thing socially acceptable.

Sometimes we try something and decide we don't want it. A long-ago wedding reception I attended offers a good example. Pleasant-looking waitresses in short dresses (funny, the things you remember) walked through the room carrying trays of delightful bacon-wrapped hors d'oeuvres, all pierced with little toothpicks. The hors d'oeuvres looked and smelled delicious, but when I popped one into my mouth, it turned out to be liver, which I loathe. The face I made was partially concealed by my hand, into which I retched the incompletely chewed food just as the bride walked up. (Good thing it wasn't the groom, who would have wanted to shake hands.) I looked for somewhere to drop the mess. It ended up in a potted plant; good organic fertilizer, I rationalized.

It just so happens that trout make mistakes sometimes, too. They occasionally inhale inedible objects, such as our flies or river debris, and expel them just as quickly. The task for anglers is that when our fly is the object of the trout's mistaken assumption, we set the hook in the short interval between inhalation and expulsion.

Our senses are often engaged in a specific order during the decision-making process. Because smells can be detected from considerable distances, aroma often excites our sense of smell long before any other sense is aware of the presence of food. Imagine the smell of freshly popped popcorn at the theater. It usually permeates the entire lobby. You may not actually crave the popcorn until you smell it.

The same pattern of food recognition is true of trout. Aroma memory is also a strong determinant in prey selection and likewise is deeply imprinted. Because their sense of smell is a long-range sense, trout are often first alerted to a potential prey meal by smell. Even though trout are visual hunters, smell is often the sense that first entices them. It may also be the first sense to alert them of fraudulence if anglers are not conscious of its importance. If a salmon can smell its natal stream hundreds of miles out in the ocean, don't think a trout is unaware of your upstream presence if you underestimate its sense of smell.

The other remote sense for trout is hearing. Sound travels well in water and fish can hear sounds from great distances, well beyond their visual range. Fishing on the flats near Key West offered a thrilling example of the underwater transmission of sound when my wife, Jo, hooked a crevalle jack. It was a nice-sized fish and my wife is slim; pound for pound, they were pretty evenly matched for first ten minutes. Then a large lemon shark showed up, attracted by the commotion of the fighting fish. Like a laser-guided missile, the shark homed in on the sound and vibrations of a fish in distress. We saw his fin from afar as he cruised right to where we were fishing. When the crevalle saw the shark, he must have figured Jo to be the lesser of two evils: he swam right to the boat just as the shark was nearly upon him. I still tease Jo about the terrified, asylum-pleading fish that nearly jumped into the boat.

For further verification of the importance of sound in feeding behavior, we need only call to mind Pavlov's dog. Ivan Pavlov was able to associate various sounds to food with such success that his dogs would begin drooling at the sounds of bells, clickers, and whistles. The same principle applies to trout; they learn to associate certain sounds with easy meals, such as the sounds made by a wounded prey fish, a streamside rodent that has fallen into the water, or a terrestrial insect thrashing on the water's surface.

I always associate the sizzle of fajitas with my favorite Mexican restaurant. Once the food hits the table, however, visual appeal takes over. Does it look enticing? Sure, the aroma and sound are intensified by the proximity of the meal, but appearance takes precedence once the plate is in front of you. The appreciation of presentation at fine restaurants underscores this. I've paid a lot for a little at some fancy restaurants, consoled by the statement, "Look! How pretty." Even a hamburger often comes with a garnish.

Once again, this is also true of trout. Once the prey is visualized, the trout become visually oriented. It is not surprising that they tend to use information provided by their senses in nearly the same order as humans when deciding what to eat—first smell and sound, and then vision and taste.

THE TROUT'S PERSPECTIVE

Since trout use information from their senses to decide what to eat, it's important to appreciate how things look from a trout's perspective. Our market analysis identifies trout as our target audience, so we need to see it the way they see it. A marketing axiom taught in business schools also applies to trout: "If you want to know why John Smith buys what John Smith buys, you first have to look through John Smith's eyes."

Obviously hunger motivates trout to eat. They need fuel to feed the biological engine. But how do they decide what to eat? Do they simply get a hankering for some Blue-Winged Olives? Is there an aquatic equivalent to a blue plate special? Or is it merely convenience or expediency?

Optimum foraging strategy is a biological theory that explains animal feeding behavior, at least most of the time. It states that animals should eat the food that has the highest caloric density and demands the lowest energy expense in its procurement. On a large scale, the theory works. If the net calorie intake exceeds the energy expense for a given period, the trout will grow and thrive. If not, it will weaken and die. Weak trout often fall victim to predators; young trout learn this maxim early or pay the price. It is easy to misinterpret the theory or try to apply it to every prey encounter. Trout cannot analyze every food decision as a return on investment because the calculation in net calories would take a computer. The theory also fails to explain why trout may be feeding on midges when larger prey is available. Since trout are disinclined to dieting, there must be another explanation.

Memory imprinting has a lot to do with it. Trout remember the smell and taste of a prey item, perhaps through recent success, and they select the smaller food item over a larger one. Perhaps the memory is stronger and raises confidence in the continued consumption of the previous prey even after a richer but newer prey selection is available. This may lead to selective feeding patterns when one food item is chosen at the exclusion of another, sometimes more logical choice.

Prey preference may also play a role in food selection. Each prey has a different taste and the trout may simply prefer one food source over another. Haven't you ever filled up on the hors d'oeuvres before the meal arrived? Maybe midges just taste better than caddis larvae.

Either way, the optimal foraging strategy theory and the exceptions to it underscore the importance of trout's senses, the mental image the trout form based on their perceptions, and their reliance upon those mental images in food selection. Their perceptions, based on information provided by their senses, are vital to feeding behavior.

When it comes to angling subterfuge, perceptions are important. If we want to fool trout, we have to make our imitation believable to them, even in ways that are beyond our own perceptions. Often our first decision when visiting the river is choosing the right fly. How do we know what is important in fly selection? Even if we have matched the hatch, do we know if the fly in our box meets the criteria of the trout?

This brings us back to the second marketing question: Based on our market analysis, does our product meet the consumer's criteria? What is most important to our consumer, the trout? Is it size, silhouette, color, or something else? Is it always the same criteria? Perhaps we are ignoring too many other aspects of the trout's template. We need to see things from their perspective—see the things the trout see and hear the things they hear.

To see things from the trout's perspective, we should look at their world through their eyes and listen to the sounds they hear. They sense things differently than we do, intrinsically as well as extrinsically.

Extrinsically, the trout's senses are affected by the different medium in which they live. Water is different from air. Things don't look the same when viewed underwater. I recently plucked a sculpin from the streambed and looked at it in the air. After photographing it in my hand, I then placed it in a shallow pool of water where I could photograph it again. The fish looked different in the water from how it did in the air. The colors underwater were more intense and even appeared to change. The yellows appeared more vibrant in the water. The same thing happens to our flies. Anglers tie flies on a vise, but these flies have a different appearance in the water.

Intrinsically, trout have some entirely different sense organs than we do, such as the lateral line and the swim bladder. Their retinas are also different from ours. Do things look the same to a trout as they do to us? Does the trout see a nymph in the same way as we see it? Since trout's eyes see contrast and color differently, they react to cues that seem absent to us.

The trout's sense of hearing is also much different from ours, providing unique information to the fish that we can only conjecture about. The transmission of sound is also different underwater than in air.

Fly tying and fly fishing use techniques to imitate food items. Our efforts must pass the trout's inspection. If we want to make sense of the trout's world and convince skeptical consumers, we need to see things from their point of view, with the information received through their senses. But before this is possible, we need to appreciate the trout's world.

chapter two

The Trout's World

Imagine the life of a trout: propelling headfirst through cold rushing water, hiding behind anything that breaks the current. Instead of legs and feet, you have a powerful tail to move you. Lacking arms and hands, you have only your mouth to grasp food (remember just how hard it is to catch a tossed piece of popcorn in your mouth, much less one that is trying to escape!). Imagine also a predator lurking behind every rock and log, ready to spring out and eat you. At the same time, you must select your own meals from the current's passing milieu. And don't forget there's some guy nearby trying to trick you and put a metal hook in your mouth! It would be like navigating a minefield surrounded by con artists.

But for trout, this is normal everyday reality. And they've gotten used to it. They were born to survive in this world. Things that seem difficult to us are second nature for them. They are just as adapted to their environment as we are to ours.

Adaptation is the process by which organisms change to meet the demands of their environment. Adaptation happens very gradually over many generations through the process of natural selection, which is Mother Nature's way of shaping organisms to fill a particular niche in the environment. For example, individuals that have a particular physical trait or behavior that blesses them with a survival advantage, such as improved underwater vision to enhance feeding efficiency, are favored to reach reproductive age and pass on a larger genetic contribution to the next generation. Individuals without the advantage are less competitive and less successful, ecologically speaking, thus contributing less. With each subsequent generation, the advantageous trait becomes more prevalent until it is a feature of the entire population.

Adaptation may be manifested in physical modifications, such as the streamlined bodies of trout that cut through the current or gills that extract oxygen from water. Without a hydrodynamic shape, resisting the force of the current would consume too much of the trout's energy; without gills, breathing underwater would be impossible.

Adaptation can also include behavioral modifications, which are important for trout to live in flowing water. Trout feeding behaviors are predicated on the current; the trout hold position in feeding lies, waiting for the flowing water to deliver their next meal. Spawning sites are situated in flowing water so the eggs receive sufficient oxygen. From feeding to spawning, trout have patterned their behaviors around the constant presence of current.

Even the trout's senses have adapted to their world. Their sensory organs are modified to meet the unique demands of underwater life. Their senses of hearing, sight, and smell are fine-tuned for life in rivers and streams. They even have unique senses that we humans lack—further evidence of adaptation to a life in water.

SENSES

When divorced from our senses, the human brain cannot function normally. When my kids were young and our house was a cacophonous world of chaos and clutter, I longed for peace and quiet. But too much peace and quiet can be a bad thing, as proven by sensory-deprivation experiments and recently outlawed torture and interrogation techniques. While mild sensory reduction for short periods can be therapeutic and create a meditative state, it requires only hours in total perceptual isolation for subjects to report bizarre thoughts, hallucinations, and depression. We need information and stimulation from our senses to function within, relate to, and respond to the world in which we live.

Senses provide information about the world. This information is perceived by the organism, after which decisions can be made. Senses connect us to the outside world. They can be defined as a means of collecting data, kind of like an IT department that provides useful information to the brain. Without the information provided by our senses, we would be literally senseless about the outside world. We couldn't live long without them.

When we think of senses, we usually think of the classic five: vision, hearing, smell, taste, and touch. The senses of vision, hearing, smell, and *five classic senses*

Vision
Hearing
Smell
Taste
Touch

The classic five senses we learned in grade school are vision, hearing, smell, taste, and touch, which provide us with information about the outside world.

taste are concentrated in specific organs designed to detect stimuli relative to those senses. For example, we have eyes to detect visual images and ears to detect auditory stimuli in the form of sound waves. Taste buds and olfactory receptors react to chemicals, either in the foods we eat or carried in the air as smells. The sense of touch is not concentrated in a specific organ, but more universally distributed throughout our bodies with sensors located in our skin. These sensors are concentrated in our fingertips, providing the constant feedback that allows for the dexterity and fine motor skills our fingers and hands provide.

While the five human senses are the most familiar, these are by no means our only senses. We get lots of information from the outside world, and a good deal of information from within our bodies, from other senses. Pain, thermoreception (temperature regulation), kinesthesia (limb position and movement), balance, and pressure are examples of other sensations we are capable of detecting, providing important internal and external feedback. Some of the internal sensory systems are under our conscious control, such as the position of our limbs, but other internal receptor-feedback systems occur entirely without conscious effort on our part. Examples of this are baroreceptors in the walls of our arteries that help regulate our blood pressure within narrow parameters and the sensory system that keeps our body temperature stable. These systems maintain *homeostasis*, or a stable balance within our bodies. So even though all sensory systems, both external and internal, provide us with useful information, much of it does not occur at the conscious level.

You might think that we consciously process all external information, but even that's not true. For instance, pain involves a reflex response, such as jerking our hand away if we get close to the fire, even before pain registers in our brain. Another example is pressure perception. Pressure changes cause our eardrums to pop and crackle, whether we want them to or not. Even though we register pressure and the discomfort created by widely and rapidly changing levels of it, our ears pop and adjust automatically for the most part, although we yawn or blow air against closed nostrils to help the process.

Sensation involves three separate components: a receptor cell to detect the stimulus, nerves to communicate the information from the receptors to the brain, and a dedicated part of the brain to analyze the data and make decisions based on it. All three components must be present to register the stimulus, which becomes important when we discuss the sensation of pain in fish. Once the information is assimilated, decisions are communicated to the rest of the body via the nervous system, perhaps instructing muscles to move away from a predator or the mouth to open for a meal.

other senses

External

Pressure

Temperature

Internal

Kinesthetic

Balance

Body Temp

Blood Pressure

Other senses provide vital information, both from the environment and from within our bodies. These include pain, external and internal temperature, balance, and other vital feedback that keeps our bodies in a state of balance called homeostasis.

A receptor is a specialized cell that is sensitive to a particular stimulus. For example, light passes through the cornea and lens and hits the retina, causing a change in the receptor cell, in this case a cone or rod. For the sense of hearing, sound waves deflect a person's eardrum, triggering a response from the auditory hair cells in the ear. Information from receptor cells is combined with signals from other receptor cells and carried to the brain via the optic nerve (or auditory or olfactory nerves for the sense of hearing or smell).

TROUT SENSES

My initiation to scuba diving occurred more than thirty years ago when I hastily arranged a certification course required to dive on an upcoming vacation to the Bahamas. Several classroom sessions adequately covered the basics and prepared me for the first underwater excursions in the pool. By the end of the course, I was comfortable with the equipment and was fairly proficient swimming along the pool's concrete bottom. No big deal, right?

Well, I can personally attest that an eight-feet-deep pool is much different than the open ocean. The pitching and rolling boat that appeared unsubstantial at the dock looked like a safe haven compared with the plunge that would thrust me into deep blue sea. Once I finally took the jump and the hyperventilating subsided, I began to look around. It was amazing! I slowly descended the sixty feet to the bottom. Looking up, there was a small halo of light from a round window of blue sky, broken and uneven in the rolling waves. The rest of the water's undersurface showed an opaque reflection of what had to be the sandy bottom of the ocean or the ocean water itself. The surface looked far away and for a moment, my breathing quickened again—it was, after all, a long way to my next breath if the tank fell off or broke.

Those fears quickly evaporated, as with wonder I began to behold the underwater world I had just entered. There were fish of all sizes, colors, and shapes. Manta rays glided soundlessly across the sand, escaping on graceful wings as we arrived at a reef along the sandy bottom. The coral was teeming with life! A moray eel poked his head from his hole and small, brightly colored fish darted through the protection provided by coral branches.

Everything seemed different in this underwater world. I could only see about fifty feet before the water faded into green. If I looked up, the small portal to the surface reminded me of a world far, far away. My breathing was punctuated with hollow-sounding bubbles that reminded me of the villain in a movie that was released around that time, with a fittingly villainous name: Darth Vader. I felt like I had entered a world just as foreign as his.

The watery world of fish is foreign to us, one we can only visit with the aid of the proper equipment. We are not designed to live unassisted in this world; the bulky scuba equipment bore witness to this, but it was apparent in other ways, too. My sense of hearing was ineffective, reduced only to hearing my own breathing or the obvious sound of the divemaster clanking a knife on his tank to get my attention. The absence of other sounds was a novel sensation. Any smells that might be present were undetected due to the inability of the human sense of smell to function underwater, and the only taste was the rubber regulator in my mouth. For scuba divers, visiting the underwater world of fish is a purely visual experience, as that is the only sense we possess that has much value underwater. The whole experience underscored the unsuitability of our senses in the aquatic world.

It is easy for us to assume that the trout's underwater experience is akin to ours—that their vision is limited, their hearing ineffectual, and their senses of smell and taste absent. But this assumption could not be further from the truth. Trout don't use our eyes to see with or our ears to hear with because our organs were designed to operate in a different environment. Just as they have developed gills to breathe underwater, their eyes, ears, and other sensory organs are uniquely adapted to operate underwater. Their senses have adapted to their environment and would be just as ill-suited in our world as ours are in theirs.

While the senses of trout are useful in every aspect of their lives, most are highly refined to aid prey capture and predator avoidance, since these are vital goals for every trout. Some of their senses are analogous to ours, such as vision, hearing, smell, and taste. Generally, their sense of smell and taste are interwoven and collectively referred to by biologists as *chemoreception*. The trout's smell and taste receptor cells perform the same function, that of detecting chemicals in an aqueous medium, and they differ mostly in the location and anatomy of the receptor cells and the nerves that carry the information to the brain. This is true to some extent for people since a large part of the sensation we experience as taste is really input from our sense of smell. For some fish senses, there is no human equivalent. The lateral line, which is actually a unique subset of

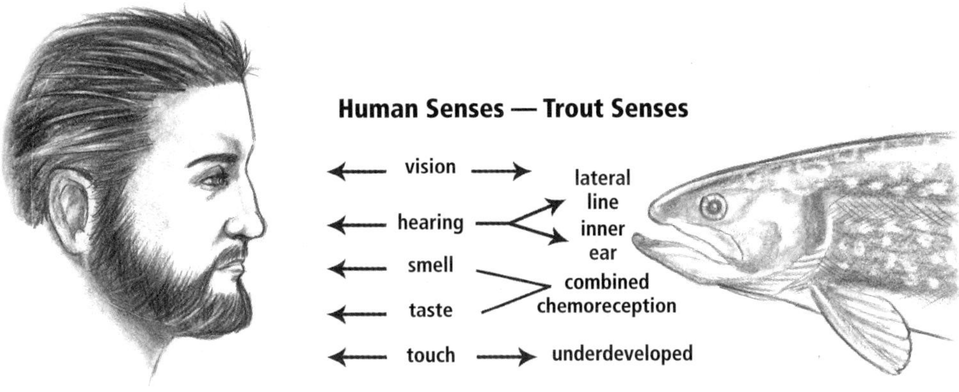

The classic five senses in humans compared to the senses of trout. Although trout lack the highly developed sense of touch we humans need for fine, coordinated motor skills, they have several sensory systems we lack—such as the perception of magnetic fields and a lateral line.

other trout senses

Thermo Reception

Magneto Reception

Internal Reception

Trout also have senses other than the "classic five," some of which, such as magnetoreception, have no human equivalent.

hearing, and the ability to detect magnetic reference, are examples

The human sense of touch is a highly refined sense that doesn't seem to have a direct correlation in trout. They certainly know when they've been bumped by another fish and they will respond to a warning nip from a more dominant trout, but they lack the sophisticated feedback from the different sensor cells we have in fingers and other sensitive areas of our bodies—the sensation we refer to as touch.

The trout's sense of touch has some similarities to that of human infants. Trout seem to experiment with feeling objects much like babies do. Babies often put things in their mouths to determine their nature or just to get more tactile information about the object. Trout also take items into their mouths, even those that lack the visual appearance of food, solely out of curiosity.

FISH AND PAIN

The age-old question of whether fish feel pain is still debated, even among modern researchers, which usually means there is no consensus. The conclusion of each new study seems to confirm the bias of the organization that funded the research. A recent report published by the Humane Society of the United States claims that fish feel pain, but a 2012 study led by J. D. Rose, a professor of zoology and physiology at the University of Wyoming, concluded just the opposite in the *Journal of Fish and Fisheries*, which has greater scientific credibility. Rose states, "Overall, the behavioral and neurobiological evidence reviewed shows fish responses to nociceptive [injurious] stimuli are limited and fishes are unlikely to experience pain." No one seems to argue the presence of nociceptors (receptors sensitive to injurious stimuli) in fish or the nerves that communicate between them to the brain, but the disagreement arises as to the cognitive recognition of pain in the brain of fish—which is the third essential component for sensory perception.

Nociception is the ability to identify noxious stimuli that have the potential to be harmful and damaging to the organism. Nociceptors allow the organism to react in a manner that minimizes the damage or moves the individual out of harm's way. Nociception is essential to survival since it is an important mechanism in preventing harm to the organism. However, reacting to noxious stimuli and perceiving pain are entirely different. The International Association for the Study of Pain defines *pain* as an unpleasant sensory and emotional experience. Nociceptors are not necessarily pain receptors; they detect mechanical, chemical, and thermal changes associated with tissue damage and inflammation that mammals register as pain. Such receptors are scattered throughout the body of most vertebrates, including fish. The signals are collected into nerves that communicate the impulses to the brain, allowing the organism to react accordingly.

While most vertebrates share the presence of nociceptors, fish differ from mammals. Even though trout and other fishes react negatively to noxious stimuli, it is not the same as feeling pain, which is a psychological experience registered in a specific area of the brain (the neocortex) that fish lack. Recall the three components required for sensation: the receptor, the communication to the brain, and the dedicated area of the brain that perceives the sensation. In regards to pain perception in fish, the third component is lacking.

Rose found that fish certainly have nociceptors that sense noxious stimuli and transmit these signals to the brain, but they lack the psychological experience of pain. Additionally, fish lack a specific type of receptor cell (c-fiber nociceptors) that is present in mammals and responsible for the sharp, excruciating pain we are capable of feeling.

Pain is highly subjective, even among people. Reaction to noxious stimuli is possible without pain in some animals, which the study concluded is true of fish. Their response to injurious stimuli is a reflex response akin to a knee jerk.

Obviously, trout resent the hook since they resist it so vigorously. Gary Borger recently told me that the fish resent getting dragged out of the water more than the hook itself. They resist the pull of the line. Gary has incorporated this into his strategy for fighting big fish, and he often reduces the pressure on them to let them settle a bit.

That fish register the hook's presence is inarguable. But it may be that the battle between trout and anglers is more an unconscious reaction and sense of self-preservation on the part of the trout than it is a response to pain.

COMMON SENSE

Our senses govern our relationship with the world in which we live; without them, we would be clueless and unable to survive. We make most of our decisions in life based on information derived from our senses. The reliance on our senses is a trait we have in common with trout and every other animal; they are just as dependent on their senses as we are on ours and, consequently, just as limited by them.

Although trout live in a world much different from ours, a lot of similarities exist. Aquatic organisms must complete the same biological processes and meet the same ecological goals as land-based species. On a cellular level, biochemical activity is remarkably similar between land-based and aquatic animals; at the tissue and organ level, there is tremendous variation. Despite these differences, aquatic and terrestrial organisms must still compete for food within their habitats. The goal of each individual is to survive and reproduce. It may be a dog-eat-dog world on land, but it is also a trout-eat-trout world underwater.

A decision is only as good as the information upon which it is based, whether it is a decision we make or one the trout makes. If we are going to be successful in the cat-and-mouse game called angling, we should know the information the trout have available to them to make their decisions. And since their sensory systems are different from ours, we need to understand their senses to know what they know.

chapter three

What a Trout Sees

Late one February afternoon on Arkansas' White River, a thick bank of gray clouds rolled in, spoiling the light for the underwater photos we were taking. But the same clouds that ruined the lighting conditions improved the fishing conditions, so we exchanged equipment and went fishing. Tom Starmack had been my "rod guy" for the pictures, setting up drifts with a pair of nymphs while I manned the camera. He even managed to accidentally hook a trout on the first drift, an event I unfortunately failed to capture on film because I wasn't ready.

Newly armed with a rod instead of a camera, I surveyed the fishing situation. Sunset was just a few hours away, so I planned a strategy to make the most of the short daylight remaining. While Tom remained in the thin riffle-and-run stretch where we had been filming, I eyed a piece of slack water just up river. Two curves below Bull Shoals Dam, the low flow from the dam offered an abundance of slack water, ideal habitat for midges.

A staple in the winter trout diet, midges are an excellent choice for winter fishing, and Tom and I both managed to fool a few trout on small beadhead midges. But where I chose to fish, the barely moving current made it difficult to approach the wary trout in the clear winter water. Long casts, well away from the trout's feeding positions, were essential. If I got too close, the trout would flee. With the smooth surface of the unbroken water, the trout had no trouble seeing. I used finer tippet to reduce the profile in the slower-moving water where trout had ample time for inspection.

In the faster run where Tom fished, vision—both his into the water and the trout's view of the surface from below the water—was compromised by the broken choppy surface and air intermixed into the water by turbulence. In fact, air bubbles in the water give whitewater its name and also its opacity. Trout often hold in current-protected lies beneath fast-water runs. Comfortable with their concealment beneath the impervious water, the trout were more approachable, allowing closer proximity for the angler and shorter, upstream casts.

The sense of vision, more accurately referred to as visual perception, is the ability to perceive and process information contained in *visible light*, which is the wavelength of light detectable to the retina, the photosensitive part of the eye. The information from the retina is then communicated to the brain through the optic nerve, creating a visual image.

THE IMPORTANCE OF VISION

The sense of vision is vital to trout. While vision plays a role in all aspects of a trout's life, including movement, social interactions, spawning, and navigation, trout are visually adapted for predator avoidance and prey capture. If the first law of the jungle is don't get eaten, then the second law is you must eat something else to stay alive. While other senses such as smell and hearing also play a role in prey and predator recognition, within the visual range of trout, vision predominates and is highly adapted to its important role. Keep in mind that each feature of a trout's vision, from the structure and placement of the eyes to the unique cellular characteristics of the retina, tends to maximize prey-capture ability while at the same time minimizing the trout's chances of getting eaten.

Just like us, trout use all of their senses all of the time. Although long-range senses may alert the trout to a feeding opportunity or the presence of an actively foraging predator, trout are primarily visual hunters and respond strongly to visual stimuli. Once the prey or predator is within visual range, the other remote senses take a backseat.

Prey detection for trout is a complex pathway involving not only the sensory organs, but also object recognition in the brain. It is not enough for trout to "see" their prey; they must recognize it as such. Otherwise, they would not be able to tell the edible from the inedible.

Object recognition or detection, for both people and animals, is an active area of research. Search-image formation, the template and method by which trout and other predators compare new prey encounters to a preformed standard, is reinforced over repeated prey encounters. A trout sees a bug, for instance, and compares the new item of interest to the search image from previous prey encounters. The trout then decides if the bug is a close enough match to eat. The more times the bug appears to the trout, the more firmly established the search image becomes. The more the trout feeds successfully and satisfyingly on the bug, the more the feeding behavior is reinforced.

Following the sequence of visual cues inherent in the search image, a predator picks out one object, say a prey species, from a background of clutter. For trout, this clutter is often a plethora of inedible debris in the current that tends to obscure and confuse the selection process. The physical characteristics of the prey in question make up the search image for trout. When we were kids, my brother and I used to play a game to pass time on long road trips. We tried to be the first to identify approaching cars in the opposite lane. The difference in size was often the first physical characteristic we could recognize, much sooner than we could tell the shape of the car. We didn't know it at the time, but we were using the automotive equivalent of a search image to tell a Corvette from a VW Beetle.

At the speed of the current, the selection process for trout happens fairly quickly. But how do trout actually differentiate the meal from the swirling debris? Astonishingly, they are proficient at feeding in the current. The visual system and search-image template allow for a quick decision-making process. But the selection process is not infallible because our flies, which are never exact duplicates of the natural prey species, are still successful, meaning they must possess sufficient visual clues to pass inspection or else we would never fool a trout. Flies are more like impressionistic paintings, having enough perceptual clues to resemble the natural prey. Determining which clues trout use in their selection process then becomes an important consideration for fishing. We can add to the effectiveness of our flies if we better understand the selection process.

A trout feeding in rhythm offers a practical example. How often have you come across a feeding trout and tried nearly every fly in the box without success? You watch rise after rise to an insect you think you have matched with your fly, yet the trout continues to snub your offerings. Something about the fly just isn't quite right. This happened to me on the Pere Marquette River one June evening during a Gray Drake spinnerfall.

The spinners rose and fell in the summer sky over the river for an hour before the first insect hit the water. Once they did, the trout rose to the occasion and I positioned myself to cast to what looked like a nice trout feeding with reckless abandon. I was licking my chops. I tried the spinner pattern I had gotten from the fly shop and cast it well above the trout, landing the fly softly on the water. I waited with trepidation as it floated over his lie. He ignored it and continued to feed unabated. Next I tied on a

Parachute Adams; the trout took a natural right next to it on the first drift, but never showed interest in my fly even though I deftly presented it right over him. Losing patience, I tried a different size. A rusty spinner was likewise rejected. I was getting a little frustrated at this point. It was a nearly perfectly tied fly, my own no less. *This trout was too stupid to know a good fly when he sees one*, I told myself. Switching again, I had to stop and add tippet since I had tied so many knots, causing another delay. The trout next refused a Borcher's Special. This dry fly, with a thick collar of hackle, looks a little like an Adams but has a more slender profile. Irritated, I cast it to him again, lining him in the process and landing the fly none too gently on the water. The trout continued to feed. What a vexing creature!

This fish had me scratching my head. On a whim, I trimmed the collar hackles from the lower half of the fly to change its footprint on the water and to let it ride a bit lower in the film. It was nearly dark and I knew this was to be my last chance.

The trout struck the Borcher's on the first pass. He was the only trout to hit my net that evening, but it was well worth the trip to the river for this invaluable educational experience. In that final attempt, something about the appearance of the altered fly passed the trout's inspection whereas previously it did not. A visual cue had changed in the modification of the fly, and it was accepted. It obviously matched the trout's search image more closely than had the unaltered fly.

People use search-image recognition every day. We use a well-defined cascade of visual parameters for recognition, whether it is the faces of other people or inanimate objects from a background designed to confuse. This happens subconsciously and automatically. In recognizing the face of a person, most people look first at the eyes, then the mouth, and then often at the cheeks and the general shape of the face.

Nearly everyone has mistaken one person for another, which happens when our initial criteria for face recognition are met by a stranger who looks like someone we know. While avoiding blatant scrutiny, we usually search the face for confirmation, which often leaves us with a feeling of uncertainty. I have been fooled to the extent that I have started conversations with total strangers, only to realize by their voice that they were not who I thought they were. But it was close enough to make me unsure. If I were a trout, I would have been hooked!

Ever see a trout do the same thing? I have seen them float under a dry fly, inspecting it just in front of their nose, probably with the same uncertainty. Trout have their own set of criteria in prey recognition and selection, which will be discussed in the next chapter.

Understanding the search-image criteria that trout use to select prey is of vital importance to angling. It answers the question of which visual cues trout use to select prey and what is important in fly design and fly presentation. Is it the color, size, or shape (profile) of our flies that elicits the strike? Is it always the same under every circumstance? This information then becomes relevant to fly selection and construction. What is the most important aspect? Once we understand the trout's sense of vision, we will be better able to answer these questions.

To be ecologically useful, the sense of visual perception must also provide accurate tracking of prey. It seems that even dragonflies, a successful predator of other flying insects, have cognitive pathways that allow for a 95 percent midair success rate for prey capture, something they accomplish with a brain measuring only 3 to 4 millimeters in size! Not surprisingly, more than 80 percent of the dragonfly's brain function is dedicated to processing visual information. It turns out that trout are similar.

Likewise essential for trout survivability, predator avoidance involves a trout's entire information network but relies heavily on vision within the visual range of trout. The unique shape and design of the trout eye allows the fish to focus on feeding without losing their visual warning system for predators. Trout always keep a wary eye out for threats, both overhead and in the water.

Trout use vision to defend their territories and feeding lies, which are both important for predator avoidance. Visual isolation is important when trout select their feeding lies; not only do trout seek concealment, they also prefer to not see other fish.

A trout will occupy the best feeding lie it can defend against challengers. Feeding lies reduce the risk of predation for medium-sized fish that rely upon a drift-based strategy as their primary mode of feeding. If they see another fish encroaching into their territory, a defensive response directed at chasing away the challenger will result. Trout are especially keen on defending the stretch upstream of their feeding lies since this is the direction of feeding opportunities. Not only has this feeding pattern evolved as the most efficient method of feeding in the current, it offers protection from predation. In the dominance hierarchy, subordinate fish not able to hold a feeding lie are at higher risk of predation and have lower survivability.

LIGHT

Any discussion about vision must begin with a basic understanding of light. Light carries a lot of information about the world, but before the visual image can form in the brain, light must first excite the receptor cells in the retinas of the eyes. Without light, there is nothing to see.

Light is electromagnetic (EM) radiation that can be seen directly from any object that emits light, such as the sun. But sunlight is so intense that it can damage the sensitive receptors in the retina if we look directly at it. More commonly, the light we see is indirect, meaning it hits and illuminates a non-light-emitting object within our visual field, and is afterward redirected toward our eyes where it excites the photoreceptors and leads to the image formed in our brain. With the exceptions of the sun, fire, and manmade objects such as lightbulbs that convert electricity to light and heat, most objects do not emit light; they reflect it. Whether it is the page of the book or the fly on your line, most objects are visible because light from another source first strikes them and is afterward redirected toward your eyes. Even moonlight is created by light from the sun striking these objects and then reflecting toward Earth. So the next time you look into the face of your beloved in the moonlight, remember that even though her (or his) face seems to glow from inner beauty, it's really a product of light that has traveled about 93 million miles through outer space from the sun and bounced off the moon before caressing her cheeks, putting the light in her limpid pools.

Like the dial on an old-fashioned radio, EM radiation varies in frequency and wavelength. In fact, radio waves are another example of the various forms of EM radiation, which includes gamma rays and X rays on one end of the spectrum and radio waves on the other (see fig. 1 in the photo section in the middle of this book). Included in between is the spectrum of visible light. Visible light is defined as that frequency of electromagnetic radiation that is detectable or visible to the human eye. Our eyes are the only organ we possess that detects any form of EM radiation, and only then in the wavelengths from about 400 to 700 nanometers (nm). Specialized receptor cells in our retinas do the job of detecting the EM radiation within this narrow bandwidth, but we lack receptors to detect other wavelengths, such as X rays, UV light, or radio waves. Manmade devices such as radios, dosimeters, and Geiger counters are designed to detect the frequency of EM radiation outside of this range.

Just outside the range of human perception, ultraviolet (UV) light has a wavelength that is not transmitted by our lens and cornea and hence not detected by our retinas. At the other end of the visual range, infrared light has a wavelength that is barely too long for our retinal receptors and therefore also undetectable to people. It is important to note, however, that just because these wavelengths are outside the range of human perception doesn't necessarily mean that they are undetectable to other species.

The wavelength of light determines its color (see fig. 2). Red light has the longest wavelength visible to us. If the light that reaches our retina has a wavelength between 650 and 700 nm, we see it as red. Violet has the shortest wavelength (between 400 and 450 nm), with orange, yellow, green, and blue in between. Every kid in my grade-school class had to memorize the acronym "ROY G. BIV" as the colors of the spectrum. The wavelength of light gets progressively shorter from "R" to "V".

When all of the wavelengths, and thus all colors, are present in light, it is called *white light*. The most abundant source of natural white light is the sun. Within the spectrum of visible light, all of the colors of the rainbow are present. When sunlight hits moisture suspended in the atmosphere, we see a rainbow; this occurs when the light is separated into its component wavelengths as it passes through the water droplets.

COLOR

Color detected by the trout's eye is influenced not only by the color of the object in question, but also by the quality of the light that hits the object and the character of the water the light must pass through. As a result, color is not always constant. A fly looks different to a trout in the late-afternoon light than it does at noon, and it looks different in stained water than it does in clear water. Color is influenced by the angle of the sun and the amount of algae, tannins, or other factors that affect water clarity or color. In general, the color perceived depends on three factors: the nature of the light hitting the object, the surface composition of the object, and the medium through which the light must travel.

Addressing first the nature of light, direct sunlight is white light since it contains all wavelengths of visible light. But not all light is white; some light contains only a narrow part of the visual spectrum. The light of a sunset, which is skewed toward red and orange, is much different than midday sunshine. When this tinted light basks an object, it adds an after-glow effect. Campfires have the same effect, as do red or yellow lightbulbs. In *John Goddard's Trout-Fishing Techniques: Practical Fly-Fishing Solutions from an International Master*, the author explains the success of the Orange Quill, a favorite fly of G. E. M. Skues, on evenings with colorful sunsets. Bathed by the glow of the setting sun, the orange-colored flies stand out starkly, attracting the attention of trout.

Black lights emit UV light and create an entirely different visual environment, which is useful in a range of applications, from rock-hunting (certain minerals fluoresce in UV light) to detecting counterfeit currency. Black lights are also used to cure resins and attract insects to bug zappers. Ultraviolet light is visible not only to insects, but also to many birds, amphibians, and reptiles as well as some mammals, marsupials, and fish.

Secondly, the surface composition of the object greatly determines the color we see. When light hits any surface, one or more of three things can occur: it can be reflected or bounce off of the object in a different direction depending on the angle at which the light strikes the object; it can be transmitted through the object if it is glass, water, or some other transparent object; or the light may be absorbed. If the object in question is not transparent, then the light that hits it is either reflected or absorbed. And as long as the object is not a mirror or other smooth, shiny surface, the reflected light is scattered in nearly every direction by the tiny, rough imperfections in the object's surface. In other words, it reflects in all directions, making the object visible from any direction in which light is scattered.

If all wavelengths of light are reflected equally, the object will appear white. If all of the light that strikes an object is absorbed, that object will appear black to us. White is the reflection of all colors, so then black is the absence or lack of reflection of all colors.

For most objects, some of the wavelengths of visible light that strike them are reflected while others are absorbed depending on the composition of the object. We see only the light that is reflected, since it is the only light sent back from the object to our retina. The color of an object depends on the wavelength of light it reflects, or in other words, the wavelength of light it sends to our eye. For instance, a leaf appears green to us because it reflects light from its surface with a wavelength of 500 to 550 nm while absorbing all other wavelengths. A blue ball absorbs light of all wavelengths but those in the blue range, which it reflects toward our eyes to be detected as the color blue.

Lastly, the medium that the light passes through also affects the color that is perceived. For us light passes through air and for trout it passes through water. If the water is stained, the discolored water alters the wavelength of light reaching the trout's retina. This causes the perceived color of an object to change according to the tint of the water.

COLOR SHIFTS

The old expression "looking at the world through rose-colored glasses" describes someone who is not seeing things as they truly are but instead holds a tinted view of how he or she would like the world to be by filtering out all that is bad. If you were to wear literal rose-colored glasses, the world would look reddish pink since all other wavelengths of light would be filtered out. Other colors would appear as different shades of pink and red. Stained glass windows have the same effect if they are predominantly one color. In the cases of rose-colored glasses, stained glass windows, or stained water, the light reaching the retina is filtered by anything through which it must pass.

Color shifts are caused by the selective absorption or selective transmission of specific wavelengths of light in different types of water. White light becomes colored light if selected wavelengths are filtered out, leaving a narrower range wavelengths. As light passes through water, it is scattered or absorbed by any solid object it encounters, even tiny particles such as those suspended in the water. If the water is crystal clear, no wavelengths of light are lost and the light is unaltered by the water. But if the light encounters any solid particles in the water, color shifts are possible. The solid particles might be algae, plankton, silt, sedimentary material, or inorganic material such as minerals. As the light interacts with the solid particles, any color that is absorbed by the individual particles tends to disappear from the spectrum of colors visualized while the reflected color tends to be transmitted. If the suspended particles are uniform in consistency, such as an abundance of green algae, the shift is profound. One green leaf absorbs all colors but green, so imagine millions of microscopic green leaves in the form of plankton and algae suspended in the water, each filtering out all but the green color. The net effect is the same as looking through tinted glasses. The deeper the water, the more pronounced the effect until only one color remains in deeper water.

The wavelength of light that is reflected by the particles—in other words, not absorbed—will remain and will be transmitted in the water. All objects viewed in the light skewed by the color shift will be tinted toward the transmitted wavelength.

The favored wavelength for transmission or exclusion differs from one water system to the next and depends on the nature of the particles suspended in the water, leading to different color shifts in different water systems. The magnitude of the shift depends on the amount of suspended material as well as the depth of the water. In the open ocean, blue light is transmitted best, whereas longer wavelengths such as red and orange are not, resulting in a blue color shift. At the surface, the effect is negligible, but it amplifies with increased water depth. My first experience with underwater photography in the ocean underscored this. All my pictures (see fig. 3) appeared in different shades of blue, as if I had worn blue-colored glasses.

In near-shore marine waters, more algae and plankton appear in the water. The suspended organisms reflect wavelengths in the green spectrum and absorb other colors, giving the ocean a greenish hue. The wavelength of light best transmitted in this type of water is not the short blue wavelengths, as was the case in the open ocean, but rather the longer wavelengths characteristic of yellow-green color; thus, the resulting color shift is in the green to yellow range. In this type of water, wavelengths of light shorter or longer than yellow and green are absorbed and removed from the spectrum of remaining light, leaving only the green-yellow. This gives objects a greenish yellow tint when viewed underwater. This also explains why the ocean sometimes appears blue while at other times or in other areas it has a green color. I noticed the change in ocean color the last time I went deep-sea fishing in the Caribbean. When we trolled from shallow water to deeper water farther from shore, the greenish water changed to blue. Rivers that carry a large concentration of algae and dissolved organic material also cause a green-yellow color shift.

Even in the absence of suspended particles, water molecules tend to absorb or scatter light. In clear water, the molecules absorb light more at the red end of the spectrum, which is more pronounced in deeper water. This leads to a sequential loss of colors as one goes deeper: first red is lost, then yellow, green, and finally blue.

I set out to document color shift using a plywood board painted across the top with the colors of the rainbow (see page fig. 4). I added fluorescent yellow, fluorescent orange, black, and white along the bottom. I took a picture of the board in natural sunlight, and the colors appeared consistent with my expectations. All appeared to be equally visible and equal in intensity.

The next step required a bit more effort, some scuba gear, and a little bribery. Using the same camera and only natural light, in an area of the ocean with blue water, my wife agreed to hold the painted board at different depths in the water while I photographed it from the same distance as I had on shore. The buoyancy of the board made her descent more difficult. The board wanted to pull her to the surface, requiring extra lead weights be added to her weight belt and a lot more effort to hang onto it. I took her out for a really nice dinner in one of Key West's finer restaurants that night to celebrate our success and to thank her for her assistance.

We photographed the board at 5-foot increments, descending to 25 feet. The distance between the camera and the board was kept as close to the same as possible to eliminate error. Several observations were apparent when we compared the underwater photographs with the one taken back on shore.

Compared to the other colors, the medium blue color was more vibrant. It seemed to leap from the board, especially as the depth increased. It showed up well because the blue color more closely matched the wavelength of light with the highest transmissibility in the open ocean water. While the other colors seem to fade, this color remained true and stood out from the others. The more dissimilar the other colors were from blue, meaning the farther in wavelength they were from the most transmissible color, the more muted they appeared. Colors most distant from blue seem to disappear. Both the red and orange, so bright on shore in the Florida sun, turned to brown at 20 feet. White gradually acquired the same color as the water. Black remained true, and the fluorescent orange and yellow were nearly as bright as they were at the surface (see fig.5).

We repeated the same experiment in the White River last spring, using the same camera and color board and under similar lighting conditions. A tailwater river, the White has an organic mass typical for such systems, with a fair amount of suspended algae and dissolved organic material well away from the dam. The water conditions the day we filmed were typical for the area: The water was not heavily stained or turbid. There were no recent rains or run-off, and the day was as clear and sunny as it was in Key West.

We selected a stretch of slow-moving water around 5 feet deep. Standing on a rock, Tom Starmack pushed the color board, which was attached to long poles, to the maximum depth of about 5 feet while I photographed it from approximately the same distance used on our previous oceanic exploits. We faced the board into the sun for the photographs.

While the water depth was obviously far shallower than we were able to achieve in the ocean, the color shift was apparent. Yellow and green seem to pop compared to the other colors. Both appear more visible than the other colors, especially the blue end of the spectrum where the deeper shades seem less distinct and blend together. The red is a little less vibrant than normal, but orange and fluorescent orange seem similar to the true color. Once again, black remained unchanged, while white was a little dull, tinted by the color of the water. (see fig. 6)

Different rivers will exhibit different color shifts depending on the character of the suspended particles in the water. Eutrophic (those with a very high biomass) rivers have a high concentration of algae and show a dramatic yellow-green color shift. Depending on the species and type of algae, the color shift can be predominantly yellow-brown, as noted in the White River. Other rivers with a different population of microorganisms can show a green color shift.

Jo and I, with the aid of fellow scuba diving and fishing friend Carl Gilmore, took the color board 20 feet underwater at a rock quarry lake near our home to show the drastic changes in visibility and color shifts in turbid water (see fig. 13). Before the dive, we walked to the water's edge. Rock quarries are supposed to have relatively clear water, right? At least I thought so. The cloudless sky offered full sun, similar to previous sessions with the color board in Key West and on the White River. The water appeared mildly turbid from the surface, but we could still see the bottom fairly clearly in 3 feet of water and we even saw a few bluegills swimming about. What I encountered once I descended below the surface, however, caught me completely by surprise. I had vastly underestimated the difference between the viewpoints above and below water! The water that had appeared mildly to moderately turbid above water was much more turbid below; in fact, the effect was profound. The water was hazy with a marked green color shift, and the overhead sun cast a fuzzy green glow. Large suspended clumps of vegetation and flecks of algae of different sizes were everywhere. They are clearly visible in the underwater photograph, but we had not seen them from above. Without the ability to see bottom as a reference, it would be easy to get disoriented in the deeper water's swirling maelstrom of suspended material were it not for the rising bubbles from our regulators indicating the upward direction.

The attenuation of light in the turbid water was also obvious; it was dark at 20 feet in the turbid water whereas it had been fairly bright at 20 feet in the ocean. The underwater visibility was about 10 to 12 feet, so we stayed close together to avoid losing track of each other.

The green color shift in the water is evident from the photograph. Of the rainbow color spectrum across the top of the board, green and yellow in the center are most visible, being the wavelength of light most transmissible in the green water. Although the brightness of these colors is diminished by the attenuation of light, the colors seen underwater are close to their actual colors. At both ends of the color spectrum, however, the color shift is drastic. The short wavelengths of light at the blue end of the spectrum are dull and drab, appearing as different shades of gray, starting with blue-gray and ending at charcoal. The red and orange at the other end of the rainbow lose their luster and vibrancy, shifting toward brown. Once again, white acquires the tint of the water while black remains true. The fluorescent colors show up well despite the color shift and light attenuation.

Rivers composed of glacial runoff have a high concentration of suspended minerals from glacial milk, the rock powder created by glacial movement. This imparts a very obvious green color shift. The Kenai River in Alaska is emerald green due to the glacial minerals suspended in its water. It is the color you might expect to see flowing from the Emerald City in the Land of Oz. The Pere Marquette is another river with a color shift; the tea-colored water is due to the tannins from dissolved peat in the river's boggy headwaters. Tannins—from the German word for "fir tree," hence the song "O Tannenbaum,"—can also arise from oak tree leaves and other organic debris in the water. They frequently impart a slight acidic character to the water as well as a yellow-brown color shift.

Rivers also show a color shift based on the geological characteristics of the watershed. The Colorado River is often a muddy red due to the suspension of reddish silt in the water, especially after heavy rains (see fig. 7). When fishing the Colorado just upstream of Lee's Ferry last spring with a group of friends, it was easy to see why. Cutting through the timeless canyon of its own creation, steep red walls track the river's meandering course. Standing at the river's edge, the rocky red landscape seems to envelop you. We filled memory cards with photographs; ancient Indians, apparently also captured by the river's beauty, carved petroglyphs on the canyon walls.

Since the magnitude of a color shift is dependent on the depth of the water and the amount of suspended particles, deeper portions of a river will have the greatest shift. Under normal conditions of water clarity, shallow river sections will exhibit less of a color shift; however, when the river carries a high sedimentary load, even shallow water will show a color shift. Even rivers with clear water and minimal color shifts can be quite different amid heavy rainfall and surface runoff.

In turbid water, anglers have to adjust their fishing strategy, especially as it concerns fly choice. Spring runoff conditions with highly discolored, turbid water offer some of the greatest angling challenges of the year. The high water flows alter feeding lanes and feeding lies by redistributing prey and predator. The amount of suspended particulate matter also alters the visibility in the water.

Seasonal variation in color shifts can occur with the summertime increase in different populations of algae and other floating vegetative organisms. This is particularly true for ponds and lakes but is also common in warmwater stretches of rivers and streams. The abundance of organisms can be profound and lead to algal blooms. Some types of vegetative bacteria produce a blue-green color and a toxin that can be poisonous to animals.

Fishing strategies and fly color selection based on color shifts and water clarity are discussed in chapter 9.

SECONDARY COLOR SHIFTS

Another surprising observation was also evident from the river experiment with the color board. The interplay of light in the broken surface of the river caused a wavy light to ripple over the board. We captured this effect on video—the light dances across the color board a bit like an aquatic kaleidoscope. The still shots we examined later that night showed an additional, unexpected effect from this interplay of light: the ripples on the surface caused the other color squares to undergo a color shift toward yellow.

The photograph in fig. 6 shows the yellow-brown color shift in the White River. Note the appearance of yellow in the adjacent fluorescent-orange square (bottom row) and the yellowish tint over the green-colored area (top row). Even small bands in the orange square on the top row show a slight shift toward yellow. In the color squares most proximate to yellow, a yellow color shift occurred, but in colors farther removed from yellow, such as blue, the ripples caused only a lighter shade of blue to appear. In other words, the closer the light was to the yellow wavelength, the more dramatic the yellow color shift.

The same surface ripples that caused the shift in colors close to the yellow wavelength had no appreciable effect in the black color square. None of the photos showed a secondary color shift in the white color square; the ripples merely appeared as dark and light shadows over the white square.

A possible explanation for this phenomenon may be the changing angle of light entering the water from the ripples on the surface. If the water's surface were perfectly flat, the light would enter the water at the same angle. But the uneven surface caused by ripples may bend or refract the light, similar to a prism, and introduce enough of a wavelength (color) shift to affect similar colors. When seen on video, the effect was eye-catching. The fluorescent orange seemed to pulse, especially as it stood in stark contrast to the unaffected black color next to it. Like a neon sign, its cat's eye–like iridescence was obvious.

THE ATTENUATION OF LIGHT IN WATER

Not only is light selectively absorbed according to wavelength as depth increases, but light is also attenuated in water, losing its strength at a logarithmic rate in relation to water depth. The deeper the water, the darker it gets, which happens more readily in stained or turbid water. In the ocean, the effect is so dramatic that in the deepest recesses along the ocean's bottom only a small number of organisms have adapted to the near-total absence of light.

River environments lack the depth of the ocean and as a result have not forced evolution's hand to develop dark-adapted species like those found in the ocean. But the attenuation of light in water still plays a role. For one thing, it has a large impact on the thermoregulation of trout. Since trout and other fish are *poikilothermic*, meaning they lack the internal mechanisms to maintain a constant body temperature, they must rely on external modifications to relieve the thermal stress caused by elevated (or drastically reduced) water temperatures. A poikilothermic organism still senses the change in temperature and suffers the effects of temperature extremes; the organism simply lacks the physiological mechanisms such as sweating, panting, or shivering that other organisms use to adjust their internal temperatures.

Trout rely instead on behavioral adaptations to reduce thermal distress. In response to water conditions that are either too hot or too cold, they move within the river or stream to find more comfortable water conditions. In the winter they seek warmer water, and in the summer they seek cooler water.

Often the most comfortable water in the summer is in deeper pools where the penetration of sunlight is less due to the attenuation of light in water. It's equivalent to our finding shade, which is much cooler than

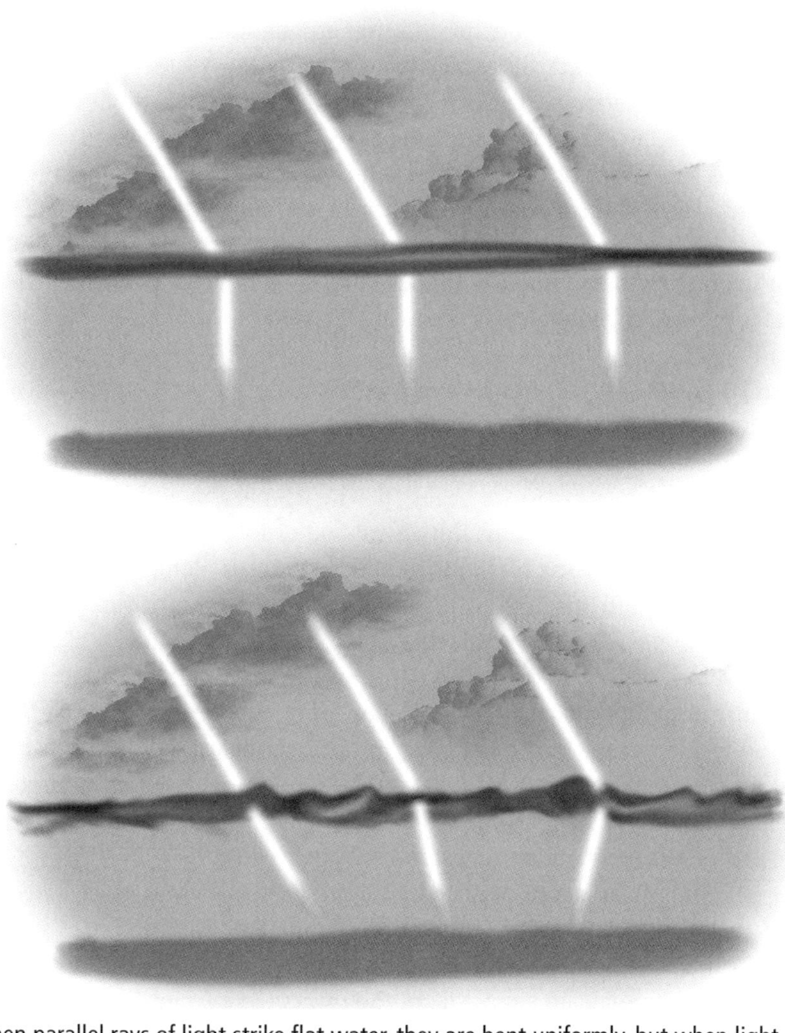

When parallel rays of light strike flat water, they are bent uniformly, but when light strikes a surface made uneven by ripples, the bending of light is inconsistent, producing shadows of ripples and secondary color shifts.

standing in the direct sun. Although the water temperature in rivers is not stratified as it is in lakes and ponds, the lack of solar rays from the sun makes deeper water much more comfortable.

Trout avoid direct sunlight in the summer when the water temperature climbs. Sunbaked shallow riffles, the springtime thoroughfares that previously held scores of fish, will be as barren as ghost town streets. Look for sections of the river where trout can find relief from the heat, such as areas with overhanging shade or deeper water where trout can get away from the sun's rays.

As the afternoon wanes, low-light conditions develop sooner in deep pools than in the shallow stretches of water. You might find large brown trout, classic low-light feeders, arousing from their slumber in these areas well in advance of other parts of the river. The deeper water also adds a layer of security to the large trout that are loafing away the heat of the day, waiting for low-light conditions to trigger their appetites. A sinking-tip line or added weight can place a nymph or streamer in front of their noses just as their stomachs start to rumble.

The way trout handle hot and cold water conditions forms the basis for summer and winter fishing strategies. Their responses to thermal stress are predictable and allow the angler to predict fish locations and patterns of feeding.

THE BEHAVIOR OF LIGHT IN WATER

Light is affected by the medium through which it travels. This holds true when light passes through a void such as a vacuum or outer space, through the air in the Earth's atmosphere, or through water. Its speed is fastest through a vacuum, slower in air, and quite a bit slower in water. Water is almost 800 times denser than air and has a different optical nature, as evidenced by its higher refractive index. As a result, light moves about 75 million meters per second slower in water than in air, which is about a 25 percent reduction. This has a profound effect on the visual world of trout, especially when they are looking up. It also affects our view from the surface as we look into their underwater world.

As noted in our discussion of color, when light encounters any surface, it can be reflected, transmitted, or absorbed, and solid objects generally reflect or absorb light, the wavelength of which determines the color of the object. The same possibilities hold true for light encountering the surface of water: it can be reflected, absorbed, or transmitted, or a combination of all three. If the water is turbid, the solid suspended particles absorb much of the light, as was revealed in our discussion of color shifts; for sake of simplicity, the following examples will focus on light that is reflected or transmitted.

When looking at a body of water, we can sometimes see the reflection of distant mountains if the water's surface is smooth enough. Other times we can see through the water, spotting fish along the bottom if the water is clear enough. What determines whether we see mountains or fish? With a

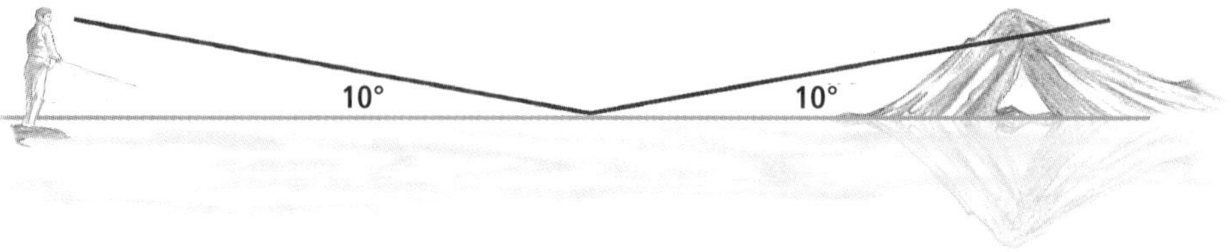

If light hits the water with an approach angle that is less than 10 degrees, most of the light is reflected, bouncing off at an angle roughly equal to the approach angle. Thus, the angler sees the mountains reflected in water.

little basic physics and geometry, it's easy to tell. Sometimes water can be a mirror while other times it can be a window, and it all depends on angles.

The angle of light as it strikes the surface of the water is a great determinant of the proportion of light that is reflected compared to that which is transmitted. If the angle is flat, generally less than 10 degrees to the surface of the water, most of the light will reflect away from the surface. In other words, most of the light bounces off at an outbound angle roughly equal to the incident angle (angle of approach). Looking at the distant mountain reflected in the mirror-smooth water of an alpine pond, the angle of incidence reflected to the viewer is less than 10 degrees. The light from the mountains glances off the water to be seen by the viewer.

Once the angle of incidence exceeds 10 degrees, reflection is less and the mirror gradually turns to a window. Our viewer is no longer able to see a reflection in the water's surface, but instead can see into the water.

If a viewer were to look straight down into the water, he would see bottom (see fig. 8). Looking into the distance, he sees a reflection. Somewhere in between, the mirrored surface of the water becomes transparent. A zone of transition separates the reflective zone from the transparent zone—the bottom is somewhat seen but the reflection of the sky is still partially present, reminiscent of a movie where one scene fades into another. This effect makes spotting trout in this zone fairly difficult, especially if the water is at all choppy.

Imagine that our viewer is sitting in a boat in the middle of a smooth lake. If he looks left or right, or even turns to look behind him, the same effect is evident in every direction; a ring of transition between the mirrored surface of the water and the window surrounds him. Closer to him, inside the ring, looking at the water allows him to see bottom. Farther

At a point where the angle of incidence exceeds 10 degrees, the mirror gradually turns into a window and the viewer will see through the water instead of the reflection of distant objects such as mountains or clouds. Because of the steeper viewing angle close to the angler, a window appears in the mirrored surface through which fish are easier to spot, as well as rocks and vegetation on the lake bottom.

away, outside of the ring, he sees the mirrored reflection of distant objects. The transition between these two views is determined by the angle of incidence, which is 10 degrees. Our man in the boat can change the point of transition by standing up or even viewing from a raised platform, since his new position moves the transition point farther away, effectively enlarging the window—the zone of water he can see through to the bottom. This allows him to see fish from farther away and is the reason Florida Keys flats-fishing guides pole their boats and spot fish from a high platform in the rear of the boat.

This photograph was taken looking upstream from a crouching position. The transparent zone is clearly evident, separated from the reflective zone in the distance by the zone of transition. JO RANDALL

By changing to a standing position, the higher viewing angle extends the transparent zone farther away from the angler, upstream, to allow better marking of fish. Note how much better you can see the bottom of the stream merely by standing up—a viewing position only a few feet higher than before. JO RANDALL

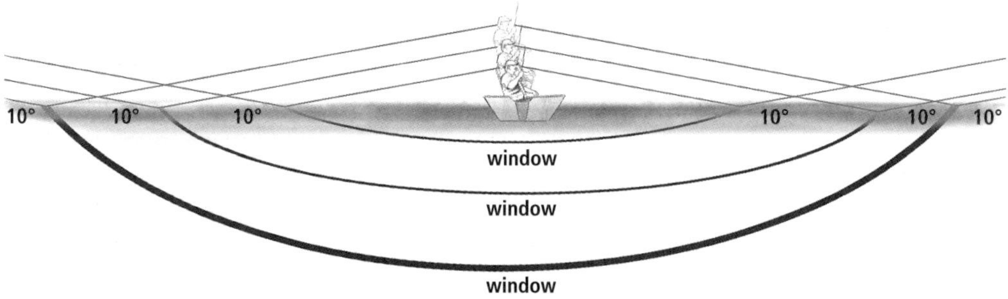

The elevated viewing position of the angler enlarges the window to the bottom, allowing the viewer to see fish from farther away.

One reason it is difficult to spot fish, especially in rivers and streams or any other water system where the water's surface is uneven, is that the rippled or broken surface changes the angle of incidence near the periphery of the window, blurring the transition between the two zones. It's still easy to spot fish if you are looking straight down into the water, but as the viewing angle becomes flatter, spotting fish becomes harder because the ripples on the surface become a mosaic of mirrored fragments interspersed in the transparent window. This occurs because the surface chop changes the consistently smooth angle of flat water into a mix of different angles.

In other words, as light strikes the uneven surface, sometimes the angle of incidence is less than 10 degrees and sometimes greater, turning

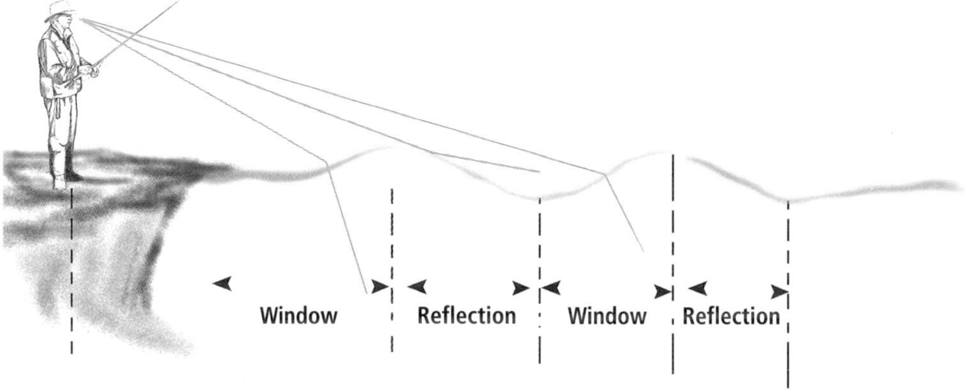

The transition between the window and the mirror is fractured by the uneven surface of moving water (or still water with waves), creating a natural camouflage that obscures our ability to see fish in the water.

the normally sharp transition between mirror and window into a broad mixed-mosaic transition area between window and reflection that serves as natural camouflage. The same ripples that produce secondary color shifts for objects seen below the surface produce a large mixed zone of transition like a shattered mirror where we can see through small cracks. Our viewing window is fractured at the periphery by ripples of mirrored sky, like a zebra-striped pattern where the bottom is visible in the dark bands but the sky's reflection is seen in the white stripes.

Because of this, it is easier to spot fish closer to you since the view is straight down through the center of the window, where the image is unaffected. When you try to locate fish that are farther away, however, you see through a window broken by interspersed reflections of sky, making it harder to locate them. It's like trying to spot a bird through the leaves of the tree; it can be done, but it takes a trained eye seasoned through practice and a focus on the subtle movements. If you are spotting fish for a buddy, find an elevated position that changes the viewing angle and allows for more effective fish spotting.

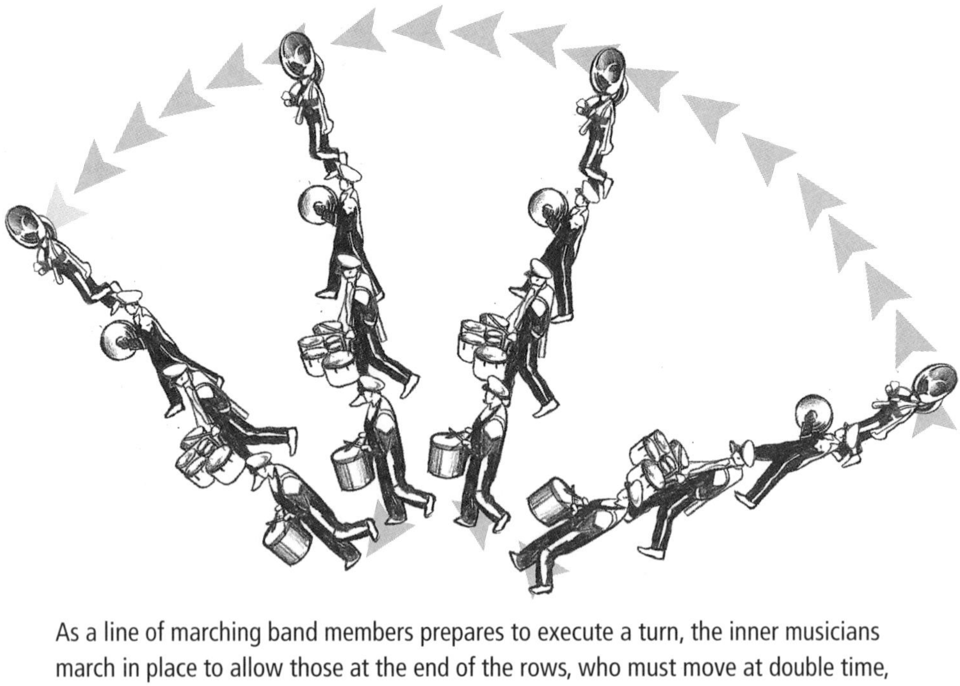

As a line of marching band members prepares to execute a turn, the inner musicians march in place to allow those at the end of the rows, who must move at double time, to catch up. Because the inner part of each row is moving slower than the outer end or the row, the formation begins to turn.

BENDING OF LIGHT

If the incident angle is 90 degrees to the surface of the water, meaning light hits the water perpendicular to the surface, most of the light will be transmitted into the water and very little is reflected away. This transmitted light illuminates the underwater world. As we learned, at an incident angle of less than 10 degrees, most of the light is reflected. As the angle of incidence changes from 10 degrees to 90 degrees, more light will be transmitted compared to the light that is reflected, but the light rays will bend as they enter the water. This phenomenon is called refraction and is caused by the slower speed of light in water compared to air.

The best analogy for understanding refraction compares a ray of light to a marching band or a row of marching soldiers. During college, I was in a military equestrian parade unit and the same principles applied there, too. To turn the column—referred to as "wheel left" or "wheel right"—the inner horses (or soldiers or marching band members) have to step in place to allow the outer line to catch up, thus turning like the spokes of a wheel around the hub, which in this case is the inside horse or band member. If executed properly, the rows remained perfectly straight, the side-to-side spacing between horses was preserved, and everything aligned as the column turned to the left or right.

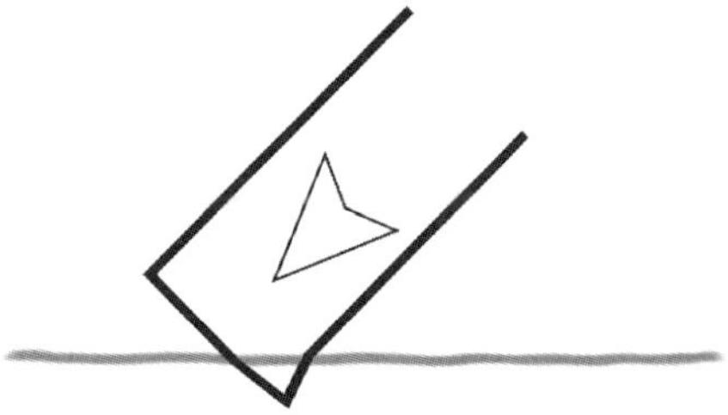

As the beam of light approaches the water, one edge of the beam (the leading edge) encounters the interface between air and water before the other (the trailing edge). This causes the leading edge to slow, much like the band members who marched in place and initiated the wheel maneuver.

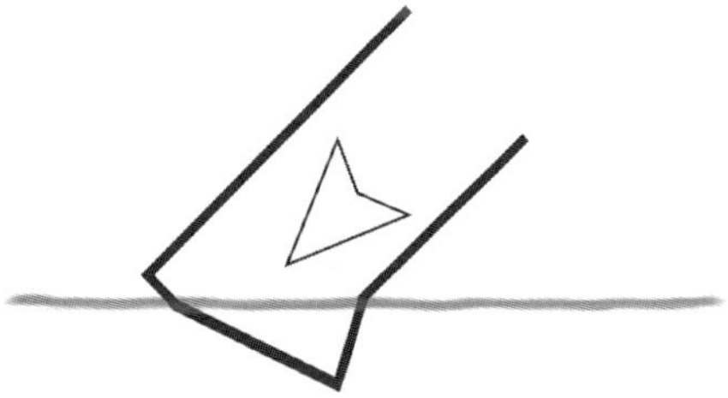

A very short time later, more of the beam of light has encountered the water, slowing the center portion of the beam.

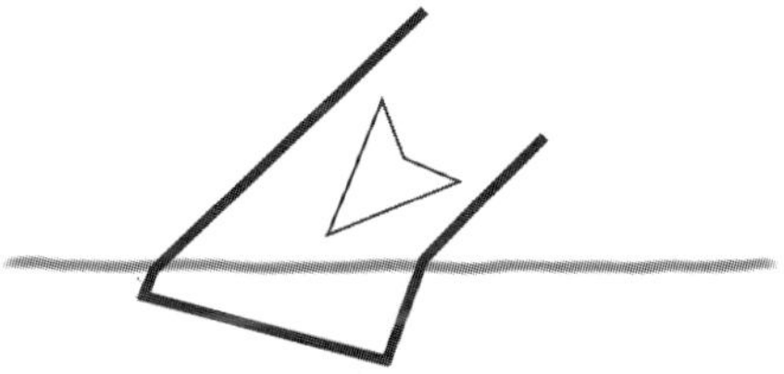

Once the entire width of the light ray has entered the water, all of the beam is once again traveling at the same speed.

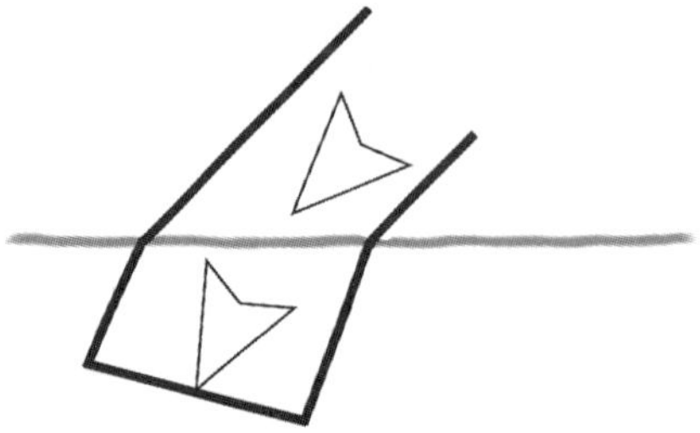

The beam of light is traveling in a new direction, bent by the relative differences of the speed of light in air compared with water. The light travels in this direction unless it encounters another object or interface.

A similar phenomenon occurs when a beam of light encounters the water at an angle. Let's assume that this ray of light has the width of a laser beam and that it has been activated by a switch. It is traveling toward the water's surface at an angle between 10 degrees and 90 degrees. The leading edge of the ray hits the water first and then slows down, much like the inner line of horses on the parade ground. The leading edge is now moving slower than the trailing edge, which is still above the water's surface. Because the trailing edge is moving through the air, it travels farther in the same time than the leading edge of light that is underwater.

As more of the light ray continues to penetrate the water, the center of the ray begins to slow and finally so does the outer edge. By that time, the leading edge lags well behind because it is moving slower. The ray of light likes to keep its formation, retain integrity in spacing, and stay as a unit, much like our parade horses; when the leading edge of the light moves slower than the trailing edge, the beam of light begins to turn, wheeling around the slower edge. Once all of the light has entered the water, it has executed a perfect wheel right.

Another analogy of the bending of light as it passes from air into water involves off-road vehicles. If a truck crosses from an asphalt surface into soft sand perpendicular to the junction between the surfaces, both front wheels encounter the sand at the same time, uniformly slowing the speed of the truck. This is the principle behind runaway-truck ramps on steep downgrades, where sand or gravel is used to stop the runaway vehicle. But if the truck hits the transition at an angle tangent to the interface, one wheel hits the sand first, slowing only that side of the truck, causing the truck to veer abruptly toward that side.

Similarly, the amount of refraction or bend in the beam of light depends on the incident angle. If the angle of incidence is perpendicular to the surface, no bend occurs. There is no leading or trailing edge since both edges strike the water at the same time. The light still slows as it enters the water, but does so uniformly from one edge to another. Since

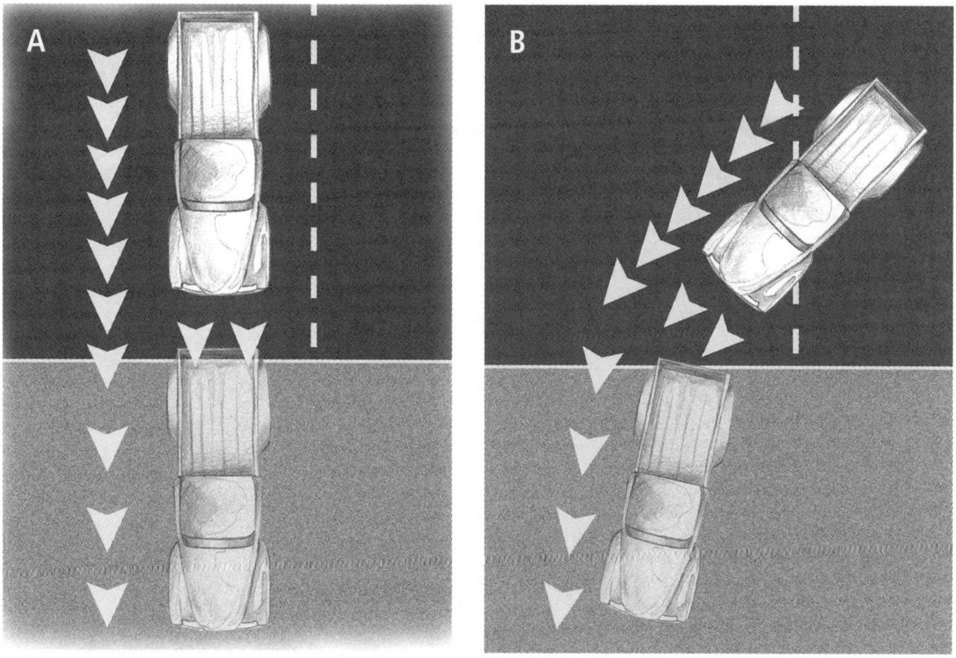

A truck driving from asphalt to sand perpendicular to the interface slows uniformly when both front wheels hit the sand at the same time (A). If it hits the interface at an angle, however, one wheel hits the soft sand first and slows considerably relative to the other wheel, pulling the truck sharply in that direction (B). By the time all four wheels are in the sand, the truck is headed in a different direction than before.

both sides are slowed equally there is no bending of the light. If the angle of incidence is flat, say closer to 10 degrees, the refraction is greatest, causing a profound bend in the ray of light.

Remember, if the angle of incidence is extremely flat (below 10 degrees), more of the light will be reflected without entering the water. Since the angle of light striking the water's surface determines the amount of light transmitted into the water, dusk comes sooner to the fish in the river than to the fisherman above. As the afternoon angle of the sun approaches 10 degrees, more light is reflected away compared to the amount that is transmitted, accentuating low-light conditions underwater. Although reflected light from the sky continues to add light to the stream, cloudy days further accelerate low-light conditions underwater as the afternoon wanes, triggering the feeding activity of larger trout that prefer to feed in low-light conditions. Lengthening shadows from terrain features such as mountains, hills, or streamside vegetation also hasten low-light

The straight pencil appears to bend as it enters the water due to the refraction of light. DARIN SAKAS

conditions in the river sooner than you might expect, which means you don't always have to wait until total dark to catch large, low-light feeding trout. Large trout begin to maraud well before sunset, hunting in shaded pools and along deep shady banks. Scout these areas ahead of time in your quest for trophy trout.

Refraction is well demonstrated by a simple experiment conducted by nearly every grade-school science teacher, at least those when I was in school. Fill a clear glass with water and drop a pencil all the way to the bottom, laying the pencil against the rim of the glass so it enters the water at a sharp angle. The pencil appears to bend, even though we know it's straight. Then move the pencil perpendicular to the water's surface. The pencil no longer appears to bend, but another effect of water is still evident: magnification. Like a magnifying glass, which also works by refracting light, water magnifies the size of an object. Water magnifies the thickness of the pencil, making it look larger and closer than it actually is.

REFRACTION FROM THE ANGLER'S PERSPECTIVE

As we look into the water, the light reaching our eyes from an object underwater is refracted as it passes from the water to the air, with some unusual consequences. Although the earliest fishermen may not have understood the cause of this phenomenon, the effect of refraction was certainly well known to those who carried spears. They quickly learned to make adjustments when they aimed at a fish and found it wasn't where they thought it was. Because of refraction, we also often mistake the actual position of trout we see in the river, which can lead to missed opportunities to catch fish.

When an angler spots a fish, the image of the fish that reaches him is carried on rays of light that are refracted at the surface of the water. Since they are bent, the image appears to be coming from a place other than the fish's actual position. The true position of the fish is deeper and closer to the angler than the image that is seen, which is why the early spearfishermen had to aim below their targets.

Since humans don't see the actual bending of light, the line of sight to the fish appears straight. The refraction of light at the air-water interface

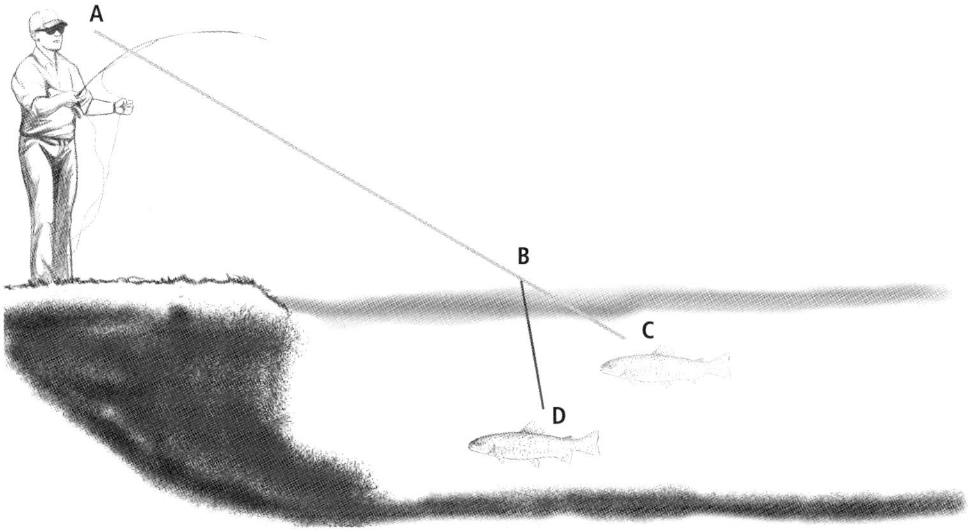

The angler's gaze is depicted by the straight line (ABC) extending from his eye to the perceived location of the fish. The actual path of light from the fish travels along the path from DBA, showing marked refraction. This means the fish is actually located at position D, deeper and a bit closer than the perceived image.

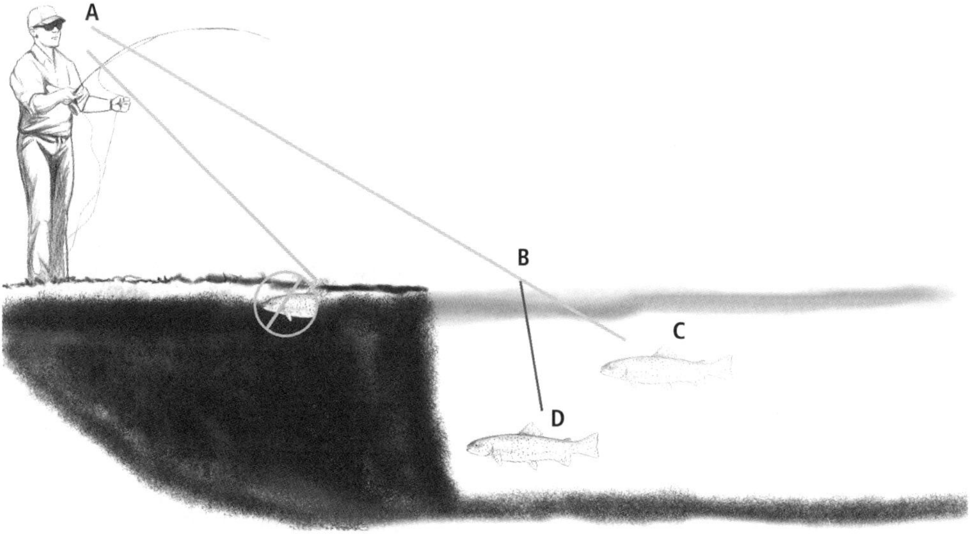

The refraction of light allows an angler to "see around a corner" and spot the fish even though the direct line between them is interrupted by the bank.

leads to the misrepresentation of the fish's position. If we are peering over the edge of a bank along the shore, we may be actually looking "around a corner," so to speak, since the actual position of the fish may be below the bank. This works in the fish's favor since it can often see you even if it is behind a rock or a bank.

The amount of refraction depends on the incident angle of light compared to the water's surface. Since a flatter angle leads to more refraction, the positioning error is accentuated when a trout is viewed from a lower angle, which occurs when the angler is farther away from the trout. Crouching down also produces a flatter viewing angle, leading to a greater estimating error. The misrepresentation of the fish's position is least when a trout is spotted from an overhead position. In fact, the only time you can be relatively certain of the trout's location is when you are positioned directly over it, since the angle of sight perpendicular to the water's surface encounters the least refraction. But even then, you would still tend to misestimate the depth because of magnification.

For this reason, the most effective technique for spotting fish involves viewing from an elevated position. A willing fishing buddy positioned on an elevated bank or (if he's young and limber) hanging from a tree can direct the angler who is at the water level, not only as to the position of the fish but also as to the strike. An elevated position also aids saltwater guides on the flats who pole the boat from a raised platform while the angler stands ready.

Keep this error in estimation in mind when casting and drifting toward fish you've spotted. I've paid for this lesson with missed strikes on nice fish, the kind where you kick yourself later. I distinctly remember a nice-sized trout on the Bighorn River last spring. I spotted him from a high bank as I approached the river and set up just below and to the side of him once

The margin of error in estimating a fish's position is reduced when viewed from an elevated position. The crouching angler (A) sees the fish as being farther away and at a shallower depth (a) than the actual position (c). The elevated angler (B) sees the same fish at (b) closer to the actual location (c), resulting in less error in locating the fish.

I got down to the shore. Caught in a crosscurrent, my first presentation drifted well to the side of his position, or so I thought. A flash of white from the inside of the trout's mouth surprised me. *No way that's my fly*, I thought.

The moment's indecision was decidedly detrimental since, by the time the strike indicator actually indicated something, the trout had spit the fly. Too late, I set the hook. I felt the heft of the trout for a split second before he was gone.

Now when I nymph fish, if a sighted trout opens its mouth or suddenly moves to one side or the other as if to intercept a food item when my fly is anywhere nearby, I set the hook. I do this even if I don't think it is striking at my fly, and even when I'm sure it's not my fly. Because of the capricious and unpredictable nature of current, combined with the magnification and bending of light, I can never be absolutely certain where my fly is or even where the trout actually is.

Another estimating error caused by refraction is gauging the water depth; the river is usually deeper than it appears to the naked eye. In other words, the bottom is actually farther away than it seems, giving us a false sense of confidence when we wade. I have often stepped into water that I thought was thigh deep only to find that it was much deeper, and more than once been surprised by a rush of cold water into my waders.

Imagine these two trout are the same distance away. One appears very thin because it is feeding at the surface, while the other trout has more balanced proportions because it is deeper relative to the first and has less vertical compression of the image.

Vertical compression of the image is also a byproduct of refraction. As "Ozzie" Ozefovich has demonstrated in his underwater videos, the closer a fish is to the surface, the more vertically compressed it is, which makes it look unnaturally skinny. The horizontal aspect of the trout is unaffected by refraction so its length is unchanged. If you spot a fish in the stream from a side viewing angle and it appears unnaturally thin, then the fish is just below the surface. A fish the same distance from the viewer that is in a deeper position is less vertically compressed and thus appears more properly proportioned, with the normal plump appearance of a healthy trout. This phenomenon aids the angler in estimating the depth of a trout when viewed from a distance.

REFRACTION FROM THE TROUT'S PERSPECTIVE

Perspective changes everything; from the trout's underwater point of view, the effect of refraction is much more dramatic than it is for the angler. From the angler's perspective above the water, refraction causes vertical compression of images and introduces error in estimating position and depth. Through the trout's eyes, the close proximity and obtrusive presence of the air-water interface make the stream a refractive wonderland complete with distorted images and mirrorlike reflections.

Some features of the trout's visual world are similar to ours: objects below the surface of the water, such as rocks and other fish, are visible to the trout through the light reflected from the surface of those objects, which passes through the water to their eyes. Although light moves slower in water, it follows the same rules as it does in air; it travels in a straight line and interacts with solid objects the trout then sees in the same manner that we see objects above the surface. A trout looking down, forward, or to either side has a visual world that is similar to ours, except for the obvious differences in scenery.

The real difference in visual worlds is the upward view of trout. When viewed by a trout, the underside of the water is sometimes a reflective mirror showing the bottom of the stream and sometimes an unusual, distorted window to the world above.

Because of his scientific research on refraction in the 1600s, Willebrord van Roijen Snell will always be known for "Snell's window," which is a circle of light that serves as a window to the world above as seen by an underwater viewer, whether that viewer be man or fish. Since many early scientific dissertations were transcribed into Latin, Snell's name is sometimes "Latinized" to Willebrordus Snellius. Seeing what happened to his name, I'm grateful that Latin translation is not likely today.

Snell's window offers the underwater viewer, in this case the trout, a distorted portal to the world above the water's surface through an interface between air and water that is otherwise visually impenetrable. The remainder of the interface is impenetrable because it shows a mirror reflection of the objects below it, such as the streambed, rocks, structure, or other fish. W. E. Frost and M. E. Brown describe the effect in their book *The Trout*: "The trout lives, as it were, in a room with a ceiling made of mirrors except for a round skylight in the middle (the window), through which the outside world is visible."

The mirror reflection on the undersurface of the water is caused by a flat angle of incidence, just as it was on the surface when we looked at the reflection of distant mountains mirrored in the water. When light from underwater objects strikes the interface with air, which is the undersurface of the water, the angle at which the light hits the surface (angle of incidence) determines whether the light ray is transmitted or reflected. If the angle is too flat relative to the interface, the light reflects. If the angle is steep enough, the light is transmitted into the air above the water. The exact point between too flat and steep enough is known as the *critical angle*, which is the basis for Snell's window.

The critical angle for total internal reflection (a mirror reflection) is the point where the light's angle of incidence exceeds the critical angle, which using Snell's formula for water and air is 48.7 degrees to an imaginary line

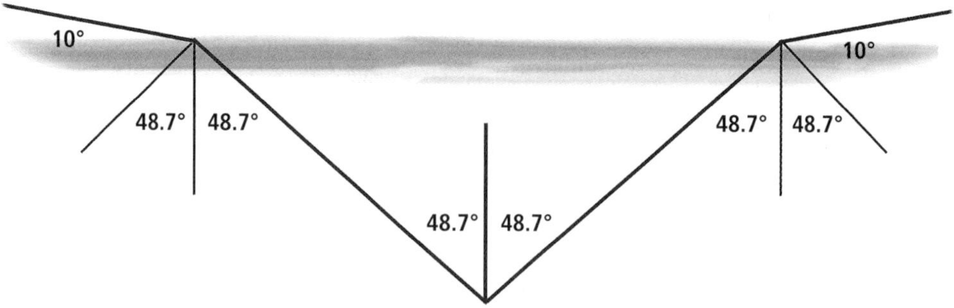

All light striking the undersurface of the water at an angle greater than 48.7 degrees to a line perpendicular to the surface will be reflected. If the angle is less than 48.7 degrees, the light will be transmitted through the interface, passing from the water to the air above.

perpendicular to the air-water interface. If the angle of incidence is greater than 48.7 degrees, the light is reflected. If the angle of incidence is less than 48.7, the light will be transmitted, although it will refract when passing from one medium to another, just as it did in the above stream example. The closer the angle of incidence is to the perpendicular line, the less it bends as it passes through the interface. The ray of light bends more as the incident angle approaches the critical angle.

Light from the stream bottom and all other objects below the water's surface that strikes the interface with an angle greater than the critical angle will appear as a mirror reflection in the underside of the water's surface, clearly visible to the trout if the water is sufficiently calm that it offers a relatively flat reflective surface. If the water is choppy, the reflective surface will be broken and images will be shattered and less recognizable. Reflections of the streambed, rocks, logs, the backs of other fish, and the upper side of our subsurface flies are visible in the mirrored underside of the water's surface.

Since light strikes the underside of the water from all directions around a single point of reference, a circular window lacking a reflection appears in the water's mirrored surface directly above an underwater viewer. This transparent window represents the zone beyond which light rays from below are no longer reflected because the incident angle of those light rays is less than the critical angle, creating the clear opening in the

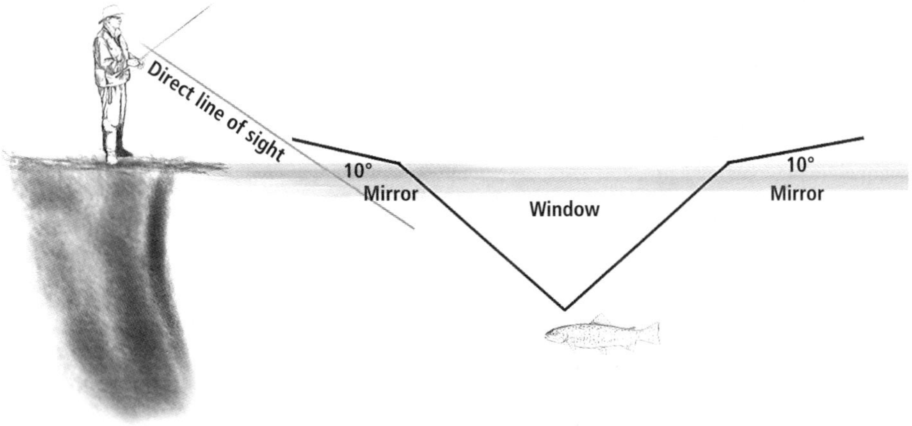

Even though the direct line between the trout and the angler is blocked by the mirrored underside of the water's surface, the trout can still see the angler because the refraction of light allows the fish to "look around the corner" of the window's edge.

otherwise mirrored barrier. Beyond the circular circumference, the water is a mirror reflection of the streambed because the angle of incidence for that entire area is greater than the critical angle. Through the window, an imaginary cone of light from the world above is visible to the trout; using a little geometry, the cone is calculated to be 97.4 degrees in width, twice the critical angle of 48.7 degrees.

Light from the world above passes through the transparent window and through refraction is condensed into a cone and funneled to the trout below the surface. So, not only can trout see the world above through this window, but because of refraction, they can actually see nearly the entire 180 degrees above the water's surface, which, again, is like looking around corners, or in this case, around the edge of the window.

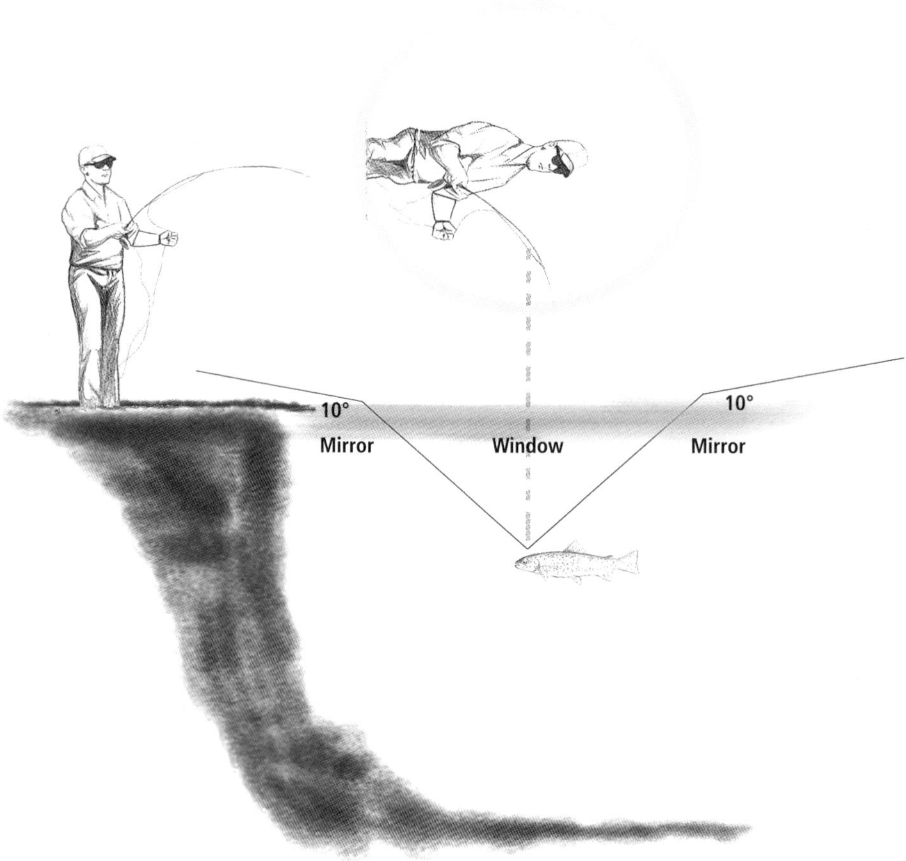

To the trout, the angler appearing low in the viewing window is distorted by the compression, creating an image that appears squat like a troll.

The image of my wife in the lower portion of the viewing window is compressed, causing her to appear short and squat, distorted by the compression of refracted light. I guarantee that she hates this picture.

This photo taken above the surface from the same location shows Jo as she actually is—tall and slender.

The image the trout sees in the lower portion (close to the edge) of the viewing window is distorted, compressed by the refraction of light. Objects directly overhead, seen in the center of Snell's window, will be unaffected by distortion and seem normal in proportion.

The size of the trout's visual window changes relative to the depth of the trout. If the trout is deeper, the window is larger because the imaginary cone from the trout to the surface is longer, making for a larger diameter when it contacts the surface. In fact, the relationship between the depth of the trout and the diameter of the window is such that the diameter of the window is equal to 2.26 times the depth of the trout. Thus, a trout that is 6 inches deep has a viewing window of 13.5 inches, whereas a trout that is 2 feet deep has a window more than 54 inches in diameter. Therefore, as a trout draws closer to inspect a floating insect, his window gets smaller. In other words, a rising trout has a shrinking window.

The size of the window must be considered when casting to trout. While landing a fly right on top of a trout is sometimes an effective way to trigger a reactionary strike, we shall soon see it is usually advantageous to have our dry fly float into the trout's visual window rather than land on it. To accomplish this goal, the angler must cast well upstream of the trout's window. Remember to account for the error in estimating the depth of the trout. Since it is difficult to estimate the depth of fish, especially from a flatter viewing angle, we often mistake how deep the fish actually is and underestimate the size of his visual window. The farther you are

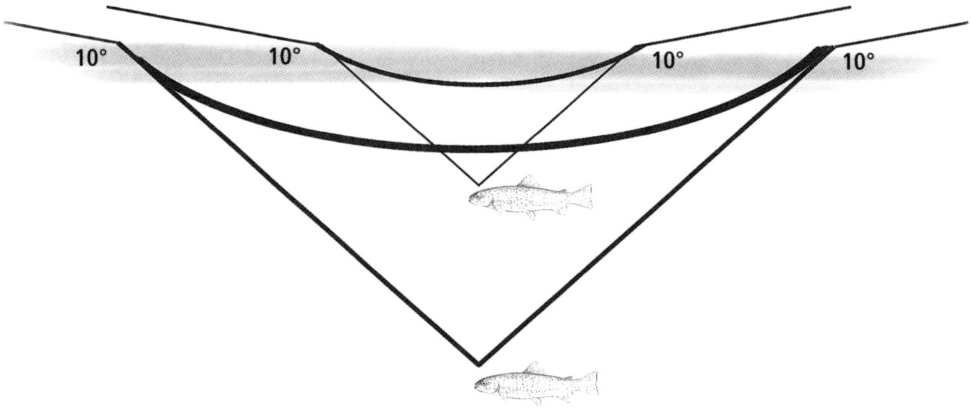

The size of the window varies with the depth of the fish. The deeper the fish, the larger the window.

from a trout, the more the depth is underestimated. Since trout like to watch a floating fly enter their window, you need to cast well upstream of the fish, farther than you think because the trout's cone of vision is much larger than you think due to the mistaken estimation of depth. The fly should ideally enter the window before your leader and line do. Casting well upstream of the window allows trout to see different features of the fly in a specific order; the dimples or footprint of the fly comes into view before the rest of it appears in the window. This sequence is often part of the search-image criteria for surface flies and will be discussed shortly.

The footprint of a floating insect or fly is caused by the indenting of the meniscus or water's surface at any point of contact. In the reflective part of the water's surface, these indents appear as pinpricks of light sparkling from the interaction of sunlight. Once the insect or fly enters the window, the points of contact with the water disappear, making the fly or insect seem to float in midair.

Although the window gets larger and smaller based on the trout's position in the vertical water column, it follows the trout wherever he goes. A circular window of visibility to the outside world is always above him in a mirrored ceiling.

WHAT THE TROUT SEES IN THE REFLECTION

In the top illustration on page 54, the fish sees the reflection of the rock in the mirrored undersurface well away from the edge of Snell's window because the angle of incidence is greater than the critical angle. As the trout moves closer to the rock, the rock's reflection approaches the edge of the window as shown in the bottom image on page 54. When the angle of incidence equals the critical angle, the reflection collides with the transparent window and the reflection disappears, as shown in the image on page 55. Once an object is close enough to the trout that the angle of incidence is less than the critical angle, its image no longer appears reflected in the surface of the water, although the trout can still see it in a direct line of sight. The trout shown can no longer see the reflected image of the rock, but can still see the rock itself.

The mirrored image often allows trout to make a more thorough inspection of approaching food items than would otherwise be possible using only their direct line of sight. When subsurface food items drift above their feeding position, trout using their direct line of sight can see the underside of the approaching food material, provided it is slightly above them. In the mirror reflection, however, they can also inspect the

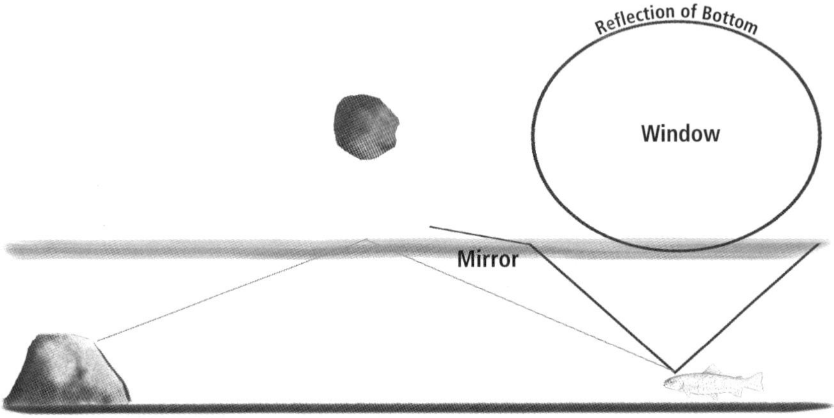

When the trout is far away from the rock, it sees the rock through a direct line of sight but also sees a reflection of the upper surface of the rock in the mirrored underside of the water. The reflection appears well away from the edge of the transparent window.

upper side of the food material. Thus, trout get two views of our flies, allowing a very thorough examination. This explains the importance of wings in flies such as the Prince Nymph and flies that have a different underbody or shell case on top. They more successfully imitate the natural two-toned appearance of many immature insects and the developing wing cases and wings of mature and pre-emergent insects.

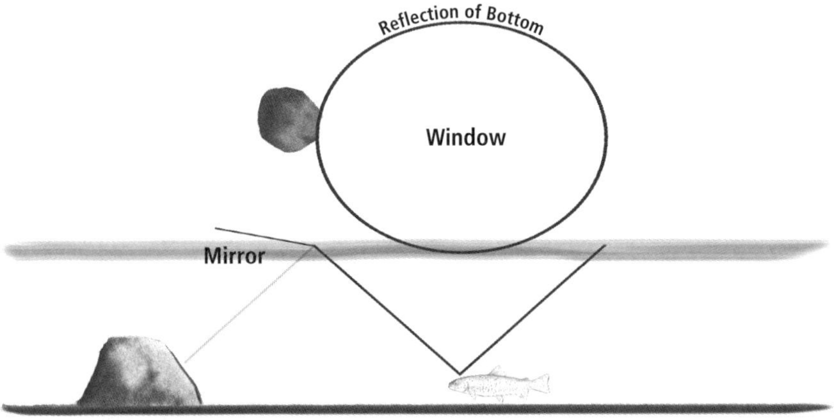

As the trout moves closer to the rock, it still sees it through a direct line of sight, but the reflected image in the mirrored surface approaches the edge of the window.

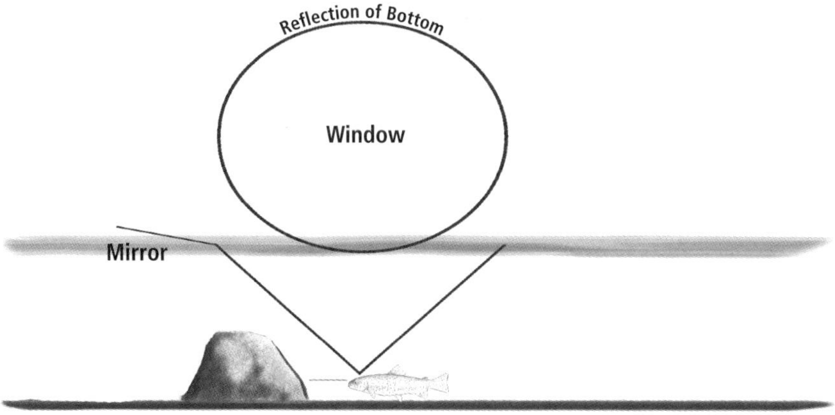

Closer yet, the reflected image disappears having entered the cone of the transparent window, but the trout can still see the rock through a direct line of sight.

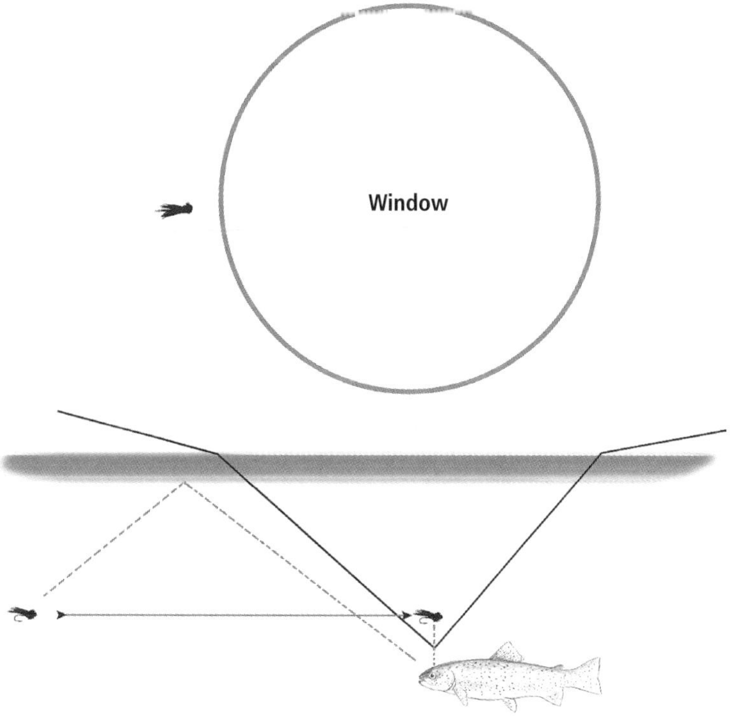

As a subsurface fly like a nymph or wet fly approaches the trout, the underside of the fly is visible to the trout, but the top of the fly is also visible in the mirrored reflection. Once the fly enters the cone of Snell's window, the reflection disappears, but the trout can still see the fly in a direct line of sight.

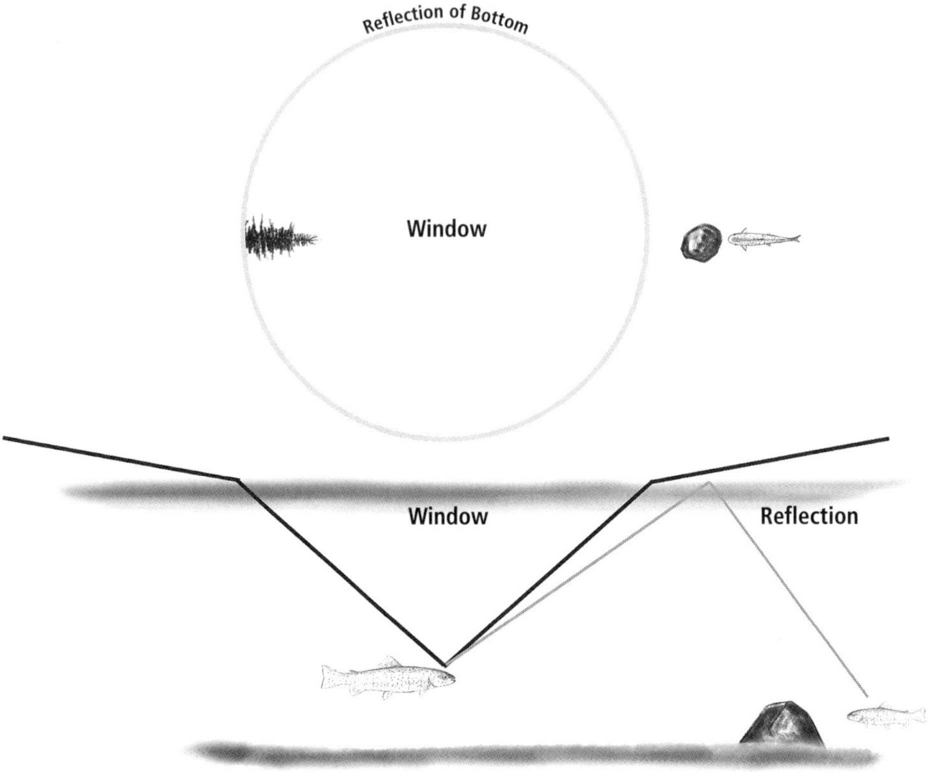

A trout can spot a larger fish lurking behind a rock even when no direct line of sight exists between them. This is done by seeing the back of the predator in the mirrored reflection of the underside of the water's surface.

The mirror image disappears as the food nears the trout's position. Once the food or fly enters the cone of Snell's window, the angle of incidence exceeds the critical angle for reflection and its reflection disappears, just as the rock reflection disappeared.

Just as a mirror can help you see around corners, the trout can see objects reflected overhead that are otherwise blocked from its direct view. Imagine two trout, one in front of a rock and one behind the same rock. The rock blocks their direct line of sight of each other. But they still are aware of each other. Providing the water is smooth enough, they are visible to each other in the mirror reflection, even though their direct line of sight is interrupted by the rock.

So, the trout really does seem to live in a world with a mirrored ceiling, where a moveable skylight follows him about, constantly overhead.

The size of the skylight changes as he moves vertically, closer to or farther away from the ceiling. In the reflection, he can see all of the features of the stream about him, including the streambed, rocks, logs, vegetation, and even other fish and bits of food. But the one thing he can't see in the mirrored ceiling is his own reflection; where that would appear, the skylight opens to the outside world.

WHAT THE TROUT SEES THROUGH THE WINDOW

If the circular opening in the mirrored ceiling were merely that, trout would see only a very small portion of the world above, a narrow circular visual field of things directly overhead. The occasional bird, or perhaps an overhanging tree branch, would cross their field of view, but they would see little else. Their risk of overhead predation would skyrocket because they would never see an osprey until it was too late and they would never see an angler fishing from the bank, which would certainly make it much easier to sneak up on a trout unawares.

Actually, we know from experience that trout are notoriously difficult to sneak up on and it turns out that their overhead portal is much more than a simple opening with a narrow field of vision; it is more like a fish-eye camera lens, collecting images from a very wide visual field extending in every direction. Like a wide-angle lens, refraction allows the trout's overhead portal to gather light from nearly the full 180-degree arc above the water and transmit it to the trout below the surface. Not only can they see the sky, but they can almost always see the angler trying to sneak up on them.

There is debate over whether a trout can see fully from one horizon to the other—the entire 180-degree field of view above the water—or if it can only see 160 degrees, a number that accounts for the loss of the lower 10 percent on each side where the angle of incidence is too flat to transmit light rays into the water. Recall that we initially assumed that light rays hitting the water's surface with an incident angle below 10 percent were reflected away.

For example, consider an angler crouching below the 10 percent angle extending above the water's surface from the trout's position—is he or she visible to the trout? According to physicists and mathematicians armed with calculations and formulas, the trout cannot see anything below the 10 percent angle. The sun's rays reflect from the water's surface when the angle of incidence approaches 10 percent, rendering any object below a 10 percent angle from the surface invisible to the trout. But experienced anglers and other researchers are convinced trout can see below the lower 10 percent and even have photographic proof of such, gathered via magnification and freeze-frame photography. But neither slow motion nor magnification is available to trout, so which opinion is correct? Since our visibility to trout affects the way we approach a trout stream, it is important to know.

Well, it turns out both theories are correct. First, let's look at the point of view of the scientist; according to optical physics, trout do not see horizon-to-horizon because of the loss of the lower 10 percent of the horizon where light reflects away. As proof of the loss of the lowest 10 percent of the horizon, merely refer back to the photos on page 51. Jo is standing on a deck almost 10 inches above the water's surface. When photographed underwater through Snell's window, the lowest portion of her leg and her ankles and feet are cut off. That's another 12 inches, increasing the entire unseen portion to nearly 2 feet. The picture was taken at a depth of 1 foot and from 25 feet away.

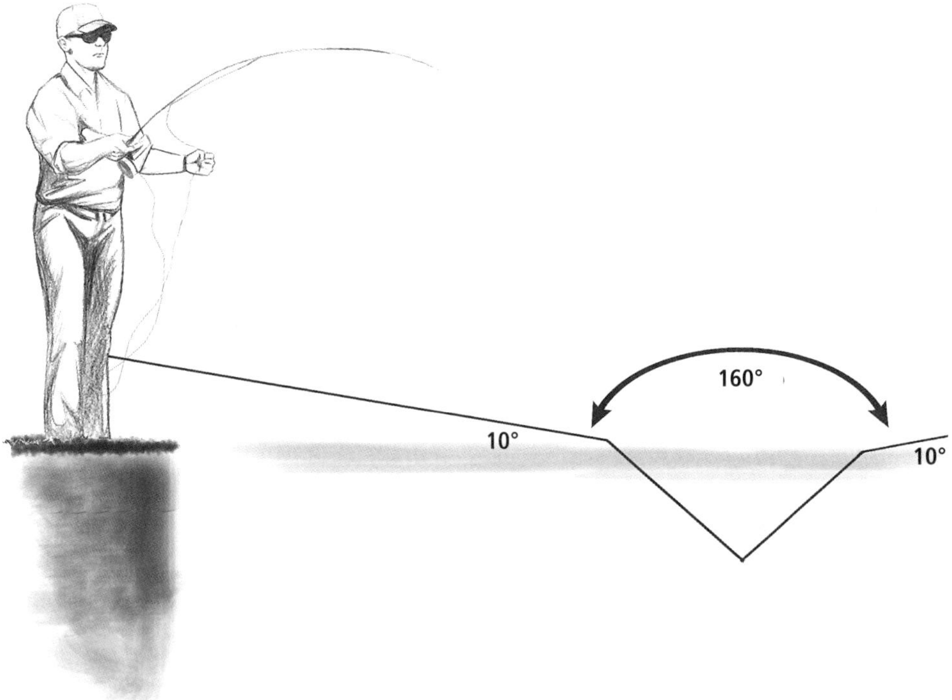

The lowest part of the entire 180-degree field of view (horizon to horizon) is lost to trout because the angle of incidence falls below the 10 percent angle of reflection.

If I were to take the camera deeper, say to a depth of around 3 feet, the enlarged window would offer a more complete view of the person on the surface. In that case, we might see the entire person, losing only the distance from the deck to the water's surface.

Additionally, every angling reference I have ever seen that discusses the subject of refraction shows the illustration of a floating insect approaching Snell's window. They show an imaginary line extending at an angle of 10 percent above the water. As the insect approaches, the tips of the wings are first visible in the trout's window before the full height of the wings are seen. Lastly, just before the bug enters the window, the insects entire body above the water is visible. If trout saw the full 180 degrees, from horizon to horizon, they would always see the entire insect as it approaches! This sequential appearance of the portion of the insect above the water's surface lays the debate to rest, at least under experimental conditions. This phenomenon never changes, as long as the surface of the water is perfectly flat. But it fails to take into account one natural fact: the surface of the water in a river is never perfectly flat.

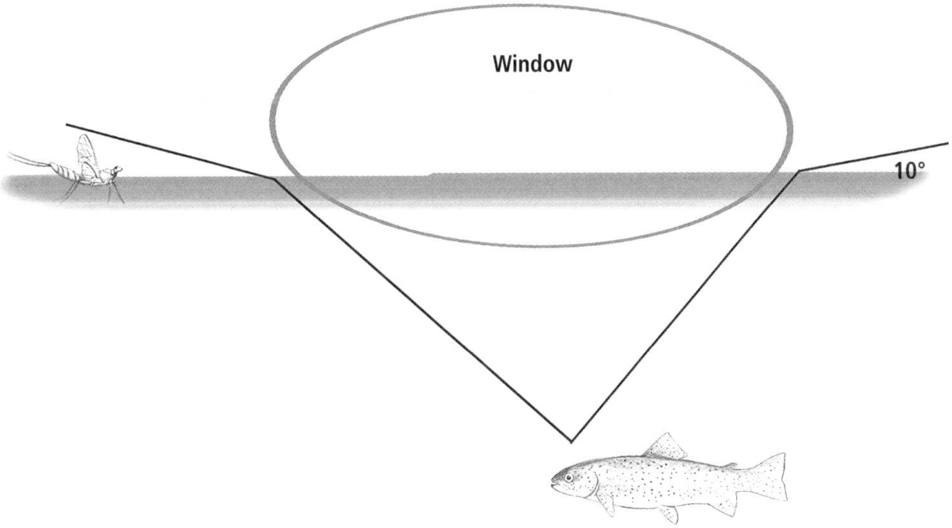

The sequence of visual images the trout sees as a floating insect approaches the window. Initially, only the portion of the mayfly that penetrates the surface film is apparent to the trout in a direct line of sight. The wings and portion of the body above the water are not seen since they are beneath the 10-degree angle below which the trout can't see.

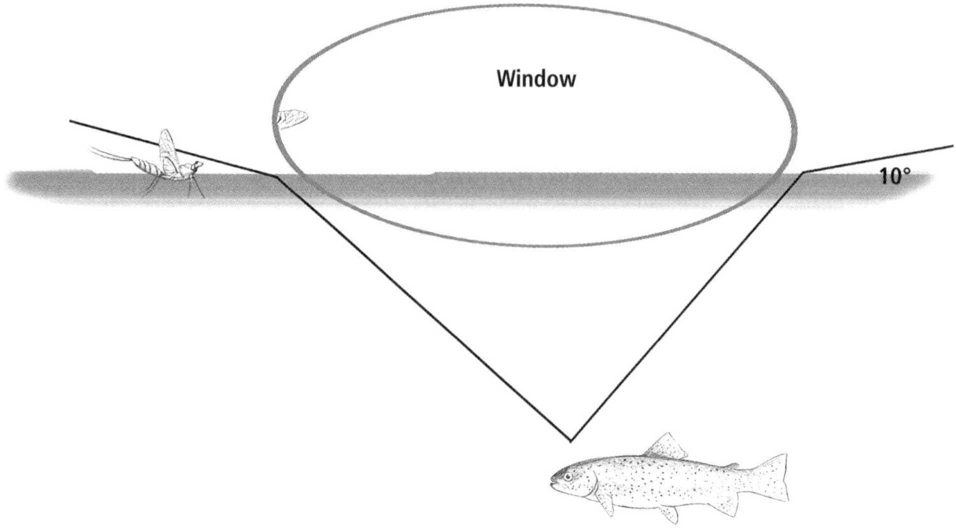

As the insect approaches the edge of the window, the tips of its wings appear in the lower edge of the window separated from the true position of the insect as indicated by its footprint—that part of the bug that penetrates the water's surface, breaking through the mirrored surface still well away from the window's edge.

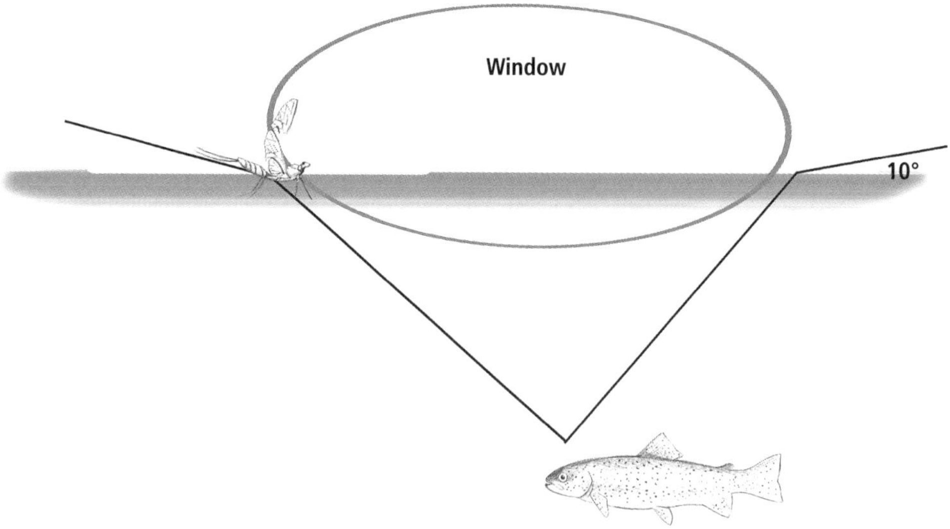

As the bug enters the edge of the window, the two images fuse together; the footprint of the mayfly and the image of that portion of the insect above the surface which has grown in size in the edge of the window.

There are ripples and undulations in the water's surface that change the flat surface of the water into subtle hills and valleys, as it were. If light strikes the upslope of a ripple or wave where the surface of water is upwardly inclined, the light that might otherwise have reflected away is instead transmitted into the water, which allows images from the lower visual field to blink in and out of view as if they were being shown by an old-time movie projector.

Imagine an angler crouching on the shore of a stream, below a 10 percent angle from the trout's position. Where light emanating from the angler hits a flat surface of the water, it is reflected away. None of this light from the angler is transmitted to the fish below and the angler is not visible to the fish. But what if the light carrying the image of the angler strikes a ripple or wave in the water's surface? This changes the angle of incidence because of the inclined slope of water near the crest of the wave. The otherwise too-flat angle is now greater than 10 percent and now allows at least partial transmission of the light, providing the trout an image of the angler, albeit a very compressed and distorted one that appears to blink in and out

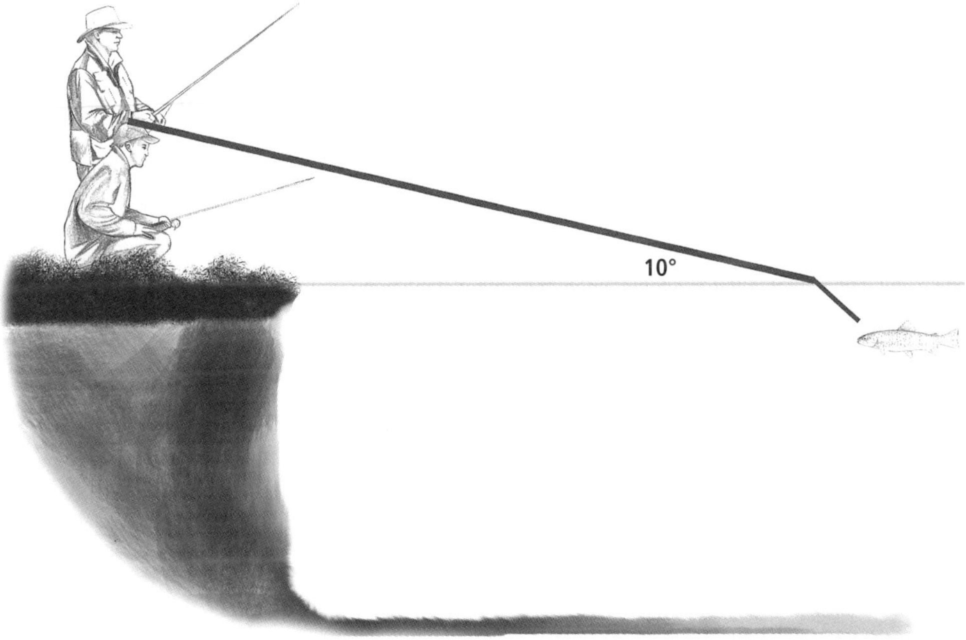

Viewed through flat water, the trout easily sees the upper portion of the standing angler but does not see the crouching angler, since he is below the 10 degree angle.

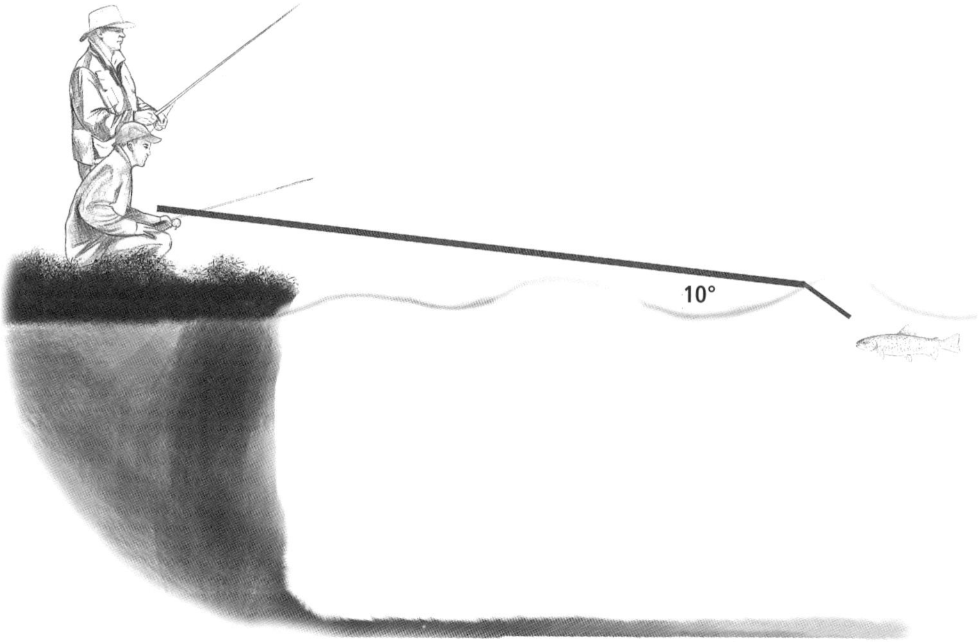

Uneven water allows a broader field of view for the trout; on the upward slope of a ripple, the 10 percent critical angle now takes the full horizon into view and allows the trout to see the full height of the standing angler on shore, and even the crouching angler next to him.

of view. If the angler is wearing a bright-colored shirt, his reflection will seem like a strobe light at a disco, sending the trout for cover.

Once again with Jo as my reluctant subject, I set out to verify this effect (see figs. 9, 10, 11, and 12). I first photographed her from above the surface of the water; she held the color board on the pool's deck, which was about 10 inches above the water's surface. I was about 6 feet away.

Next, I photographed her and the color board from a depth of about 12 inches below the water's surface. In these images, the space between the deck and the water's surface is greatly compressed, appearing as a thin white line indicating the wall of the pool just below the thinner brown line of the wood decking.

I backed up another 6 feet, to a distance of 12 feet from Jo and the color board. I approximated the same 1-foot depth and repeated the picture. This time the image of Jo was compressed, making her look short and squat, but both she and the color board are readily recognizable.

At a distance of 20 feet and the same depth, I can make out the blurred and distorted image of Jo and maybe the upper portion of the color board, but I would be hard pressed to identify them as such if I hadn't already known what they were. The colors on the board are indistinct and not easily recognized. But looking carefully, I can see the rainbow color pattern of the board in a ripple below the edge of the window—an image captured in a narrow sliver of transparency on the surface.

Caught in a ripple on the surface of the water, an angler crouching below the 10 percent angle from the trout will still occasionally blink into view, warning the trout of the potential threat. The bright, reflective colors of the angler's clothing, coupled with movement, is probably enough visual stimulus to alert the wary trout.

Crouching to minimize your visual image certainly makes you less obtrusive to the trout. Even though your image will still wink into the trout's view, it is blurred, compressed, and largely unrecognizable as an angler. But it still may be viewed as a threat by trout. Wear earth tones that blend into the natural surroundings. Moving slowly and judiciously will also minimize the likelihood of attracting the trout's attention and alarm. Moving quietly, as we shall discover in later chapters, also helps.

This winking into view becomes doubly important when considering flashes of light from shiny objects such as a rod, a reel, or a watch. As an Eagle Scout, I had to learn a wide variety of outdoor skills, which later in life I had the privilege to pass onto my son during his path to Eagle. Outdoor survival skills were emphasized, and I received an emergency survival kit. One of the many things in the pouch was a signal mirror. Reflected light from a signal mirror is highly visible even from long distances, capable of attracting the attention of planes overhead. Rod flash and reflections from other shiny objects are like signal mirrors to trout, even when they arise near the 10 percent angle.

Because of refraction, the images trout see in their window are often distorted, especially near the margins of the window. If the light is perpendicular to the water, little refraction occurs. Images in the center of the window appear normal. A bird seen in the center of the window is properly proportioned. At the outer edges of the window, however, the compression of light rays leads to dramatic distortion of the image. The same bird when caught in the edge of the window is flattened and squat, looking more like a toad than a bird.

An angler standing on the bank offers a practical example: The portion of the angler's body below the 10 percent angle from the water's surface is invisible to the fish, assuming the water is perfectly flat (which we know it really isn't, but it simplifies the illustration). The fish only sees the man from the knees up, but the man's thighs appear compressed, making him seem like a squat troll. The width of the torso is unaffected, but the man appears vertically challenged—squashed, in other words. The compression is accentuated in the angler's legs and waist, but his head, which appears farther from the edge of the window, begins to have more appropriate proportions. The farther the image is from the edge of the window, the less distortion, so if our angler wears a hat, it has a more normal appearance than the head it rests on.

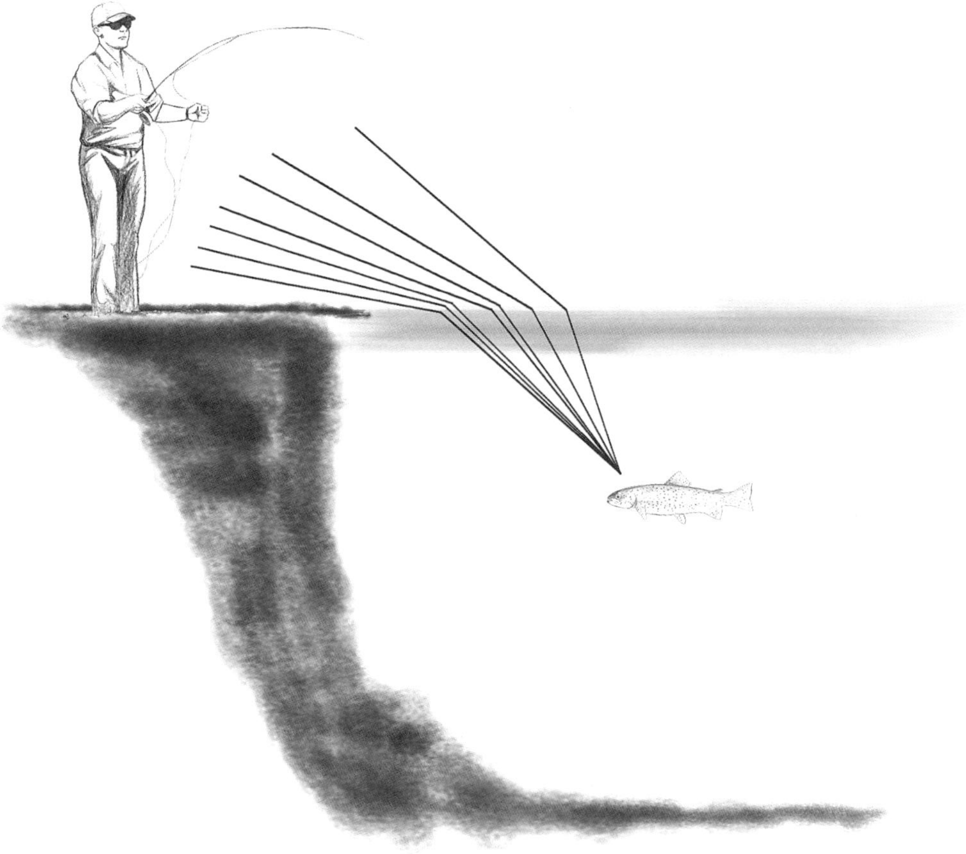

The angler standing on an elevated bank is fully visible to the trout underwater, but the image the trout sees is distorted by refraction.

The portion of the image the trout sees in the center of the window, which in this case is the angler's head, has proportions closer to normal. The part of the image that appears closer to the edge of the window is compressed vertically, making the angler appear to have a short torso. His legs, at the very edge of the window, show the greatest compression, making him appear to stand on very stubby legs.

If our angler steps into the water and moves a bit closer to the trout—and assuming the trout does not skedaddle—the image the trout sees will be slightly different. If the angler stands in knee-deep water, his lower legs will be visible to the trout in a direct, unrefracted line of sight through the water. If our 10 percent angle still strikes our angler at the waist, the portion of his body below his waist and above his knees will not be visible to the trout. The torso above the waist will still appear as a vertically compressed image to the trout, but the chest will seem to elongate as it approaches the

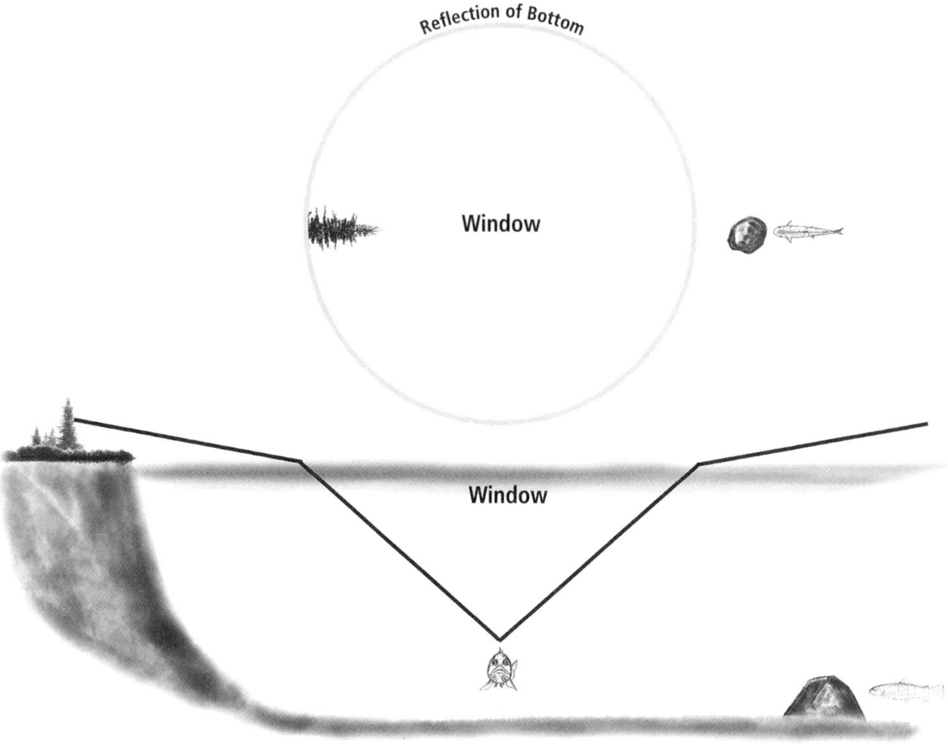

A panorama of visual images, reflected in the mirror or seen through the fisheye portal to the world above the water, is available for the upward-looking trout.

shoulders and the head. Since it is farther from the edge, the head will appear to loom out of the neck, leaping into the center of view.

WHAT A TROUT SEES

What a trout sees depends on which way it is looking. The trout sees the streambed below when looking down, and perhaps a crayfish scuttling among the rocks if luck would have it. If it is looking forward, it might see other fish or food material approaching in the drift of the current. Looking upward toward the underside of the water, however, offers a unique perspective: a view of windows and mirrors based on the refraction and reflection of light.

If you still have trouble visualizing Snell's window, put on a mask and snorkel and look at the water from below the next time you visit a swimming pool. Also remember the same phenomenon occurs from the angler's perspective, although the angles are different from the surface than they are from below. I remember standing, coffee cup in hand, at the end of the dock at our family cabin in Michigan one summer morning. The water was like glass in the still morning. Looking across the lake, I could see the wooded treeline of the distant shore reflected in the water's surface. In the water a bit closer to me, I saw the reflection of the sky. Looking straight down into the water below me, I could see the bottom through the shallow water. Because my angle of sight was nearly perpendicular to the water, I had no trouble seeing into the water, and even spotted a few bluegill. Looking a short distance away, however, I saw a point of transition between where I could no longer see through the water and where I began to see the sky reflected in the surface. This was the edge of a window to the bottom, a circular transition between a zone close to me where light was transmitted from the bottom and the rest of the lake where light was reflected from the sky above. Farther away, I could still see the reflection of the tree-lined shore. In a sense, this was Snell's window in reverse, since it was a circular zone of visibility into the water in an otherwise mirrored surface.

I'll address the trout's search-image criteria again in chapter 5, emphasizing refraction and reflection in respect to food selection. It turns out that refracted images and the order in which they appear and change are important deal-closers for trout. First, though, we must understand *how* a trout sees.

chapter four

The Anatomy of a Trout's Eye

Lefty Kreh once told me that he could always tell if a fish in a photo was alive or dead when the picture was taken. He said that a live fish looks longingly down at the water from which he came and to which he'd like to return; the eyes of a dead fish stare straight out from their sockets as if the fish is looking at the camera. I've made a point to observe this and I now agree: the eyes of living fish are always cast downward when the fish are held out of the water. I've also heard another explanation for this—out of the water, the weight of the fish's eye causes it to drop, but only if the fish is alive. For some reason it doesn't happen if the fish is dead. Either way, whether it is aquatic envy or simply a matter of weight, this idea seems to hold true.

While the eyes of trout allow for movement, when trout are in the water, their eyes mimic those of a dead fish, looking straight out from the socket unless they are focusing on a bit of food, which makes them appear cross-eyed. Their eyes flick nominally to and fro as items catch their interest, but for the most part, their eyes remain directed to the side, which allows them to be on the lookout for potential prey as well as potential predators.

The placement of the eyes in the skulls of animals reflects the ecological priorities of the particular animal's lifestyle. The visual requirements of a predator are much different from those of prey species, and the position of the eyes reflects this. The main visual goal of a predator is to identify and track prey, so it needs visual acuity and accurate depth perception, both important in prey identification and capture. As a result, the eyes of predators tend to be forward facing. On the other hand, since the goal of prey species is to avoid getting eaten, they require a wide field of vision to alert them of a predator's approach. Their eyes are located on the sides of the face, as with deer or rabbits, to afford the largest visual field even at the expense of binocular overlap.

There's a saying in comparative zoology: "Eyes in front, likes to hunt. Eyes to the side, likes to hide." The owl and the tiger, both predators, show the typical placement of the eyes in a forward-facing arrangement. This arrangement allows the largest possible overlap in the visual field of each eye, which is called binocular vision. This improves visual precision and depth perception—both vital to prey capture. In other words, in the zone where the visual field of the left eye overlaps that of the right eye, depth perception and acuity are much better.

Try a simple experiment: Cover one eye and then turn your head to a new visual environment to negate the effect of visual memory. Identify an object and reach out to touch a specific point on it. You'll find it's harder to judge distance and even direction with only one eye, since acuity and depth of field are reduced with monocular vision.

The forward-facing eyes of an owl are typical for a predator. They allow a large field of binocular vision in the forward field, permitting accurate prey tracking and depth of field.

The lateral eye placement of a horse is typical of an animal that has evolved under the constant threat of predation; the eyes are situated to allow the largest field of vision possible, even at the expense of a wider binocular field to the front.

A horse or deer, with its eyes placed along the side of the face, can optimize the overall size of the visual field at the expense of binocular vision. These animals can see nearly the full 360 degrees around them, but the size of the binocular zone is limited, reducing depth perception and visual acuity. But it's not like the grass is trying to escape, so they don't require the focus and depth perception that a predator needs to accurately track prey.

Trout are unique in the animal kingdom because they change from prey to predator over the course of their lifetimes. As trout mature, their default diet changes from bits of plankton at the onset of their lives to invertebrates and finally to piscivorous activity (eating other fish) after they reach maturity. With each dietary change, they climb one rung up the food chain. They begin their life as prey, eaten by larger fish and birds, but end their life as the most feared predator in their ecosystem, a unique occurrence in the animal kingdom. Most predators, such as wolves, are born as predators and stay that way. Most prey species, such as antelope and rabbits, are born as prey and stay that way throughout their lives. Antelope don't suddenly become predators, and you'll only see carnivorous rabbits in reruns of old Monty Python movies.

As trout ascend levels in the food chain, adaptations occur that facilitate the change from prey to predator. Their mouth gape, the maximal size of the mouth opening, widens and allows them to target increasingly larger prey species. As trout mature, a groove in their snouts develops just

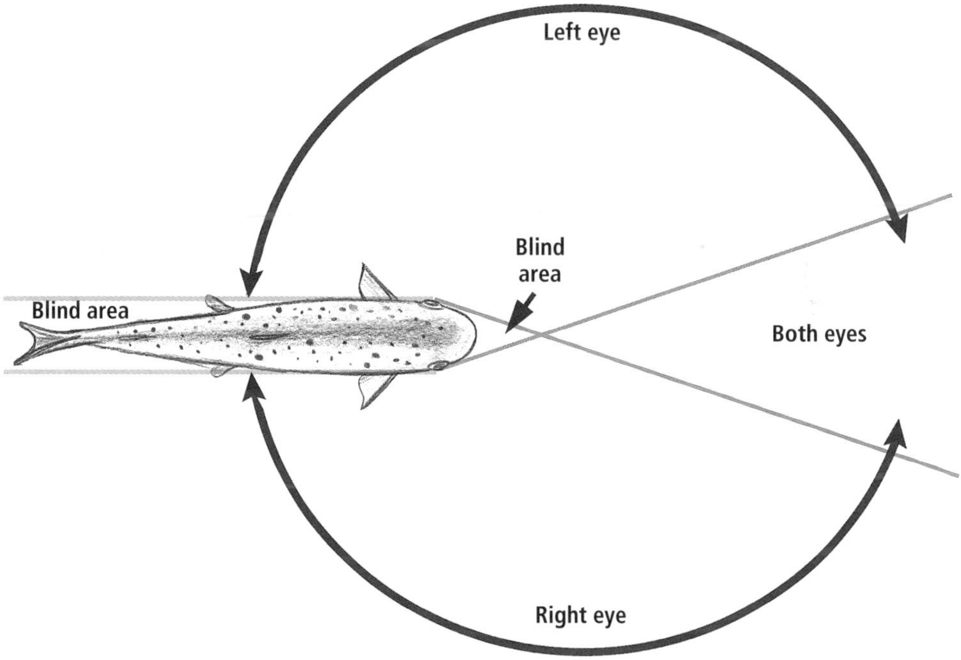

To the front of the trout, the overlapping field of vision from the left and right eyes—binocular vision—creates a zone with improved visual acuity and depth perception. The trout examines and chooses food in this zone. The trout has a larger field of monocular vision laterally (to the side), above, below, and to a limited degree to the rear, allowing for early predator detection.

in front of their eyes; this groove gradually deepens and widens, allowing expanded overlap of the visual field of each eye and broadening binocular vision in the forward visual field. The groove, similar to that found in a mature eagle, is another adaptation for a predatory lifestyle.

Trout, however, retain many characteristics and behavioral features of prey long after they become predators, making large trout even harder to

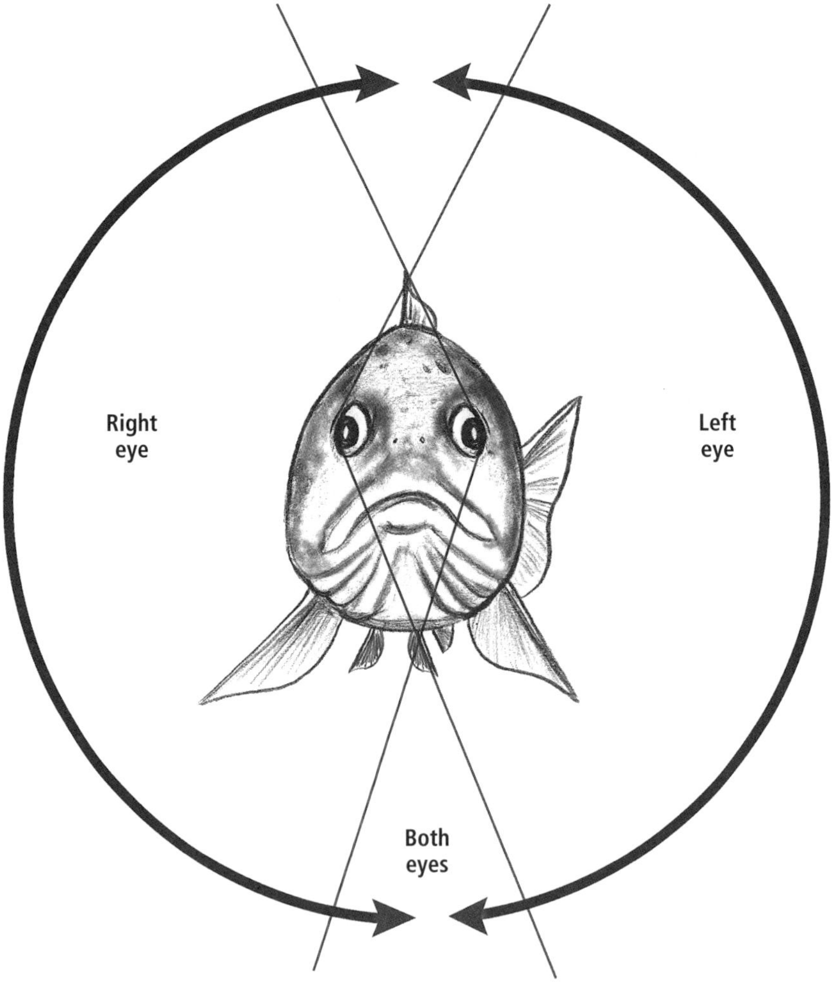

The binocular field of vision allows the trout to clearly see approaching food while the lateral placement of the eyes maximizes the field of visual perception, even extending above and below the fish.

catch. Many predators are bold and aggressive, fearing little, but trout retain the innate wariness they learned as smaller fish, when they were the hunted rather than the hunter.

Since trout spend part of their lives as prey and part as predator, they have visual characteristics of both prey and predator. Their eyes are placed on the side of the head like a prey species, but because of the shape of the eye and the relationship of the lens within it, trout have a large zone of binocular vision where the visual field of each eye overlaps with the other. They not only have the wide field of vision characteristic of a prey species, but they also have the visual acuity and depth perception of a predator in the forward visual field. These adaptations provide the best of both worlds to the trout's vision: the fish retain the very wide field of visual perception to protect against predation while keeping the visual capacity to capture elusive prey.

Since a trout's head is immobile, meaning the fish can't turn its head to study approaching prey, a wide range of binocular vision is a modification that allows it to track prey more accurately without turning its body, which would otherwise expose it broadside to the current. Additionally, while the trout's eye is somewhat moveable within the hard orbit of the skull, it lacks the range of movement our eyes enjoy. Muscles, similar to human eye muscles, attach to the outer surface of the globe of the trout eye and provide for limited eye movements. A wide area of binocular overlap helps offset the limited capacity for eye movement. A trout's best visual acuity, however, is straight in front; as prey approaches, a trout will turn its entire body to face the prey just before committing to eat it, keeping the item of interest in front to afford the best visibility. In strong current, the commitment is quick because of the exposure to current. In slower water, trout often study prey more closely, even following it right in front of their noses, before crossing their eyes at the last moment.

Except for the immediately proximate region either just above or just below their bodies, trout see very well in an upward and downward direction, turning their eyes only minimally to do so. The field of view for trout leaves very few blind spots, none of which has much more than theoretical significance. Much is made of a small blind spot above their snouts, but it has little actual significance in getting food in their mouth. Humans also have a small blind spot just below our nose that prevents visualization of the mouth, but that has never interfered with my ability to eat. Another blind spot occurs directly behind the trout, but it also has little actual significance.

EYE ANATOMY

The shape of the trout's eye is elliptical rather than round, with the long axis oriented parallel to the trout's body and the short axis perpendicular to it. The shape is much different from the round shape of the human eye. As a result, the distance from the lens to the retina is different in the long axis of the eye than it is in the short axis, creating different focal lengths in each direction. This important defense mechanism allows images from the far field to remain in focus to the side of the trout while at the same time approaching food remains in focus in the forward viewing direction. Trout can be watchful for predators even while focused on feeding. To accommodate feeding activities, the elliptical shape of the eye provides a larger forward field of vision than would otherwise be possible.

Because of the constant presence of water, trout have no need for eyelids to keep the eyes moist, as we do. But trout lack another important function eyelids provide—that of protecting the eyes from injury and excessive exposure to sunlight.

Since the eyes are important sensory organs, protecting them from injury is important. The blink response is a reflexive, protective mechanism of the body to avoid injury to the eye. It is an involuntary closing of the eyelids triggered by contact with or tactile stimulation of the cornea. The lids snap shut to protect the eyes from damage. The lids also close to protect the eye in anticipation of injurious contact, such as when we flinch at the approach of an object before contact is made.

Imagine dropping to the bottom of a drift boat and landing on your face without the ability to protect your eyes by closing them or by shielding the blow with hands and arms. Imagine also your eyes scraping against a stiff net as you are scooped into it or while you are flopping around inside. Or the leader abrades them as it winds around your face. This is what happens if we are not careful in how we handle trout when we land them. Their lack of eyelids serves them well when they are underwater, but out of the water, their eyes are very vulnerable to damage.

Secure trout quickly in the net to prevent their thrashing and damaging their sensitive eyes and gills while you remove the hook. Once the hook is free, drop netted fish back into the water while you get the camera. Keep them in the water to avoid drying the corneas and gills. Use a mesh glove to hold them for photos to avoid losing your grip; this also helps avoid the tendency for a finger or two to slip under the gill plate and contact the gills, which are very fragile. Return fish to the water as quickly as possible, taking extra time to revive them if the water is warm.

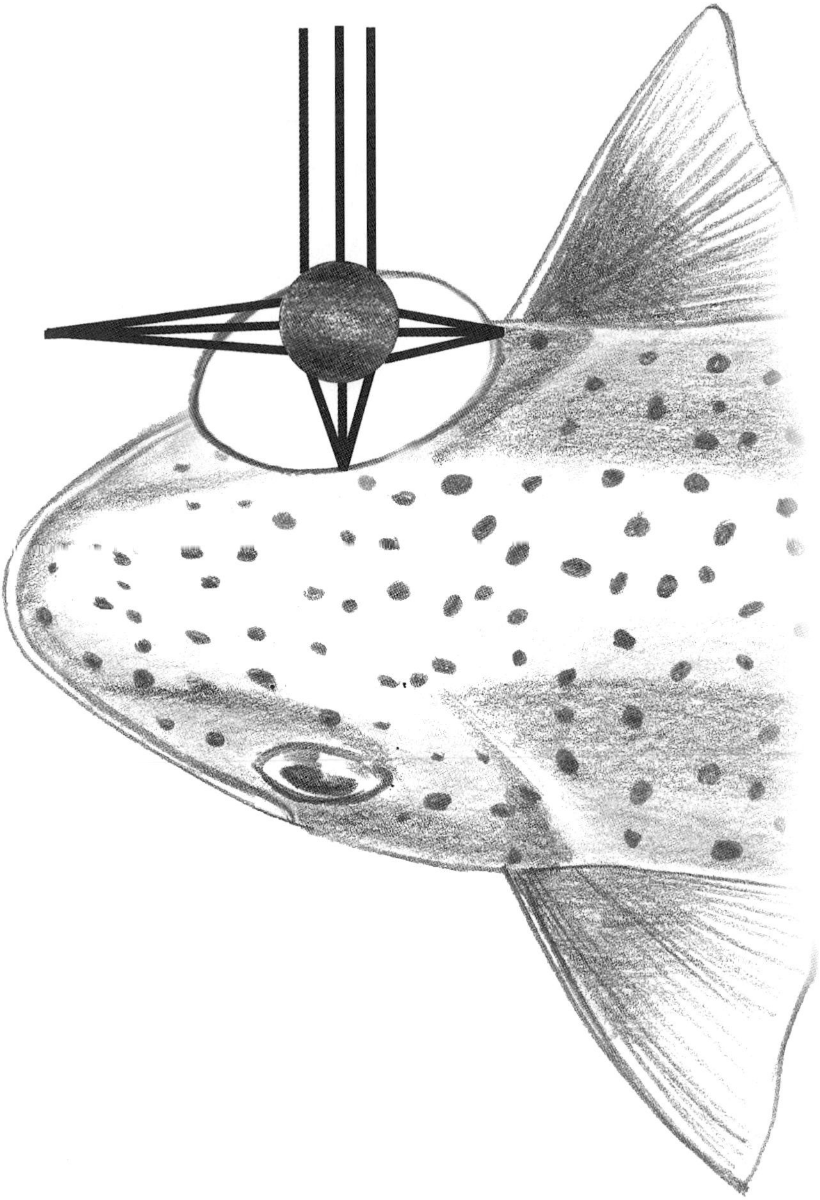

The trout's elliptical eye, with the long axis parallel to the length of the fish and the short axis perpendicular to it, allows two focal lengths. Food approaching from the front, projected on the posterior (rear or toward the tail) aspect of the retina, is in focus at the same time a predator seen from the side, projected in the central part of the retina, is also in focus.

The eyelids of terrestrial animals also protect sensitive eyes from excessive light. In bright glaring sunshine, we squint our eyelids to reduce the amount of light entering the eye, at least until our eyes adjust by constricting our pupils to block the light's intensity. Most of us also reach for the sunglasses as well. But trout don't have eyelids or sunglasses, and their pupils don't constrict in response to bright light, either. The pupil of the trout is fixed; it doesn't change to let in more or less light. Because of the absence of constrictive muscles around the pupil, the opening always stays the same size, neither dilating nor constricting. Like a camera with the aperture stuck open, a trout's eye has the approximate equivalent aperture of f/1.4, which lets in about three times more light than the human eye (which has a maximum aperture closer to f/2.4). This allows trout to see much better in low-light situations than we do. Even starlight offers plenty of light to nocturnally marauding trout.

So, if trout can't squint and their pupils are locked in the open position, how is it that they are not blinded in sunlight? Rather than light-limiting pupils and eyelids characteristic of most other animals, the retina itself limits the light intensity hitting the sensitive photoreceptors. Amazing adaptations are incorporated into the retina, as we shall soon see, that protect the sensitive light receptors from the damaging effects of intense sunlight.

The protective mechanisms trout use to guard against bright light hitting the retina are less effective and take longer to respond than the constrictive pupils and squinting mechanism that other animals employ. By the study of adaptive mechanisms and behaviors, biologists can deduce the conditions for which an animal is best suited. From the way trout respond to intense light, it is evident that trout are ill adapted to bright-light conditions. Conversely, further study of the trout's retina will show how perfectly suited trout are to low-light conditions. Keep this in mind the next time you bring a trout to the surface from deep murky water or from a shady lie, both habitats trout prefer. The sudden jolt of bright, dazzling sunlight after the darkness of shadows must be quite a shock and it is potentially uncomfortable to the trout. It is like a human rushing from a movie theater into blazing sunshine, but without the ability to squint, constrict your pupils, or even shade your eyes. When landing a fish on cloudless days, turn your body away from the sun to keep the fish in the protection of your shadow. Resuscitate the fish in the shadow of the boat or in a shady location along the stream.

As the outermost structure of the trout's eye, the cornea serves as a protective barrier for the rest of the eye. In humans, the curvature of the cornea also begins the process of focusing the rays of light, but the trout's flatter cornea does not allow this. For them, the entire responsibility for focusing a sharp image onto the retina rests with the lens.

Unlike human pupils, the shape of the trout pupil is not perfectly round. A slight anterior (forward, toward the nose) notch can be seen in the pupil, which broadens the scope of light entering the pupil from the forward field of view, once again improving the range of the binocular vision that facilitates feeding activities.

The lens in the trout eye is much different from that of people; it is rounder in shape and less malleable. Accommodation, which is the process of finely focusing the image of an object onto the retina, particularly as the object moves closer or farther away from the trout, is accomplished differently than in humans. For us, the lens changes shape, either becoming thicker or thinner by the action of muscles attached to the circumference of the lens. It's like having one lens for close-up and another for faraway images. As we age, the lens becomes stiffer and less compliant, like our

A notch in the anterior (forward) aspect of the pupil serves to improve the range of binocular vision in the forward field.

joints and muscles, and the lens loses some of its focusing ability. It is usually about that time that we seek the services of an optician and obtain glasses and bifocals to assist our stiffening lenses.

In trout, the spherical shape of the lens does not change, but it still projects an image onto the retina that is free of spherical aberration. Accommodation in fish happens when muscles move the lens forward and backward along an axis, anterior to posterior (toward the snout or toward the tail). Just like holding a magnifying glass closer or farther from the newsprint to bring the words into fine focus, trout move the lens closer or farther away from the posterior part of the retina where the forward field of vision is projected. The distance from the lens to the central portion of the retina does not change in the process of accommodation. In other words, accommodation only affects the focal length in the forward field of vision. The focus never changes in the lateral fields, including the fields of vision above and below the trout. These regions remain in focus to alert the trout of predatory threats even when the forward field of vision changes to facilitate feeding.

At rest, the position of the lens is such that the forward field of view is accommodated for near-field focus. Since trout inspect and identify food material at close range, this makes the most sense, ecologically speaking. Muscles actively move the lens when the trout changes the focus to see objects farther away. Interestingly, in cartilaginous fish such as sharks that identify their prey from greater distances, the muscles function in an opposite manner, meaning they are relaxed for farsighted vision and must actively accommodate to focus in the near field. The distance between the lens and the central part of the retina does not change in the process of accommodation, so lateral vision is always set for far-field focus. In fact, to the side, a narrow zone in the near field remains out of focus and cannot be brought into focus. Since the lateral (side) field of vision is statically set for distance and the forward field of vision defaults to the near-field focus, the trout is often said to be nearsighted anteriorly and farsighted laterally.

The elliptical shape of trout's eye, and thus the retina, makes possible the simultaneous far-field focus in the lateral field and the near-field focus in the forward field. Trout can clearly see food items approach from the front while at the same time they can remain alert to approaching predators above, below, and to the side of them, serving as an advance warning system for threats. And don't forget that a large part of their brain is dedicated to processing visual data—all of which makes them pretty hard to sneak up on!

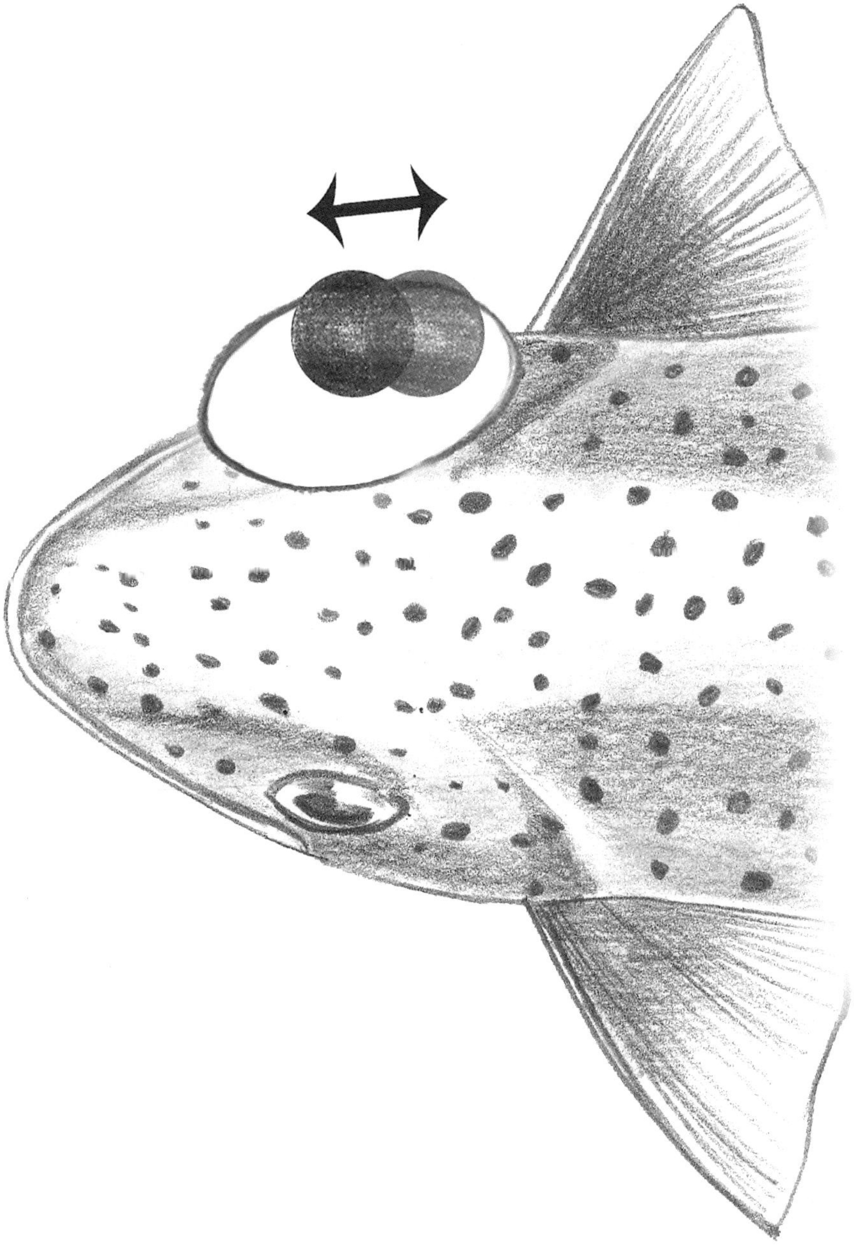

The trout's lens moves anterior to posterior (nose to tail), changing the focal length and focus point from near to far in the forward field of view. It remains equidistant to the central part of the retina where the lateral field of vision appears, so it remains focused for far-field vision irrespective of the movement of the lens.

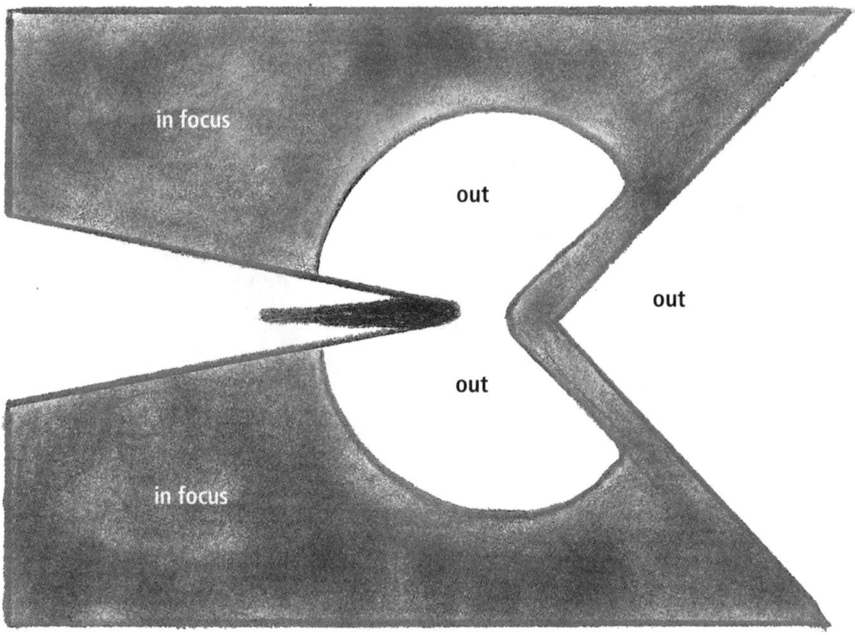

The near field remains in focus in the forward visual field but is out of focus in the lateral visual field. The opposite holds true for distant images; the far field is out of focus in the forward direction but is in focus to the side of the trout.

In his book *Trout Fishing Techniques*, John Goddard states that trout have a visual acuity of 20/200, much less than that of humans. In fact, their fine resolution is many times less than ours, especially for distances beyond more than several feet in the forward field. Some sources estimate the distance for useful, sharp vision as short as 5 feet, since trout's forward vision is preset for the close distances of feeding. They can see farther, although less distinctly, but remain *very* sensitive to movement. Although this is a subjective estimate, since trout are unable to answer the questions on a vision test, it underscores that they possess less resolution power for fine detail, especially at distances beyond their near-field range.

What does this mean for fly tiers? Can trout discern the painstaking detail we often use in fly construction? The answer is yes, but not until the fly is within the fishes' near field of vision; they often subject flies to close inspection from short distances. It is the final deal-sealer. The visual acuity of trout comes into play again when we consider the important features that contribute to search-image formation.

Trout's visual acuity is limited not only by their visual capacity, but also by the optical nature of the medium in which they live, which is frequently stained or turbid water. They see less distance and with less clarity in murky water and a bit better in clear water. With limited visibility in most streams, trout would gain little advantage from highly refined far-field vision.

While trout are visual predators, their sense of vision is obviously not the first to be engaged in the feeding process. Compared with their sense of hearing and smell, vision is a relatively short-ranged sense. Even though search-image formation generally applies to visual cues, an angler can blow it with an inadvertent disrespect for the trout's sense of hearing and smell, or if you are not cognizant of their sensitivity to movement as you approach the stream. The trout's innate wariness for predators means that no matter how pretty and convincing your fly is, it'll be ignored—they'll have run for cover. The sale we must make to the trout begins the moment we arrive at the stream and the way we make the first cast. Ideally, to follow the correct sequence in feeding, the presentation of our fly has to sound like a meal and smell like a meal before it needs to look like a meal. While we may never perfectly imitate all of these feeding cues, we should at least avoid the alarm cues of potential danger. After all, if you are on full alert for a crisis or catastrophe with adrenaline coursing through your veins, the last thing on your mind is a cheeseburger and fries.

THE AMAZING RETINA OF TROUT

After the lens focuses the light, it passes through a transparent liquid in the center cavity of the eye and is projected to the retina, which lines the outer orbit of the eye like a coat of paint on the inside of a basketball. The retina of trout has the same primary function as the retina of humans: it contains the receptor cells that detect light.

The retina is composed of many different cells organized in well-defined layers. The layer of the retina that light first contacts is a network of tiny nerve fibers that course across the surface of the retina and ultimately collect to form the optic nerve. After passing through this layer, the light next encounters ganglion and bipolar cells, which are the equivalent of middle-management cells. They collect the input from receptor cells lying beneath them and ultimately send the signals through the optic nerve to the brain. The extensive interconnecting network of these middle-management cells, a characteristic shared by many predators, allows the

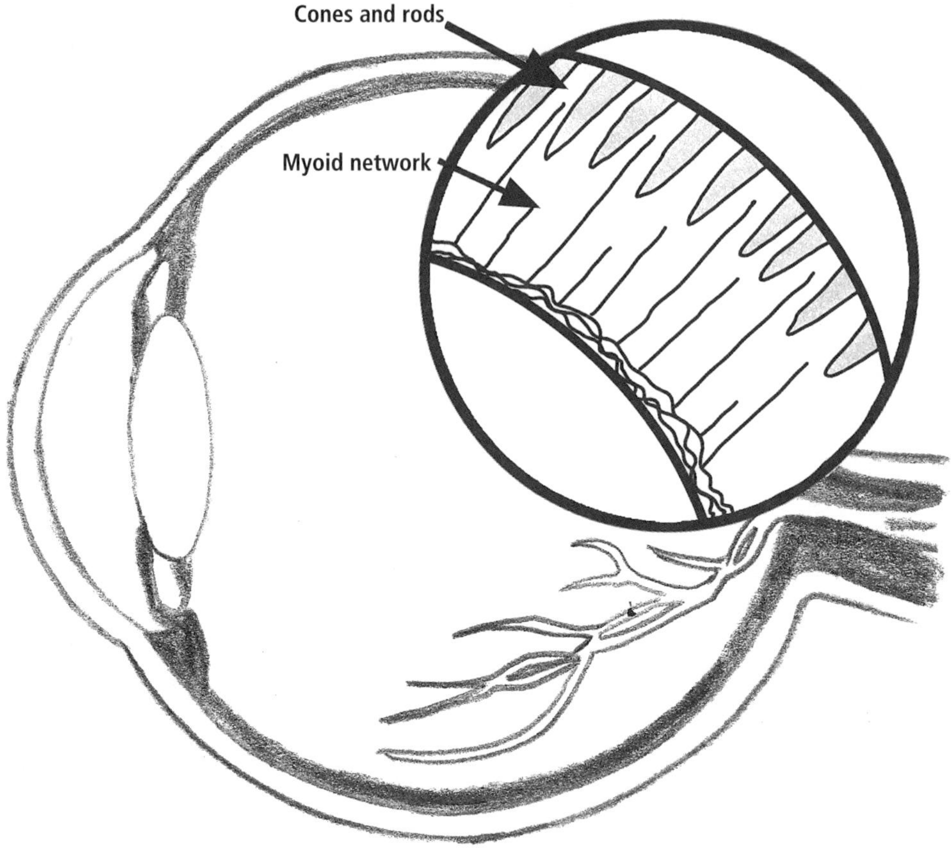

The trout retina is organized into layers. The light-sensitive cones and rods are in the outermost layer, which the light contacts only after having first passed through all other layers.

detection of even subtle movements, either associated with feeding or for predator detection. The trout's acute perception and tracking of objects is vital to feeding on the moveable feast that rushes by them in the current. In the deepest layer of the retina, the cones and rods, which are the light-sensitive receptor cells, are adjacent to an outer pigmented layer. So, it seems that the retina is built inside-out: the light contacts the receptors in the deepest layer of the retina only after first passing through all the other layers.

The two types of receptor cells, cones and rods, respond to different characteristics of light and provide different pieces to the visual puzzle. Cones respond to the wavelength of light, allowing for color vision. They provide high visual acuity, both spatial, for the accurate detection and location of prey, and temporal, for accurate tracking; both are vital for daylight feeding. Their acuity also results in a sensitive predator-alert system, working in conjunction with the middle-management cells. But the cones lack the sensitivity to light to be effective at night, which is when rods come into play. Rods do not detect color but instead are much more sensitive to the intensity of light. They are able to detect light with minimal intensity but at the expense of acuity and color perception. They provide the low-light visual capacity that is essential for nocturnal feeding.

The relative incidence of these two photoreceptors in the retinas of different animals is a strong indication as to whether that animal is active during the day, at night, or both. Owls, for instance, have an abundance of rods, reflecting their nearly exclusive nocturnal feeding habits; in owls, cones are rare, allowing only limited color vision. The preponderance of light-sensitive rods makes them averse to bright light. Like owls, cones are all but absent in fish species living in the depths of the sea. Fish that live most of their lives in the uppermost layer of the ocean have a higher proportion of cones. Trout have a mixed population, reflecting a lifestyle that requires them to function during the day as well as at night.

The composition of the receptors in the retina changes as the trout matures. Cones develop first in the retinas of most fish embryos, well before the rods appear. Since cones provide visual acuity in the daylight-feeding youngsters, their presence is mandatory at the earliest stages of life. The rods appear later in development. By the time the fish reaches the young juvenile, rods outnumber cones significantly. The combination of a wide aperture pupil that lets in large amounts of light and a high concentration of rods in the retina ideally suits the mature trout for nocturnal predation, and night becomes their preferred time to feed as they enter adulthood.

Light rays enter the trout's pupil from the entire scope of the visual field and are focused by the lens onto different regions of the retina. Images from the lateral part of the visual field follow a path parallel the perpendicular to the long axis of the eye and project onto the central part of the retina. The forward visual field is directed along the long axis of the eye to the posterior or temporal part of the retina. Each area of the retina is different, with a population of receptors suited to carry out its specific task.

In the human eye, our most accurate vision for detailed work is provided by a small depression in the retina called the *fovea*, which is a specialized region of densely packed cones. Rods are virtually nonexistent in this area. The fovea provides sufficient acuity for tasks such as reading, tying flies, and other activities where visual detail is vital. It is the area of the retina we use when we concentrate on a task demanding sharp, focused vision. Although trout lack a fovea, regions of the trout's retina differ in the ratio of cones and rods depending on the task they perform, which is based on whether they receive light from the forward or lateral fields of vision. The temporal region, receiving light from the forward field of vision along the main axis of feeding, has the highest density of photoreceptors to provide the greatest visual acuity needed for the discriminant vision of feeding. The central area of the retina that receives light from the lateral visual field has a higher incidence of cone receptors since this is the most sensitive visual system for predator detection.

CONES

Not all cones are created equal. Cones can be single cells, but also appear as double cells, which is when two cones are apposed together and are thought to enhance visual acuity. All salmonid fishes even have triple cones, the number of which varies from species to species. Triple cones amount to less than 1 percent of the total cone population and their function is still unknown.

Cones differ from one another in the wavelength of light they detect, falling into one of three categories for humans. In our retina, one type of cone preferentially detects light in what we perceive as the red range, another cone responds primarily to the blue wavelength, and yet another to green wavelengths. To be precise, cones do not detect color; color is an interpretation of the brain arising from variable stimulation of different cone types in the retina. The cones themselves are just luminosity detectors, each type best stimulated by light within a certain range of wavelengths. All cones absorb from their maximal wavelengths down to ultraviolet wavelengths, but their maximal sensitivity is only for a narrow range of wavelengths. For example, a red cone is maximally sensitive for light that has a wavelength that we perceive as red light. Trout have an additional cone that detects light in the ultraviolet range, at least for very young trout.

ULTRAVIOLET LIGHT

Many organisms can see UV light, and many have a UV cone at some stage in their lives, including birds, amphibians, reptiles and insects. The source of UV vision in trout, however, has been a hotly debated topic, even among scientific researchers. Some of the earlier studies have been refuted by many of the newer ones, creating confusion in the scientific world as well as in the angling community. Earlier angling authors wrote entire books on the subject, but in fact, the ability, sensitivity, and actual significance of UV photosensitivity to adult and young adult trout has often been overestimated.

Ultraviolet light is shorter than the shortest wavelength of the visible light, falling between 100 and 400 nm. Recall that light just above 400 nm is in the human visible spectrum and we perceive it as violet (*ultraviolet* literally means "beyond violet"). Ultraviolet light is further subdivided into three categories based on its biological effect. UVA is the closest to visible light, just outside the visual range. It falls in the wavelength range between 315 to 400 nm. UVB varies from 315 to 280 nm and UVC from 280 to 100nm. Animals that possess the ability to see ultraviolet light have receptors sensitive to UVA; these animals do not visually detect UVB and UVC because the lens does not transmit light below the UVA range.

Fortunately for both humans and trout, most UVC is filtered out by the Earth's atmosphere since it is considered harmful and detrimental to most organisms. Don't forget that UVC light is right next to X rays on the electromagnetic spectrum and is similar to X rays in terms of its detrimental biological impact. UVB has biological significance in the conversion of Vitamin D in our skin, and also causes tanning of the skin, but has no visual relevance. So, for our purposes, the discussion about UV light perception focuses on a narrow range of light: UVA, just below the violet color on the visual spectrum.

I must admit that I was initially frustrated by the conflicting scientific data regarding UV light vision in trout, but things were clearer after I had the opportunity to discuss the subject with one of the world's leading authorities on trout vision: Dr. Iñigo Novales Flamarique of the Department of Biological Sciences at Simon Fraser University in British Columbia, Canada. He has researched salmonid vision extensively, specifically the topic of UV photosensitivity. His research is published in scientific journals, many of which are listed in this book's bibliography. What follows is a synopsis of our conversation.

All trout have the capacity to detect ultraviolet light at a very young age because they have a type of cone photoreceptor that is specifically tuned to wavelengths in the UV range. In fact, young trout have three basic types of cones in their retina when they hatch, each maximally sensitive to a specific wavelength of light—UV, green, or red. As the trout grow, the UV dedicated cones transform into blue light-sensing cones (which maximally sense blue light in the same manner as human blue cones), such that by the time they reach the late smolt stage, which is a few inches in length, the animal no longer has UV cones. From that point on, the cones that were previously maximally sensitive to UV light now sense primarily blue light.

The early ability for UV photosensitivity is especially important to young trout given their feeding preferences. When they initially leave the redd, which is the site where the females lay eggs during spawning, trout fry feed on plankton and are referred to as *planktivorous*. Plankton includes both tiny vegetative organisms as well as miniature crustaceans such as *Daphnia*, also known as the water flea, and many others. As they forage, trout fry pluck plankton that is attached to rocks and gravel on the streambed, attached to larger vegetation, or floating in the water just above the bottom. The fry's small mouth size and inability to chase quicker prey species limits their choices to a diet that is small and cannot flee. The ability to detect UV light is an asset to the young trout feeding upon these otherwise mostly indistinguishable tiny organisms because it creates additional contrast in the visual field, making the plankton stand out against the background.

Young trout are just as selective in feeding patterns as older trout, and apparently not all plankton are created equal in the UV-sensitive eyes of the young fish—they often favor one type of plankton over another, and UV-sensitive vision aids in telling the prey apart. Contrast is one basis for the trout's visual discrimination; with the aid of UV analysis, they can tell apart the different plankton species. For instance, *Daphnia* and *Diaptomus*, two species of plankton, have different patterns of UV absorption. Although they appear similar under normal conditions, they look completely different in ultraviolet light.

As the trout mature, their diet shifts from plankton to invertebrates, comprising immature insects, larger crustaceans, and other prey species common in the stream. By the time they have reached maturity, they have switched their feeding preference again, this time to other fish, small streamside mammals such as mice and voles that accidently fall into the river, and other energy-laden prey. The UV light sensitivity that was a tremendous asset to the young trout has much less practical value to the mature trout.

Does this mean that mature trout cannot see UV light at all? The answer is no, but the perception of UV light is much reduced from its level prior to the conversion of UV-sensitive cones to blue-sensitive cones. The reason trout retain limited UV perception as adults is that all cone types, regardless of whether they are UV, blue, green or red, absorb UV light to a small degree. But it is only the UV cones in the very young trout that are *maximally* sensitive to UV light. The sensitivity of the other cone types—blue, red, and green—is much less, so that the adult trout has only limited UV photosensitivity.

The reason for the limited UV detection of other cone types (blue, red and green cones) is based on the specific visual pigment proteins in the cells of the photoreceptors, called *opsins*. Each cone has a specific opsin bound to a molecule called a chromophore, which together have a main absorbance in the region of the light spectrum corresponding to the cone's namesake. In other words, it is the opsin and chromophore (together known as the visual pigment) that determines what color wavelength a cone is fine-tuned to. For instance, a blue cone absorbs maximally blue light at 430 nm, a green cone is maximally sensitive to light at 520 nm, and a red cone at 565 nm because of the specific visual pigment within the photoreceptor. When the change from UV to blue cones occurs as the trout ages, the opsin of the visual pigment in the cones that previously detected light maximally in the UV range shifts to a slightly longer wavelength in the visible violet-blue color range, like changing settings on a radio dial.

But in addition to its main peak absorbance, each opsin has a secondary absorbance peak, called *beta bands*, in the range of UV light, between 320 and 400 nm. It is the beta bands that offer the adult trout its limited UV sensitivity.

In summary, according to Dr. Novales Flamarique, "All trouts and all salmonids that have been thoroughly studied are visually sensitive to ultraviolet light throughout their lives, but their sensitivity is much reduced after the smolt stage because the ultraviolet cones have disappeared. As for the use of ultraviolet vision in young salmonids (with UV cones), the UV cones enhance the contrast of zooplankton prey and improve the fish's foraging performance. Nothing is known about the function of UV vision in salmonid fishes at later stages in nature and it is doubtful that it serves any ecological purpose once the UV cones are gone."

In other words, UV light seems to have limited practical significance to the adult trout. The weaker secondary beta absorption bands available for UV detection in mature trout are much less sensitive compared to the main bands of UV-dedicated cones of immature trout, and so UV light plays less of an environmental role after the smolt stage.

Many objects, including insects and the feathers of birds, reflect UV light. But given the limited UV photosensitivity of adult trout and the high absorption of UVA light in many water bodies (which means that it is not well transmitted), the UV reflectance of insects seems more relevant to other insects that can actually see UV light than it does to trout. The same holds true for UV-reflecting bird feathers; they are very ecologically significant to other birds that see UV light, playing a role in identification and courtship, but not so much for trout.

So, will a trout take a fly constructed with UV materials over an identical fly tied with non-UV materials, based solely on the material's UV properties? I don't know, but I suspect not given the trout's limited UV sensitivity. The contribution of the UV component to their total visual information is probably negligible.

Trout may take a UV-constructed fly based on other visual features of the fly's material, however, which means that I'm not going to throw away my UV dubbing and tying materials. In addition to reflecting UV light, these materials have other visual properties that make them fish-catchers. The success of these materials, erroneously attributed to UV light properties, may in fact be caused by other optical properties of the material. These features will be discussed in the final chapter.

POLARIZED LIGHT

Polarized light is light that vibrates in only one directional plane, as opposed to unpolarized light, which oscillates in all directions perpendicular to the path of the beam of light. This is best understood by looking at light as a wave. Light has wavelike properties in its movement, behaving just like a wave moving across the surface of the ocean toward the shore. Imagine standing in the surf watching waves approach; as each wave reaches its peak, its crest is high and the trough is low. The water rises and falls relative to your body as the waves approach and pass, making the up-and-down oscillation in water height pretty obvious. Thus, the wave of water can be described as oscillating vertically. Since it only oscillates in one plane, its movement is similar to polarized light.

Contrast that movement to that of unpolarized light, which vibrates in every plane perpendicular to the path of light. It's like a wave of water moving not only up and down, but also side to side at the same time. Imagine a ray of light coming at you in super slow motion. Unpolarized light oscillates up and down and side to side and in every direction in between—all at the same time.

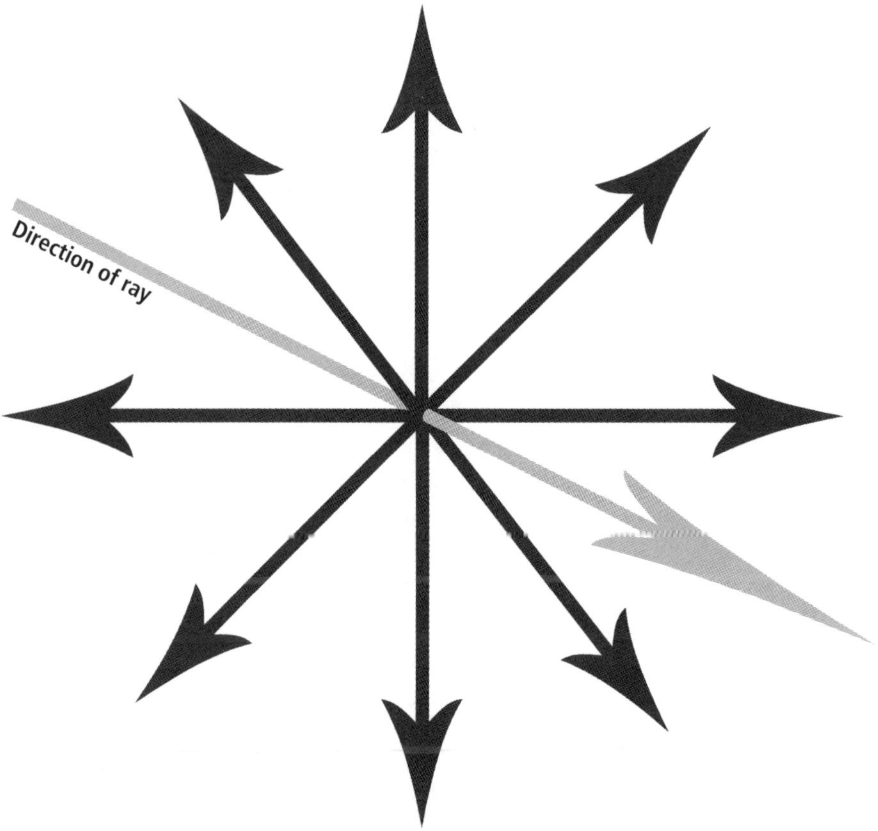

Unpolarized light oscillates in every direction as it travels, moving right, left, up, and down and every plane in between.

A common analogy for the polarization of light is light passing through the slats of a picket fence. As a ray of light approaches the fence, it vibrates vertically and horizontally and every direction in between. When passing through the fence's slats, only the light's vertical waves pass through since they align with the slats. The waves vibrating along the horizontal axis will be blocked. Passing through the vertical openings in the picket fence polarizes the light, and so afterward it is oscillating only in the vertical direction.

Light from the sun is unpolarized, at least initially. Partial polarization of light occurs as it passes through the atmosphere. When light strikes and reflects off a flat surface, whether it is water, asphalt, or any other flat surface, it becomes horizontally polarized, which is the main source of glare.

The light reflects as a polarized, horizontal sheet. That's the reason glare can arise from the road, making sunglasses a necessity for driving on sunny days. The glare is even worse from highly reflective surfaces such as streams, rivers, or other bodies of water.

While the reflected glare is strongly polarized horizontally, the rest of the light reaching our eyes from the other objects we see when we are visiting the river is mostly unpolarized. This includes trees and brush, our fellow anglers, and even other areas of the water away from the angle of the sun's reflection. So, in order to reduce the glare, polarized glasses are designed to remove all the waves of light oscillating in the horizontal plane. Most polarized sunglasses contain long molecules that are oriented vertically like our picket fence, only on a much smaller scale. They screen out all horizontally oscillating waves; this includes nearly all of the glare, since it is primarily horizontally polarized. Polarized sunglasses also block the horizontal component of the unpolarized light from other sources. The resultant light that reaches our eyes is now vertically polarized, meaning

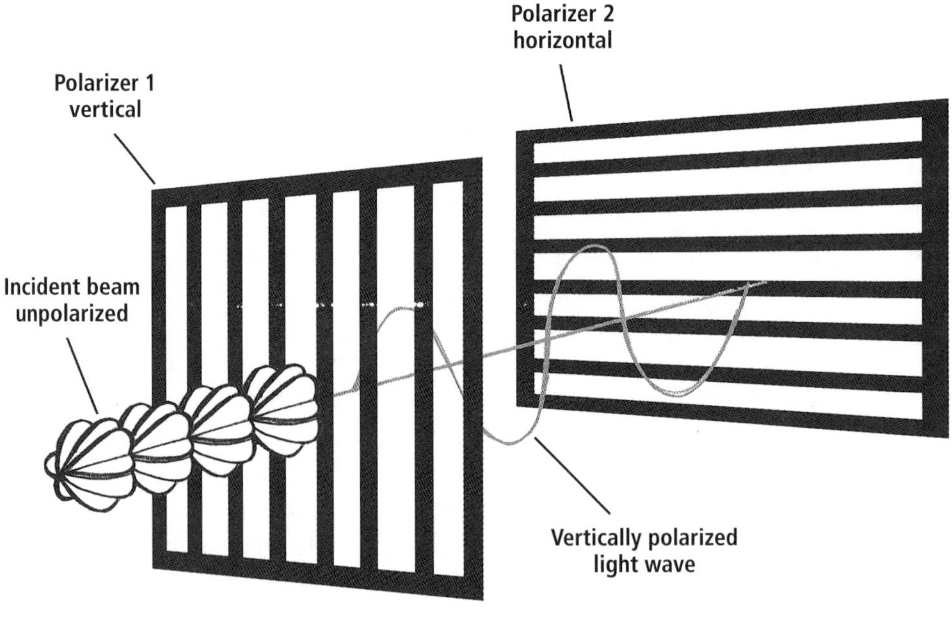

The polarization of light follows the simple analogy of the picket fence: light passes through the slats of the fence, resulting in light vibrating only in a single plane rather than oscillating in every direction. If the light passes through a second polarizer aligned 90 degrees to the first, only a single tightly focuses ray of light remains.

Polarized sunglasses work in the same manner as our picket fence; long, vertically aligned molecules filter out the horizontal component of light, which includes most of the glare.

we see only vertically aligned waves. Since polarization filters block out approximately half of the available light, the image seen through polarized glasses is darker by that amount. Without the glare, anglers can see into the water to better identify structure and locate fish.

The sensitivity of trout to polarized light has been debated among researchers. Some of the early research seemed to show that trout respond to polarized light and will change orientation in response to changes in polarization, but the exact mechanism of detection or the actual receptor was never identified. Current research has shown that the capacity for detection and the effect of polarized light on adult trout was probably overestimated.

Present scientific research shows that the detection of polarized light by adult trout does not play a significant ecological role in feeding or migration.

Similar to UV light, polarized light may facilitate the feeding success of young trout, but this is also subject to debate. The ability to detect polarized light would clearly be advantageous to immature fish in the planktivorous life stage in the same manner as UV-light detection does—by adding contrast. Zooplankton may be more conspicuous to a fish that senses polarized light because of the pronounced birefringence that the calcium carbonate exoskeletons of zooplankton exhibit.

Early research also postulated that polarized light detection might assist in navigation since the polarization of light varies with changing angles of the sun. In other words, it would serve as a directional aid to orient the fish during migration. The role polarized light may play in migration is still under investigation, but it is not thought to be significant.

As yet, no known mechanism for the detection of polarized light has yet been determined and a specific receptor or neural processing network has not been identified. Research is ongoing but the most recent scientific publications question the role of polarized light detection in salmonid fishes altogether.

RODS

When you mention the word *rods* to most anglers, they start listing their favorite manufacturer, weight, and tip action. But for purposes of our current discussion, rods are the retina's highly sensitive photoreceptors that lack the color capability and visual acuity of cones. The information they send to the brain is interpreted as black and white imagery, with shades of gray. Less refined and detailed than the information from cones, pure rod vision is a little coarse, but contrast will be evident. It is analogous to night-vision goggles; the image is monochrome (green in the case of most manufacturers' military-grade goggles) but contains sharp contrast.

Rods outnumber cones in the retina by the time the trout reaches maturity and switches to larger prey species. At that time they also shift their lifestyle to nocturnal or low-light feeding conditions, for which the ultrasensitive rods are ideally suited. This helps make large trout the quintessential nocturnal predator.

Rods detect such low levels of light that mature trout can even feed effectively in starlight. Stripping and swinging streamers at night can be an effective strategy for targeting large trout, since that is when they are actively feeding. As the smaller prey fish head home at night, the big boys are just rousing from their slumber. It is one of the best times to land a trophy trout.

Because of the roaming, mobile nature of piscivorous (fish-eating) trout, it is more effective to target their home sites, which they visit periodically between nocturnal feeding excursions, than it is to predict which of several hunting grounds they may occupy at any particular time. Ideal home sites are usually located in deeper, soft-bottom sections of the stream, with slow but steady current. Deep undercut banks and pools are often well suited for home sites, particularly in logjams that offer safety and concealment. Think of a hidey-hole in the game of hide-and-seek—that's where you'll find the big trout. If no one is home on your first attempt, check back later; large trout visit their home site many times through the night.

With the peak of the invertebrate drift (the occurrence of invertebrate species floating in the stream—a major food source for young adult and juvenile fish) occurring at dawn and dusk, smaller- and medium-sized trout and other prey fish are moving about during transition times. Older trout with a higher numbers of rods in the retina have better night vision than immature fish, which gives the predator a clear advantage in nocturnal marauding. During transition times, tie on a streamer that imitates an immature trout, chosen to represent the age of the young trout occurring at that time.

Streamer selection is important and is made much easier when some basic scientific principles are kept in mind. Since older trout are willing to prey upon younger members of their own species, imitating young trout moving to and from feeding stations at transitional times is a good strategy. Large trout frequently roam intercept routes, hoping to catch smaller fish on the move.

It is important to imitate the correct stage of immature trout, matching it with the prevailing season. In other words, don't tie on a streamer that imitates a parr in April, since there are few naturally occurring parr at that time of year. (A parr is a trout that is several months old and has vertical bars or stripes along the body.) Since immature trout of all species leave the redd in late winter or early spring, they will have a flash of red or orange at their neck that is a remnant of the recently disappeared yolk sac.

The parr is an immature trout and can be identified by vertical bars along the body.

The parr markings will appear later in the summer or early fall. The late summer and early fall is the time to imitate parr with a streamer that has three or four vertical stripes.

In the quest for your trophy, a sculpin-imitating streamer is also a good choice for night fishing. Also nocturnally active, sculpins make up a significant portion of the diet of large trout. Bottom grazers that lack a swim bladder, they often lie motionless along the bottom of the stream, moving only as needed to forage or flee. A Clouser Minnow bounced along the bottom can bring home the bacon, so to speak. I like to vibrate the rod as I lift the streamer from the bottom to imitate the swimming movements of the fish. I then let it drop to the bottom again. You should be ready for a strike on the drop, so don't let too much slack develop in the line as the streamer falls.

LIGHT AND DARK ADAPTATION

As noted earlier, we and most other animals have an adjustable pupil and eyelids that can reduce the amount of light entering the eye. When we go from a dark movie theater to bright sunlight, the pupil constricts to close the diameter and if needed, we squint or even close our eyes. We can even use our hands to shield our eyes or reach for sunglasses. In the opposite scenario, when we leave broad daylight and enter a dark room, our pupils dilate to let as much light as possible enter the eye. Our eyes rapidly adjust to changing light conditions, which protects our sensitive retinas against bright light and also makes the most of all the available light to help us see in darkness.

Trout, on the other hand, have an entirely different way of adapting to changes in light intensity. While we have an adjustable pupil; they have an adjustable retina! It happens involuntarily, like the change in our pupil, just not as fast. Trout engage and disengage the retina's rods and cones according to the amount of available light. The sensitive rods are hidden during bright light of day when only the cones are exposed. This protects them from harm. At night, it is just the opposite: the cones are covered and the rods are engaged. Trout exclusively use cones for bright daylight conditions and use rods for nighttime vision requiring low-light sensitivity; thus, the retina is configured for either darkness or light. Trout use the same photoreceptors as we do—cones and rods—but just not at the same time. Their photoreceptors engage and disengage by moving in and out of a protective pigmented layer as needed according to the amount of prevailing light.

During bright daylight conditions, the cones are engaged by pulling them out of the protective layer, allowing light access to the photosensitive

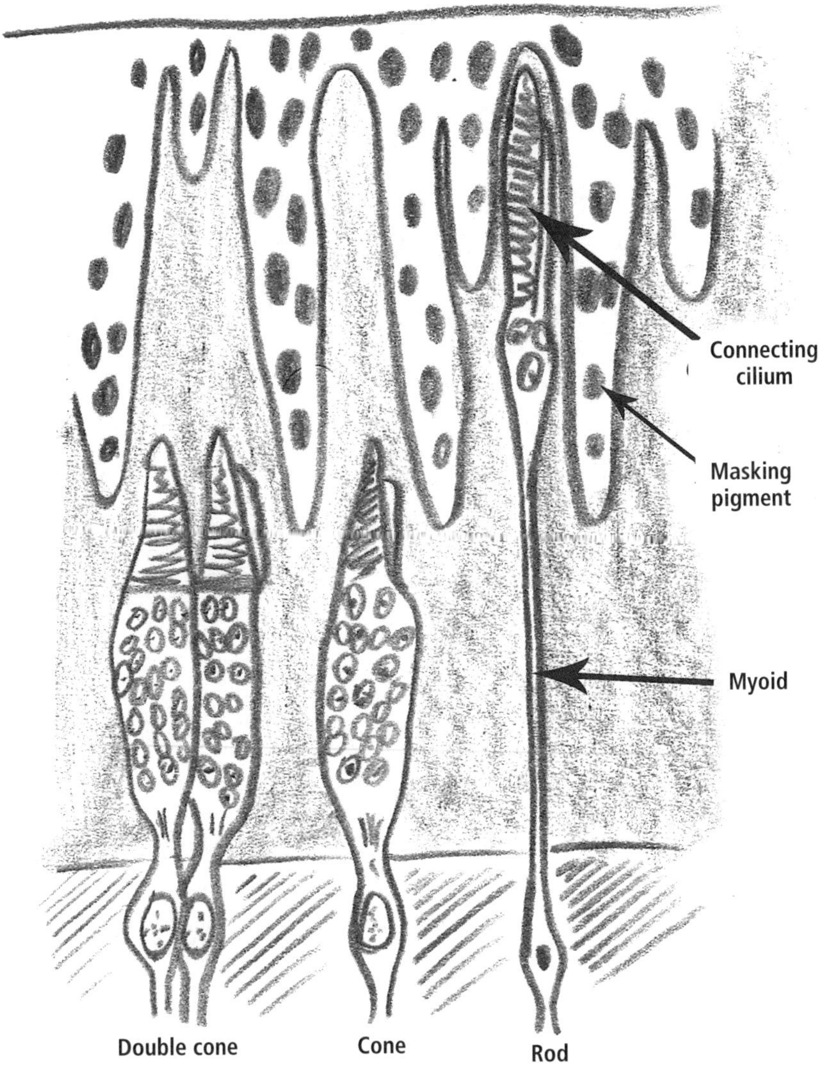

The light-sensitive rods are not needed in daylight. They are embedded in a pigmented layer at the back of the retina to shield them from the intense bright light of day.

portion of the tip of the cone. At the same time, like an ostrich sticking its head in the sand, the sensitive rods are inserted into the protective layer to keep them out of contact with the intense light. Additionally, a retinal masking pigment moves within the protective layer to enshroud the rods, further shielding them from light.

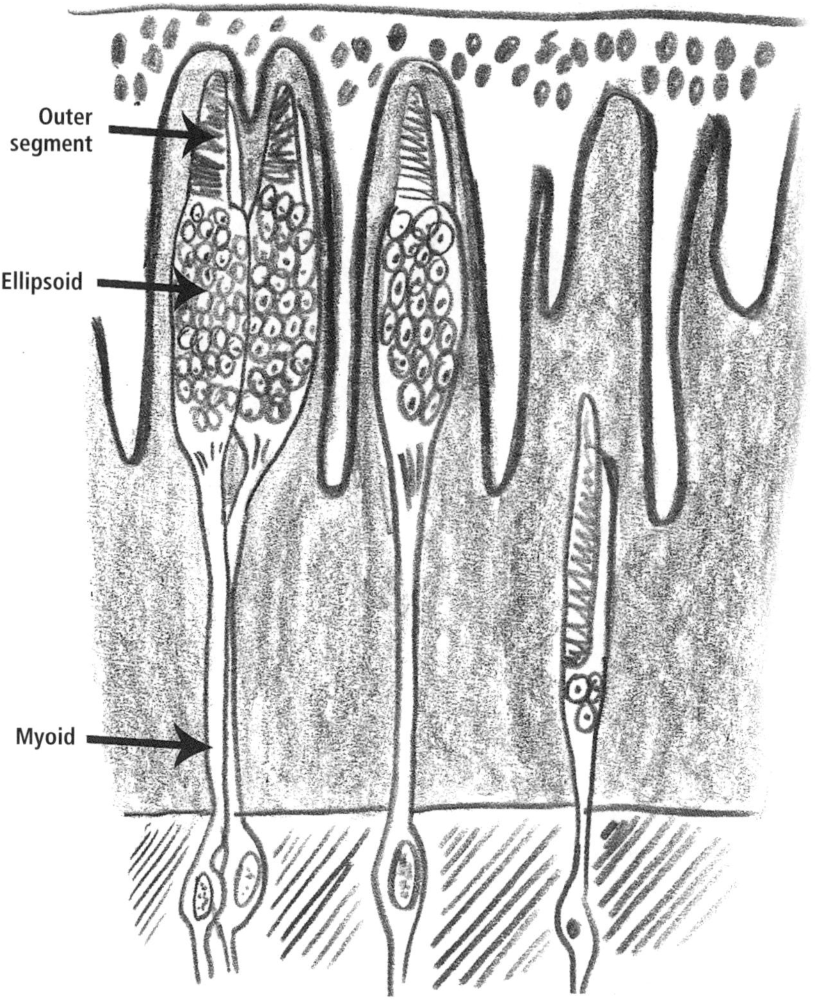

At night, the light-sensitive rods are withdrawn from the protective masking layer for low light vision and the cones are inserted into the protective layer until the next day.

When darkness falls, the masking pigment migrates away from the ends of the rods to uncover them and they are lifted from the protective layer entirely, making them available for light detection. Like the night shift coming on duty, as the afternoon sun wanes, the rods gradually begin to lift from the protected layer, switching places with the cones. The sensitive rods will be needed to enable the trout to see in the dark. The cones, as if done for the day, are advanced into the protective pigmented layer to lie dormant until the next day. After the change to dark-adapted vision, the trout no longer sees in color.

The transition from light-adapted vision to dark-adapted vision does not happen as fast as our pupil dilates. Our pupil adjusts in seconds; the adjustment for trout, however, usually takes twenty-five to thirty minutes and sometimes longer

During the transition from light to dark conditions and vice versa a brief period of overlap occurs when both the cones and rods are active, which potentially improves visual performance. This may account for the increase in trout feeding at dawn and dusk.

With their rods fully engaged and active, large trout prowl the night-time stream with the equivalent of night-vision goggles. Like the owls of the ecosystem, they are on a search-and-devour mission. The unfortunate prey fish caught out after curfew will likely not live to repeat the mistake.

NIGHT FISHING

The night vision of trout requires some adjustment in our nocturnal fishing strategies. In the trout's black-and-white night vision, contrast is sharply defined. Even though we can't see at night, they can. Against the dark foliage of the shore, white or other bright-colored clothing will stand out like a neon sign. Instead of light colors, choose dark or subdued clothing that blends into the background. The actual color is unimportant since trout can't tell one from another with their cones disengaged, but dark greens, browns, and blacks will allow you to blend in with shoreline vegetation.

Remember to move about the night stream with care—not only for your personal safety, but also to avoid scaring the very trophy you seek. Even though you may think you have the advantage under the cover of darkness, remember that they see much better at night than you do. What's dark to you is ideal to them. You are easily seen silhouetted against the night sky. Also remember to soften your footfalls; sound is just as noticeable to them at night as it is during the day.

Another tip for night fishing is to avoid unguarded lights as much as possible. A bright flashlight at night must seem like a bolt of lightning to a dark-adapted trout. When night fishing, I always use a red filter over the lens of the flashlight. Since trout can't see color at night, this appears as a muted, dull glow. It's not as easy to tie on a tippet in the subdued red light, but I think the red light is less obtrusive to trout. Their highly sensitive, pure-rod retina allows them to see even the dimmest light.

One of the challenges of fishing the *Hexagenia limbata* mayfly, or Hex to those in the know, is getting used to fishing in darkness. Adding tippet and tying flies is hard enough in daylight, much less at night! Early in my love affair with Hex fishing, after what seemed like endless waiting one June evening, a decent fish started to rise just below the position my buddy and I had taken along the shore. It was closer to him, so he got the opportunity to catch the first fish. He listened intently to gauge the direction and distance in the scant starlight. After a few rises, he had it and he had also established the rhythm of feeding. He timed his cast perfectly—right into the bush behind him. With friendly mirth, I ended up catching his fish, but he evened the score a short time later when he hooked a better one. I had the first laugh, but there's certainly something to be said about getting the last one.

Our biggest mistake that night was that we were unfamiliar with the river and had not done enough scouting ahead of time. Now, if I am fishing new water, I scout the section in daylight. After choosing an ideal section, which for the Hex often includes low banks with cattails and a mucky bottom, I walk the shores to find the best angles, carefully checking the backcast lanes. I look for trees and bushes, marking ideal fishing positions along the shore. I also estimate the distance to the center of the river, which is nearly impossible to accomplish after dark. I am also sure to arrive well in advance of sunset and have my rigging complete before the light fades.

THE PINEAL GLAND

Sometimes called the third eye of trout, the pineal gland (also referred to as the pineal body) is part of the brain, yet also considered part of the hormonal system because it secretes the hormone melatonin into the bloodstream of the fish. It lies in the upper part of the brain under a small, specialized area of the head that allows for at least partial transmission of light through the skull. The pineal gland responds to light independently of the information provided by the eyes.

The pineal gland seems to have two separate, functional modes: one that is quicker and more dynamic, and one that is a slower or tonic mode. The dynamic mode may be facilitated by direct communication to the brain and serves as a shadow detector that alerts the fish to the threat of overhead predation. Even blind, cave-dwelling species of fish can detect shadows through the light-sensitive pineal gland, allowing them to instantly react to the threat of overhead predation.

Trout are extremely wary of overhead shadows because the threat of overhead predators is a significant concern for much of their lives. Large birds of prey including herons, osprey, and eagles are capable of preying upon relatively large trout. I have seen 18-inch trout in the iron grip of a raptor's talons, lifted from the water with ease on powerful wings. If you want to send trout fleeing for cover, just let your shadow suddenly cast across their feeding lie.

Because of this innate fear, angler position relative to the sun becomes an important consideration. Gunfighters like to keep the sun at their backs, but if anglers adopt the same strategy their shadows will likely fall across their casting targets, possibly spooking wary trout. Trout love stationary shadows cast by riparian trees, brush, and overhead structures like bridges. Their sun-sensitive eyes and poikilothermic bodies make them crave these sun-protected lies. Trout do not, however, like shadows that move or appear suddenly. Approach angles to potential feeding lies need to be made in such a way as to keep the angler's shadow from hitting the target.

This also applies to boat position, which should be oriented with respect to the sun to allow anglers to fish the ideal thread of the river without placing the shadow of the boat or the people in the boat over the trout lies. The shadow of a passing boat must seem to trout like the mother ship of the eagle clan.

In its tonic mode, the pineal gland helps establish circadian (day-night) and seasonal rhythms in the fish. For it role in circadian rhythms, the pineal body has also been termed a "dusk detector," because it prepares the fish for changing lighting conditions associated with day-night transitions. The pineal body possibly initiates the changeover from cones to rods in the retina. The tonic mode is more likely mediated through the slower means of hormonal secretion. Melatonin levels increase during the night, reflecting increased activity of the pineal gland. Interestingly, the same nighttime rise in melatonin levels occurs in people as well, regulating our sleep cycles and causing us to get sleepy at night even though we might try to stay awake. The persistence of these high levels at the wrong time is a major cause of jet lag.

Circadian rhythms are essential to trout. Circadian cycles regulate feeding activity, resting times, and other daily cyclical activities, synchronizing cycles of activity to light cycles in the environment. The pineal gland functions in place of an internal clock, coordinating the trout's biorhythm with the ebb and flow of the river.

The overall secretion of melatonin also varies on a seasonal basis and helps regulate seasonal rhythms in trout. The seasons are hallmarked by changing photoperiods—the relative length of day and night—which is detected by the pineal gland. The coordination of seasonal rhythms regulates the growth of the trout, including sexual maturation and smoltification, which is the process of internal changes that prepares the young anadromous fish for the marine environment. The pineal gland also plays an important role in the timing of migration patterns and spawning activities.

If you've ever witnessed a salmon spawning migration, you come away with a sense of wonder and awe. Annually, during summers on Alaska's Kenai River, tens of thousands of sockeye salmon enter the river from the ocean that has been their home and breadbasket for the previous few years. They move en masse to their spawning beds upriver with a coordinated synchrony that would make a water ballet team envious. Two weeks later, the shores of the river are littered with their red carcasses, their strength spent but their goal realized. If it were not for the pineal gland regulating the salmons' seasonal cycle, this synchronized event would never take place at the right time.

WHAT A TROUT SEES

So, in summary, what does a trout see? In the absence of a talking trout, we can only surmise about what we think they *should* see. Science allows us to at least draw some logical conclusions. The most apparent realization is that their visual system is well adapted to the world in which they live and the lifestyle they've acquired. When their lifestyle undergoes drastic change during the maturation process, such as the shift from a diet based on plankton to one based on invertebrates, their visual system changes also, swapping the UV light sensitivity of UV-dedicated cone receptors that aided them as alevins for a more appropriate visual system with blue cone receptors better suited for the new environment and visual tasks. When trout make the next dietary leap from invertebrates to nocturnal piscivory, the visual system is again well prepared with a rod-dominated retina which facilitates night-vision, turning the trout into the ultimate nocturnal predators. Their vision encompasses the best of both worlds, those of prey and predator. They have the motioned-based visual system to be a successful predator yet retain the visual warning system characteristic of prey species. This makes them a very worthy opponent in the contest of wits that we call angling.

chapter five

Search-Image Formation

Jamie Clous and I sat with several other friends on the porch of the North Branch Outing Club one midsummer morning debating the nuances of night fishing. The club's rambling Victorian-era building overlooking the shores of the North Branch of the Au Sable River hails back to a time when the likes of Henry Ford drove up from Detroit to fish the fabled waters. This particular morning was flavored with black coffee, easy contentment, and retold fishing lies. We had spent the previous night drifting mouse patterns along grassy banks and swinging large sculpin streamers in front of logjams, through deep pools, and among other large-trout habitat.

Each of us had a favorite pattern from the previous night's fishing, one that had proven itself over and over. We discussed the importance of the shape and size of flies, especially for night fishing. By the time breakfast was served, we were talked-out and hungry. We didn't solve all the problems before breakfast, but at least we had each raised a few good points.

If anglers could ever figure out the specific criteria trout use to select food, we'd certainly catch a lot more fish. It's all a matter of giving them what they want, which goes back to basic salesmanship, but exactly how do they judge our offering? Now that we are armed with the knowledge of what trout see, a clearer idea of search-image formation comes into focus.

Search-image formation is a characteristic of predators. As previously mentioned, the search image is the template that trout establish for feeding, and against which they measure future prey encounters. Our imitation must meet their criteria or it will be refused. We may think we have matched the hatch, but have we effectively matched the search image?

Luuk Tinbergen wrote in a 1960 paper, "Many prey species rely on hiding or camouflage to keep from being captured. As a result, prey species are often difficult to spot for predators, but predators can enhance their capture rate by looking for specific clues of a certain prey type. This is called the formation of a search image by a predator." Although Tinbergen's research applied to birds, other researchers have since broadened the term to apply to nearly every predator. It addresses the clues predators use when evaluating potential prey meals, especially a template that has been reinforced over multiple prey encounters.

The predator must eat to stay alive. The prey, on the other hand, has the equally important goal of not getting eaten and uses every method at its disposal to avoid such a fate. Most prey species have the ability to detect the approach of the predator. Many also have the ability to flee, and so they try to escape to safety. Others hide, trying to blend into the surroundings. To avoid predatory birds, many moths "disappear" when they land on the trunk of a tree, so well do their coloring patterns match that of the bark. A good example of a well-camouflaged prey fish is the sculpin, whose mottled body is difficult to distinguish from the gravel streambed as it lies motionless on the bottom. Other prey species, particularly aquatic insects, use blitzkrieg tactics for emergence and egg-laying activities, running the gauntlet en masse to ensure that some individuals survive to propagate the species. If emergence or egg laying happened at a more leisurely pace over a longer period of time, most if not nearly all of the insects would be eaten. These synchronized events, called *temporal prey clumping* by stream biologists, overwhelm the ability of trout or other predators to eat all the prey items. These temporally clumped events also expose trout to repeated prey encounters, which reinforces the search image template. The trout are conditioned to a particular food item through repeated exposure. This leads to prey exclusivity, in which trout will only accept a very narrow range or even specific stages of a particular prey species. Woe be to the angler who under these conditions fails to match the search-image criteria—it'll certainly be one of those fishless days.

The concept of search-image formation applies on a large scale to overall feeding patterns of trout and on a small scale to individual prey encounters. On a small scale, which occurs every time a trout selects a food item, the size, profile, color, and behavior of each prey item, including our imitations, is scrutinized against predetermined parameters. This is discussed in greater detail in the next section on search-image criteria.

On a large scale, search images explain feeding patterns, which can be classified as either opportunistic or selective. This was described by Doug Swisher and Carl Richards in their landmark book, *Selective Trout*. When trout have a search image that is strongly reinforced through multiple prey encounters, they become inelastic in their prey choice, which Swisher and Richards called "selective feeding." This occurs during temporal prey clumping events such as an insect emergence, behavioral drift, and egg laying; the prey species gain an ecological advantage, as exposure to predation is limited by compressing the prey activity into as short a time period as possible. It is a survival tactic employed by many other prey species, not just insects. It also applies to scuds during the behavioral drift, which is the simultaneous release of many individuals from the streambed into the current to redistribute their population. They reduce the attrition from predation by synchronizing the event with numerous individuals, overwhelming the trout's ability to eat them all. The trout feed on them heavily, though, which establishes the trout's focus on this prey species and solidifies the search image. When the search image is so firmly entrenched, trout are much less willing to deviate from it.

The search image is established through *operant conditioning*, which is learning through positive reinforcement. Successful behaviors are rewarded. A trout selects a food item; it tastes good and satisfies the trout's appetite, so the trout feeds with enthusiasm, lessening its wary defenses. The more the behavior is repeated, the more ingrained it becomes. Typical of operant conditioning, the more recent the exposure, the stronger it is; the longer the exposure, the longer it persists even after the prey source has dwindled.

During this time and for a short while afterward, the trout is looking for this food type and will be less likely to consider alternatives, even those that may offer a larger energy incentive. As the prey source declines or shifts to another species, the trout will modify or alter the search image.

In the absence of multiple "same prey" encounters, the search image is less firmly established and trout are more flexible in their prey choice. Swisher and Richards described this feeding pattern as opportunistic, which sums it up it pretty well. Rather than seeing the same prey species over and over to establish a narrowly focused search image, the trout are seeing multiple prey species in the drift and are feeding more indiscriminately. You might think of them as more broad-minded about their prey choices at these times, as they are considering multiple prey types.

When the search image is less firmly established, not only will trout deviate according to species, meaning that they may take a scud, a nymph, or something else altogether, but they are also less discriminant as to the specific criteria of the search image, such as size or color. They are more flexible in their feeding choices because the lack of repeated exposure has not reinforced the conditioning of a narrow search image. Think of an assembly line worker who is trained to spot deviations while observing a conveyor belt bringing a constant flow of identical items past his gaze. In the steady flow of uniformity, aberrance is easy to spot. But if the flow past his inspection station were to become intermittent with only the occasional item appearing for inspection, quality control would suffer—not necessarily intentionally, but because inconsistencies would be harder to spot. In other words, the comparisons he makes would be less exact because his search image would weaken.

So the first order of business when approaching a feeding trout is to determine which prey species is the object of its attention. You can't get to second base if you don't first get to first base. If there is a predominant food source available, this is usually, but not always, the subject of the search image for the trout. In other words, in the age-old mantra of angling, you should match the hatch.

The second order of business is to match the specific features of the search image. The concept of search image for each individual prey encounter describes what is important to a trout as it evaluates each food item. Breaking it down, we can improve our success if we know the size, profile, color, stage of development, and any other nuances of the natural prey (such as its behavior in the environment). We can usually determine most of this with close visual inspection.

You may need to collect some samples of whatever the trout are eating in order to do this. Sometimes we get the insect right, but we imitate the wrong stage for that insect, which would be a major blunder for matching the search image. How are we ever going to approximate the search image if we choose to imitate the wrong stage entirely? We see insects popping off the surface and are often too eager to assume the trout are eating floating insects when they may be feeding on emergers at or just below the surface film. The stage of the insect that the trout are eating can sometimes be inferred by the nature of the riseform. Marinaro described more types of rises than I'll ever remember, but it pays to be observant. The small bubble that remains after a surface rise has cued me more than once to switch to dry flies.

Other times it's not so obvious and figuring it out requires getting samples from the feeding lane, which must be done with care to avoid upsetting the trout's feeding activity. When this is necessary, approach downstream from the feeding fish, since their attention is focused upstream. This also keeps you from kicking up clouds of silt and debris across their feeding lie. A seine net held at different levels in the water column will offer a more representative sample than looking under rocks, which while interesting is not as indicative of the drift composition. Don't forget to check the lowest layer just above the streambed; most of the feeding occurs in this layer, but it is often underestimated due to lack of visual evidence from the surface.

SEARCH-IMAGE CRITERIA

Once you have matched the food type and the correct stage of development, what else is important? Even though trout use all their senses in selecting food, they are primarily visual predators and rely heavily on visual input for their search image. So it follows that within the range of trout vision, the visual aspects of our fly and how we present it are the deal makers or deal breakers. Using what we know about the visual capabilities of trout, we can considerably improve the odds of our success.

Our flies are never exact duplicates of the natural prey they are designed to imitate, which means that trout are not using a photocopy of the natural for their search image. If that were the case, no fly would be accepted simply because of the obvious presence of the hook. Since our subterfuge is obvious, the trout already has all the justification it needs to refuse the fly without further inspection. But the hook doesn't deter the trout from eating the fly—meaning our fly is not necessarily refused for what is present, but more often for what is lacking in our fly or presentation. In other words, a hungry trout is looking for a reason to eat your fly rather than a reason not to. It must eat to stay alive and is not looking for a reason to reject any potential meal, including your fly. Instead, by comparing our fly against its search image, the trout is looking for reasons to accept it. A trout's search image has certain criteria our fly must possess to be accepted. It is a list for approval rather than a list for rejection. If we identify what's on that list, we'll certainly catch more fish.

The search image is not always the same under every circumstance. For instance, trout use different criteria at night than during the day for the obvious reason that they can't see color at night. Snell's window and the refraction of light dictate that the search image is also different for subsurface flies than it is for those floating on the surface. Let's look at each specific component individually.

The size, profile, color, and behavior of prey species are four factors that form the basis of the search image for trout and are important criteria used to compare our artificials to the trout's natural food source. Therefore, these are the factors we must consider when we select and present our flies. Profile not only includes shape, but also proportion, silhouette, and for dry flies, impact on the surface film. Behavior includes movement; this refers to large-scale movements such as the ability to move through the water or across the streambed, and also to small-scale movements that make the large-scale movements possible, such as the twitches of fins, the moving legs of a crawling mayfly nymph, or the flicking and thrusting of a grasshopper's legs as the insect attempts to return to the safety of land.

Size and profile are the first criteria trout notice, since these physical attributes can be estimated accurately from a greater distance than can color. The same applies to our far-field vision. Think of a row of cars and trucks in a parking lot; you can make out the size and shape of each, especially as compared to the others, well before subtle differences in color or shade are apparent. The colors are often attenuated by distance, especially if haze or air quality obscures our vision. Can you tell a dark blue car from a black one from far away? I can't.

From their first impression of our fly, it is easy for the trout to estimate its size and profile as it approaches in the current and compare it to their search image. As individual criteria, it is hard to separate size from profile since they are both evident from the first moment a trout sees the fly and thus are equally important. If the size and profile of our fly are off at this first assessment, the fly will be refused long before it gets close enough for further evaluation.

The first impression trout have of our fly will not include much detail since trout are nearsighted in their forward field of vision. In other words, they wouldn't be able to read the license plate of an approaching car but could tell the difference between a sedan and an SUV. Detail comes into sharp focus once the fly is close to the trout.

For trout, color is influenced by water quality and therefore subject to color shifts whereas size and shape are not. For this reason, color alone is a secondary consideration. It is important only after the fly has passed the test as to size and profile. Contrast between colors, however, is a strong criterion in the search image and more important than the individual colors.

Trout constantly see contrast in the natural prey they feed on. Most of the prey species trout encounter are two toned, with a darker color or pattern on the upper half of the body and a lighter color for the underside. Both insects and prey fish use this form of camouflage. When seen from above, the darker color on top of the animal blends in with the background of the streambed. When seen from below, the lighter color blends in with the lighter sky. This is why there are contrasting colors on the bodies of many prey species. Sometimes the tones are different shades of the same color while other times the colors are completely different.

A perfect example of two-toned natural camouflage is the brown trout. The spotted top of the fish blends into the cobble and stones of the streambed to confuse overhead predators. It also makes them harder for us to spot. The underside of the brown trout is yellow or a variation of yellow. You might think that the yellowish underbelly would be easily spotted from below, but it makes sense when we remember the yellow-brown color shift of fresh water. If you look up from a deep pool, the yellow tint of the water is obvious—even the sun looks like a hazy yellow-brown glow.

Since contrast is a strong element in the trout's search image, it becomes an important feature to add in fly design. The colors don't even have to be naturally occurring in the prey species, such as a fluorescent hot spot tied into a scud pattern. There's nothing natural about it, but the element of contrast makes it a "plus" on the search image and, in fact, improves the performance of the fly compared with the same fly without the hot spot.

When matching a hatch, I would rather miss the color of my fly by a shade or two, but get the right size and profile, than get the color right but blow it on the size and shape. When I was fishing on Pennsylvania's Spring Creek last year, a nice number of tan caddis began to emerge in the late afternoon. Searching through my fly box, the closest fly I had that matched the size and profile of the natural was an olive-bodied x-wing caddis with a trailing shuck. I tied it on and caught several nice fish. Could I have caught a few more if the color was a perfect match? Maybe, but I would have caught none if I had the right color but missed the size by two hook sizes or if the profile was wrong.

Although insects come in many shapes, sizes, and colors, the physical characteristics are remarkably uniform for each species, at least during a particular hatch on a particular river. Once you match the search image, you should be good to go. There is, however, tremendous regional variation in the size and shape of insects; a sulphur mayfly in Michigan is much different from a sulphur in Pennsylvania. They may match in profile, but not in size or color. What matches the search image for a particular insect on one river may not match it for another. The same applies to other prey species: sculpins, for example, vary widely in coloration from one river to another. I like to buy local flies at local fly shops for that reason. I'm not against online fly sites, but I think a local tier has a better feel for his or her river.

Behavior is a vital component in the search image. Trout feed on living organisms—grasshoppers struggle in the water, worms wriggle, insects undulate, and prey fish swim. Not only do their individual parts move, but most prey species are also capable of locomotion in the water. Since movement is inherent in the natural prey, it should be incorporated not only into the design of our fly, but also included in the art of presenting the fly.

Movement includes not only the proper animation of the fly as a whole to imitate the large-scale action of the natural, but also the movement of individual components within the fly itself, which includes the materials used in the construction of the fly. If a beautifully constructed fly is rigid and stiff, instead of imitating a living organism it will float like a plastic toy. To appear natural, the fly should interact with the nuances of the current, like a breeze through your hair.

Incorporating movement into the design of flies has been realized through the addition of materials specific to that purpose. Rubber legs on grasshopper and beetle patterns wiggle as the fly navigates the ripples and swirls of the surface current. The palmered hackles of many wet flies and nymphs add a natural element to the fly by interacting with the current. Natural products often add lifelike movement, creating streamers that flow and billow as they are stripped and paused. These little additions can be the selling point to a wary trout.

The large-scale animation of the fly imparts a vital element of realism. Making an artificial fly behave like a living organism involves the art of presentation that in my opinion is the mark of an accomplished angler. If you are to reach that pinnacle of angling prowess it is not enough for the fly to merely look like the natural, it must act like the natural. If the natural is drifting motionless in the current, so must our imitation. Line control and mending are necessary skills for a dead drift. But if the natural is swimming, wriggling, or crawling on the bottom, the angler who best imitates it will have the most fish at the end of the day.

Movement is one of the most important search-image criteria for trout; theirs is a motion-based visual system typical of predators. Predators are attracted to movement—the twitch of a deer's ear or the flick of a tail can draw the attention of a mountain lion. The same is true for trout. The target of their predatory focus is a living organism, one that is usually moving. Whether it is a grasshopper kicking its legs while trying to gain purchase in the water or the swimming movement of a prey fish, the trout's food sources are usually animated and frequently trying to escape. If a sculpin lying motionless among the rocks and gravel of the streambed flicks a pectoral fin, it is enough to attract the attention of a nearby trout. Animation of our presentation is an integral element for anglers and one that is often overlooked, but it is frequently the difference between catching a few fish and a lot of fish. To be realistic, it has to act real; it must catch their eye.

It is important to match the movement of your presentation to that which is characteristic for the prey species you are imitating. If you are imitating a swimming nymph, try adding a rhythmic, undulating movement to swim the fly. But the twitches need to be size appropriate; small pulses rather than large rod movements will better imitate the motion. The same applies to leeches. I know anglers who are deadly with a Woolly Bugger by adding lifelike animation at the end of the dead-drift period as the slack tightens and the fly swings. Short jerks on the rod during the swing make the Woolly Bugger swim like a leech. Angling pioneers also appreciated the need for animation: "Leisenring's lift" was an early technique for adding natural animation. It causes subsurface flies to elevate in the water column at the end of the drift like an emerging insect rising

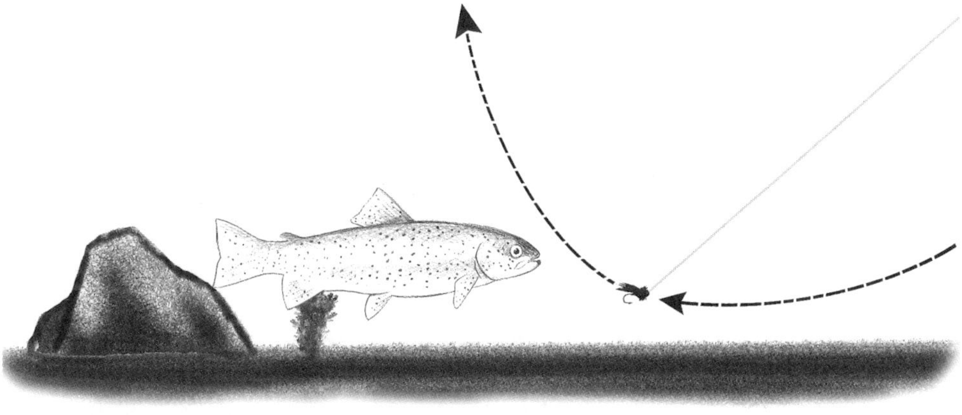

Leisenring's deadly lift adds a lifelike rise to drifting nymphs that mimics the emerging insects' rise in the water column. If the lift is timed relative to structure and likely feeding lies, it is even more effective.

to the surface. Like a carrot dangled in front of a horse, Sawyer's induced take also tempted trout with lifelike animation.

Ray Bergman was one of the earliest anglers to address the importance of animation with his hand-twist technique for retrieving nymphs. His technique imparted an erratic movement to his weighted flies and nymphs. He accomplished this by first grasping the line with his thumb and index finger. Holding it, he then extended his bottom three fingers forward to pull the line down by rotating his hand. Lastly, he held the line in the three fingers as he reached forward to a new point with his thumb and forefinger, ratcheting his hand in this repeated manner to retrieve the line.

Most wet flies can also be enhanced with lifelike animation. After a period of initial dead drift, the current eliminates the slack and the flies begin to swing. Twitching the rod tip during the swing can make the flies move more naturally and trigger strikes from wary trout. Remember to keep rod movements size appropriate—if the wet fly mimics an insect, keep the movements slight. A little jiggle can make the flies move in an undulating manner like a swimming nymph.

Animating the retrieve for your streamer is just as effective, but adding the correct animation is important. Too often, we lob our streamers at structure and strip them all back with the same short strips of line, regardless of the streamer type. Since not all prey fish swim the same, neither should all retrieves be the same.

In other words, don't retrieve a sculpin-imitating streamer in the same way you would a Muddler Minnow. A Muddler Minnow offers a good imitation of dace, darters, and other common stream minnows. Short, intermittent strips of the line imitate their stuttering movements. A sculpin, however, spends more time lying motionless on the bottom than it does swimming about. Sculpins graze the bottom, foraging for immature insects and other small invertebrates by "belly crawling" along the streambed. They lift from the bottom to relocate to a new area, rising in the water column; lacking a swim bladder, they glide back to the bottom once they stop swimming. They have impressive burst speed when startled, but they are safest from predators when they meld into the bottom.

A weighted nose cone built into a sculpin streamer offers lifelike animation; cast it slightly upstream and allow it to sink to the bottom, even mending if necessary to allow it to do so. Once the slack is removed, lift the rod tip slowly, twitching or vibrating as you do in order to mimic the waggle of the fish's tail as it rises in the water column. Drop your rod to allow the streamer to sink back to the bottom. Be careful not to introduce

To effectively fish a sculpin-imitating streamer, be sure to match the way the natural fish swims. They graze along the streambed, crawling between rocks, but rise in the water column when they swim. Their lack of a swim bladder means when they stop swimming, they sink back to the bottom and settle among the rocks, resulting in an up-and-down swimming style.

too much slack or you may lose contact with the fly and miss strikes and hookups—trout often hit during the drop.

Try varying your streamer retrieve. Use a strip-and-pause technique as an alternative, especially if you are mimicking a wounded baitfish. I like spun deer head flies with blunt, shovel-shaped heads and long flowing bodies for use with this technique. The head displaces water to create noise. When using a sinking-tip line, the exaggerated, abrupt strips yank the streamer down, but enough slack is introduced so that during the pauses the buoyancy from the deer hair makes the fly rise to the surface like a dying baitfish.

Animation is sometimes even important in dry-fly fishing, a style dominated by the dead drift. The dabbing action of an egg-laying caddis can be better imitated by skipping your fly on the surface than with a dead drift. This can be accomplished at the end of the drift when the leader tightens to the fly. By your lifting the line from the water, the fly can skitter and bounce on the surface chop of a riffle. Be ready for a splashy strike as the trout slashes at the fly.

I also tie a deer hair caddis, which lacks the blunt tuft of hair typical of an elk hair caddis. The tapered profile can be pulled underwater at the end of the dead drift, swimming like an emerging pupa. This often tempts finicky trout that have been reluctant to rise to a dead-drifted dry fly.

I often twitch a hopper fly when it lands, especially if a dead-drift presentation has been previously ignored. An additional feature of the search

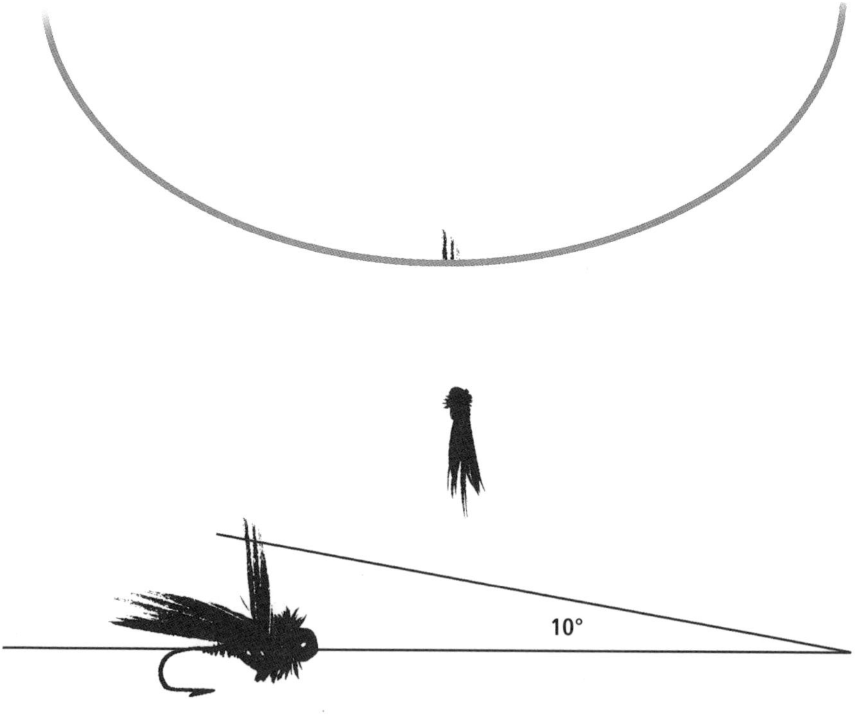

As a dry fly approaches the window, at first the only portion of the fly that's visible to the trout is the lower aspect of the abdomen and thorax, since the rest of the fly is below the 10 percent drop-off of what trout can see above the surface horizon. Once the tips of the fly hit the 10 degree angle, they are visible in the window.

image for hoppers often includes a "splash landing" for the insect, which can be mimicked by making an overpowered forward cast, directed slightly downward to slap the fly onto the water. This often entices wary trout.

The search image for floating insects and dry flies involves the footprint in the surface film and the correct sequence of visual clues as the insect or fly becomes visible in the window. Different aspects become visible to the trout in a specific order. At first, as the fly drifts toward a waiting trout, the only visible part of the fly is what breaks through the surface film. This is the footprint of the fly, which mimics the depression or dimple in the surface film made by the legs and abdomen of the natural floating insect. None of the fly above the surface is visible because it lies below the 10 percent drop-off in the trout's visual horizon, below which light is reflected and not refracted. For the dry fly, the footprint is created by the hackle tips, either collared or parachute style, and the part of the abdomen in contact with the water. For spinners, the wings also press into the water's surface.

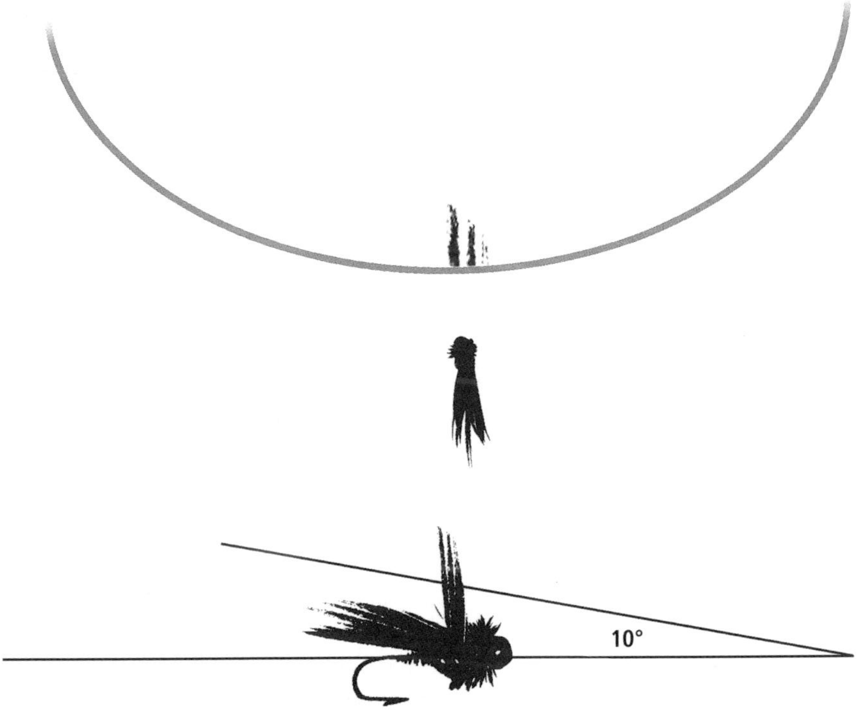

As the fly floats closer to the edge of the window, the tips of the hackle post elongate.

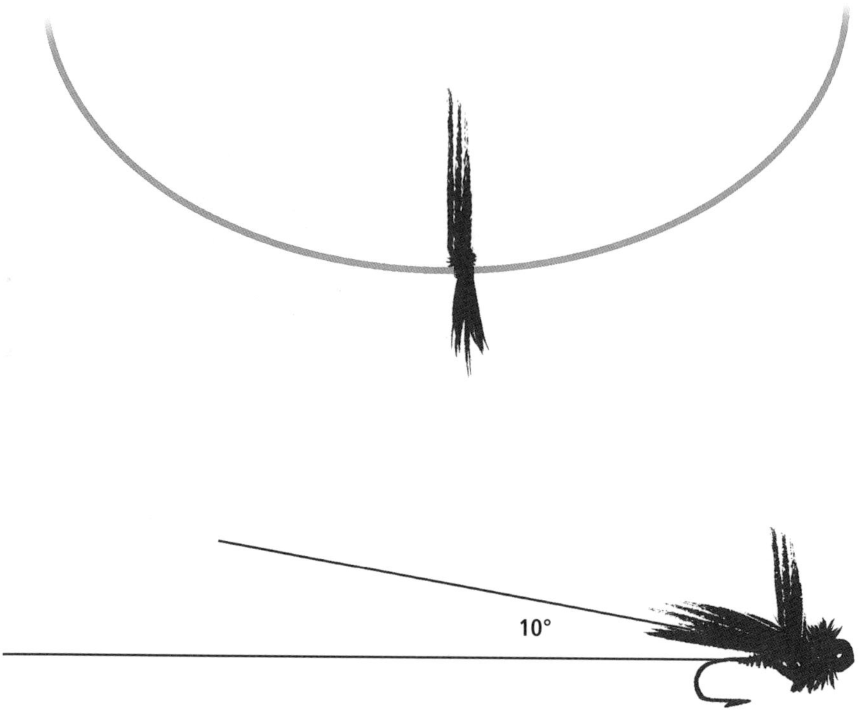

At the edge of the window, the approaching fly meets the lengthening image of the wing tips, causing the fly to momentarily appear larger than it is. Trout often float just below a fly, keeping it in this makeshift magnifying glass to inspect it closely.

As the tips of the hackle post first reach the 10 percent barrier, they become visible at the edge of the window. The two images, the footprint and the wing tips, are separated by the length of the reflective mirror between them. The footprint is the actual location of the fly even though the wing tips appear at the edge of the window. As the fly moves closer to the window, the wings grow in length because more and more of their height is above the 10 percent cutoff. The two images grow closer together until they eventually merge at the point where the fly enters the window.

At the very edge of the window, a magnifying effect occurs as the entire wing, body, and underside of the fly come into sharp focus for the trout. At the edge of the window, the fly magnifies vertically for a brief moment as the two images meet. At that point, the fly appears larger than its actual size and the trout really get a good look at it. Ozzie Ozefovich calls this "vertical magnification." For this reason, the trout often views

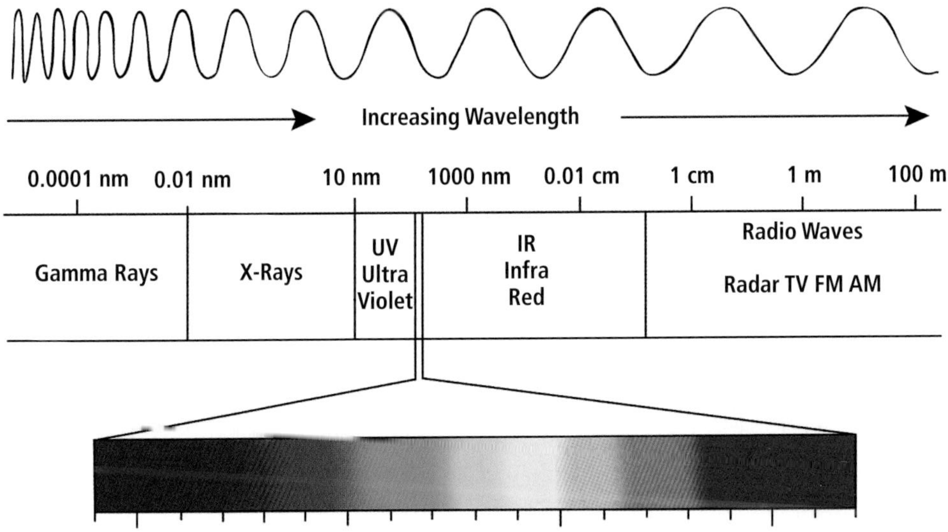

Fig. 1. The narrow range of visible light is near the center of the spectrum of electromagnetic radiation, with the longer-wavelength radio waves on the right and short wavelengths of UV light, X rays, and gamma rays on the left.

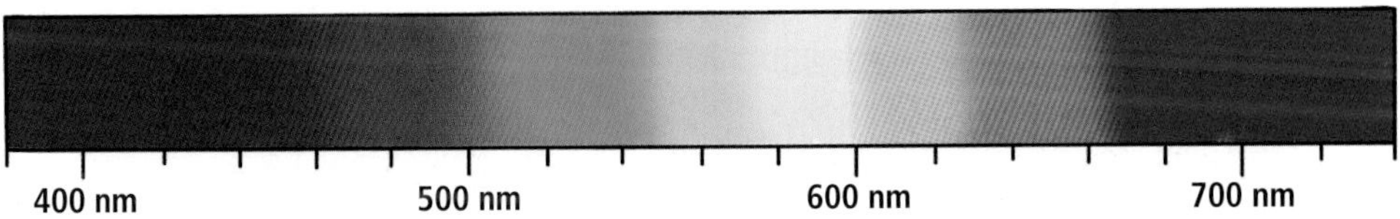

Fig. 2. Within the range of visible light, the wavelength of light determines its color. Electromagnetic energy with a wavelength near the upper end of the visible spectrum, close to 700 nm will appear to us as red, while a wavelength approaching 400 nm will appear to us as violet. The other colors are distributed in between these two according to their respective wavelengths.

Fig. 3. The color shift in this photo, which was taken with only natural light, illustrates the selective absorption of light in the ocean since the warm colors of red and orange are absent. The water was clear, visibility was around 50 feet, and the depth was around 15 feet.

Fig. 4. This colored board was photographed in full sun to serve as a baseline to compare with photos taken in different water systems. Each photograph was taken with the same GoPro camera in a waterproof case.

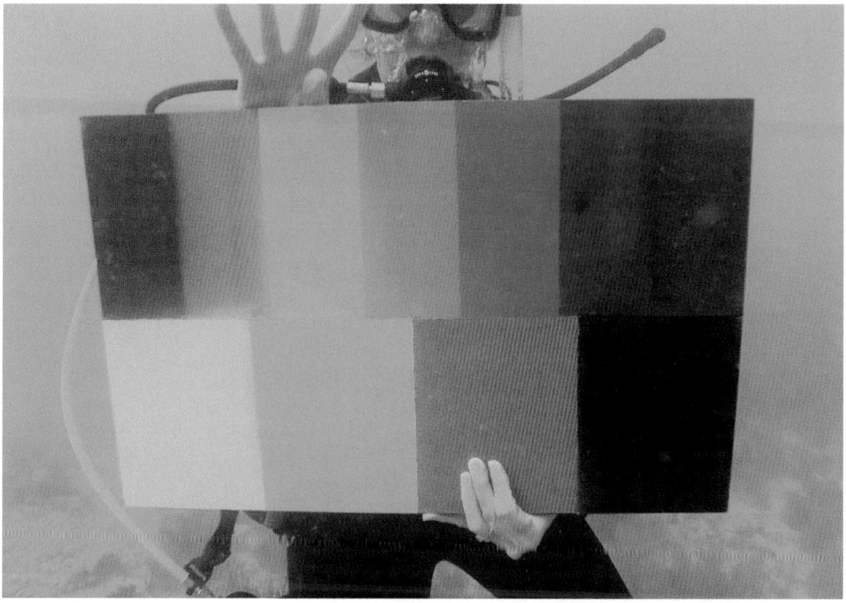

Fig. 5. The color board photographed at a depth of 20 feet in the ocean shows the blue color shift. The blue color, although slightly affected by the reduced light available at that depth, remains closest to its true color as seen on the surface.

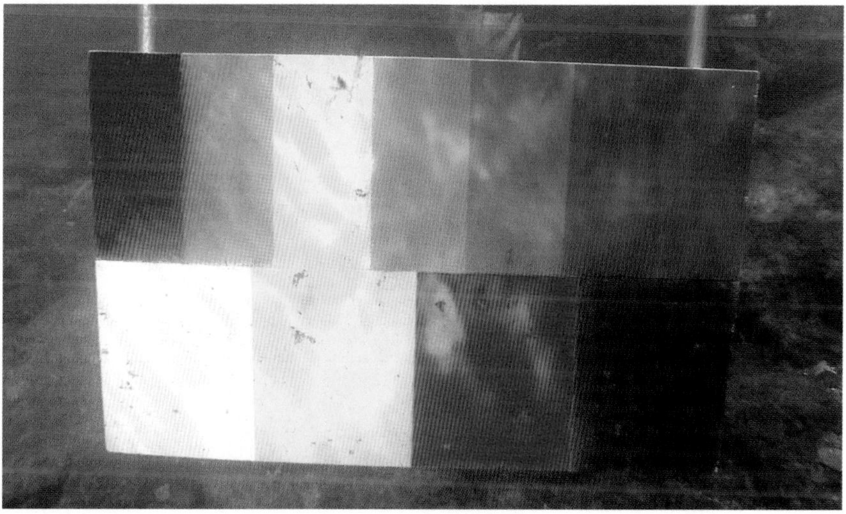

Fig. 6. In Arkansas's White River, the yellow-brown color shift caused by the suspended bits of algae and debris was apparent. Also note the secondary color shifts created by the uneven, rippled surface of the water. Small blotches of yellow color appear in orange, fluorescent orange, and green. In other color squares, the secondary shift causes a change in the tint of the color but appears as dark shadows in the white color square.

Fig. 7. The red landscape surrounding the Colorado River bleeds into the water during heavy rains, producing a reddish color shift.

Fig. 8. The lower portion of this photograph shows the river when viewed straight down from a bridge. You can easily see the sandy bottom and clumps of vegetation along the streambed. Farther away, just before the river rounds the bend, the water shows a reflection of the far bank, the sky, and the clouds. In between is a transition area where both the reflection and the bottom are visible.
JO RANDALL

Fig. 9. Jo held the color board on the deck of the pool while I photographed her and it through Snell's window from 6, 12, and 20 feet away. Each photograph was taken at a depth of 1 foot.

Fig. 10. The first shot, taken from 6 feet away, shows Jo and the board with minimal distortion of either.

Fig. 11. From 12 feet away, distortion has compressed the image at the edge of Snell's window, but Jo and the board are still recognizable. JO RANDALL

Fig. 12. The wildly distorted image is no longer recognizable in the broken edge of Snell's window. Only if magnified and with foreknowledge can one discern that it is Jo and the board. In a ripple below their image, however, the rainbow pattern of the color board is caught in the sliver of transparency created by the ripple. JO RANDALL

Fig. 13. In 20 feet of water, the green color shift is evident. Because green and yellow (the center of the visual spectrum) closely match the wavelength of the water color, they remain closest to their true colors while the colors farther in wavelength have the greatest color shift and attenuation of intensity.

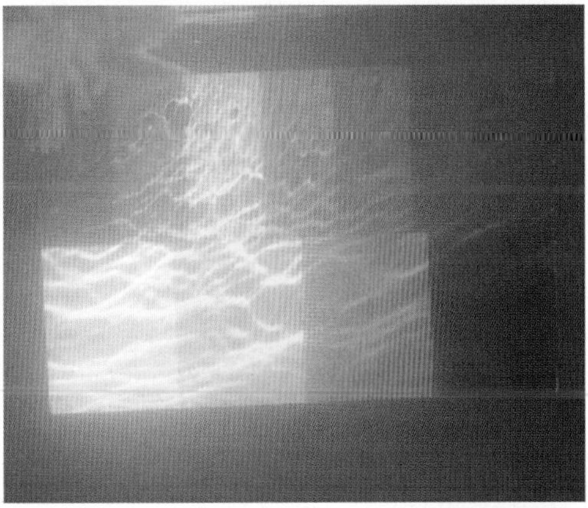

Fig. 14. Color shifts occur in even in shallow water if objects are viewed at a distance. Here the color board is held just below the water's surface and photographed from a distance of about 3 feet in turbid green water.

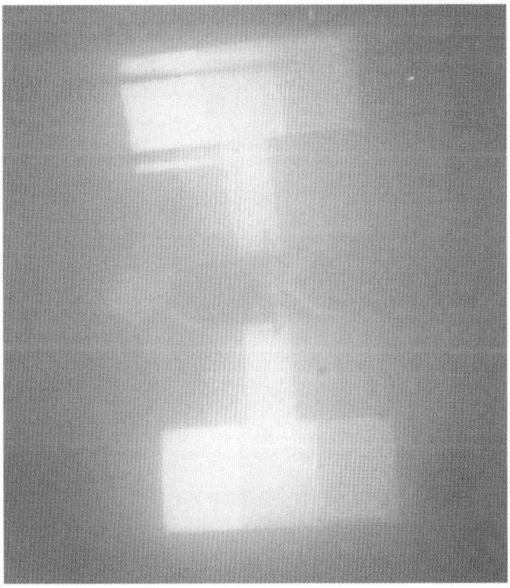

Fig. 15. Photographed at the same depth in the same water, but from a distance of 8 feet, a marked green shift in the colors is obvious. The shades of blue and violet have nearly disappeared; red and orange have shifted toward brown. Since their wavelengths most closely match the color shift, green and yellow are easily recognizable and the fluorescent colors really show up well. The reflected image of the color board is seen in the mirrored undersurface of the water.

Fig. 16. The MW Scud is ideal for use during the brown color shifts that arise from high water. The fly is highly visible in brown water and the fluorescent hot spot adds contrast. DARIN SAKAS

Fig. 17. The Gunni Special has the right stuff for green stained water; its sharply contrasting colors show up well in the green color shift. DARIN SAKAS

Fig. 18. Timber Coulee Creek in the Driftless Area of southwestern Wisconsin shows a marked green color shift by late August from the proliferation of vegetative organisms suspended in the water. JO RANDALL

the fly at the edge of its window to get the best look at it, just as Marinaro claimed more than thirty years ago.

This is the same sequence previously illustrated when the mayfly approached and entered Snell's window in the preceding chapter. Notice how well our dry flies, with upright posts or feathered wings, mimic the same chain of events of the natural insect. It was a hot August afternoon when Jo and I paid a visit to our neighbor's pool to photograph a fly as it approaches and enters the trout's window. The pool offered good visibility for the photos and was a great way to spend a hot day. But it wasn't all play and no work. We got a lot of good shots.

Through Snell's window, a water slide is seen in some of the photos while in others silos at the neighbors' farm loom in the horizon. The blue sky and white fluffy clouds are seen as clearly as if you were laying on a grassy hill, surrounded by a few trees. In the mirrored underside of the water's surface outside of the window, the mottled blue pool bottom is reflected. The window really does look like a skylight in a mirrored ceiling!

The series of photographs shows the sequence of visual cues a trout sees as a fly approaches. Initially, only the footprint is seen. It is followed by the tips of the wing post as the fly approaches the window. At the edge of the window, vertical magnification is apparent as the fly seems to grow in height. Once the fly enters the window, it seems to float freely in space.

Another observation, also captured in the photos, is the striking footprint the fly makes in the mirrored surface before it reaches the edge of the window. At several contact points where the fly dimples the water's surface, small glimmering points of light break through from above in the otherwise mirrored surface. The depressions made in the water's surface by the fly change the angle of incidence with light and open miniature windows, letting pinpoints of sunlight break through. They catch the light and sparkle like diamonds on black velvet. The surface sparkle is, of course, affected by the angle of the sun and is less apparent on cloudy days.

Different flies have different footprints. Parachute flies ride lower in the film than collared hackle flies, which tend to ride higher on their hackle tips. Spinners, with their outstretched wings, also ride lower in the water, similar to a parachute. Because of the similar footprint, parachute-style flies can often be used to imitate spinners, especially in a pinch.

Leader and tippet lying on the water's surface also makes a footprint on the water, outlining the monofilament with glowing light and drawing attention to its presence. This is best seen in the final photograph of the series, in which coils of slack lie on the water in the bottom left. Where

In the fly's initial approach, only its footprint and the portion of the fly that is visible below the water's surface is evident to the trout. The footprint is striking, however, appearing as tiny sparkling dimples that let in sunlight from above.

Once the tips of the hackle enter the trout's 160-degree cone of vision above the water, the very tips of the fly appear at the edge of the window as if growing out of the meniscus. Here they appear between two silos seen in the distance. The actual position of the fly is still accurately indicated by the footprint, even though it is still a ways from the window's edge where the wing tips appear.

As the fly nears the window's edge, the wing post seems to grow taller as more of its height is above the 160-degree cone of surface vision. Once the fly reaches the window's edge, a momentary elongation of the fly occurs, dubbed vertical magnification, which allows the trout to closely inspect the entire fly. Note how much taller the wing post appears.

Once the fly enters the window, it is seen in proper proportion, but appears to float in midair since its contact with the water is not apparent.

the tippet lies outside of the window, it is highlighted by sunlight in the otherwise uninterrupted reflection of the pool bottom. The tippet is less obvious where it lies within the window.

The search image for subsurface flies differs from that for surface flies. For one thing, the entire fly is visible to the trout from the onset rather than coming into view incrementally. Additionally, both the upper- and underside of the fly can be seen by the trout if the water's surface is smooth enough to allow an unbroken reflection of the upper part of the fly in the undersurface of the water. The reflected image disappears as the subsurface fly approaches the trout, leaving the trout to focus only on the actual. Once it enters the cone above the trout, the window replaces the reflective surface and the fly is silhouetted against the overhead sky.

The nocturnal search image is different from the search image for daylight conditions. Color and detail are much more important during the day when trout are able to perceive them through use of the high-acuity cones rather than rods. Color is unimportant in the black-and-white visual panorama of a night-adapted trout, so the actual color of the fly we use is unimportant compared with its size and profile. With the loss of acuity associated with rod vision, size and profile are important but detail is less important and color is relevant only in terms of its shade of gray.

Even without the sun to accentuate dimples of contact points, the footprint of the fly is still critical at night. With night vision several times more sensitive than ours, the dark that seems impervious to us is ideal to the dark-adapted retina of trout. Underwater photographs of floating insects in low-light conditions show the insect in stark contrast against the dim sky, even to my less-sensitive eye.

When fishing at night, think contrast! The profile and silhouette of the fly will be outlined in contrast against the night sky, which is much brighter to the dark-adapted trout than it is to you.

DEVIANTS

There are times when it pays to deviate slightly from the search image of trout. During a heavy hatch, when a trout is presented with your fly among countless natural insects, a fly that is a size larger than the rest or has a bright fluorescent hot spot can attract the attention of the trout when otherwise the fly might be lost in the crowd. The ability of predators to discriminate based on prey size is well documented in many species of predators, including many species of predatory birds. Just like our assembly line worker whose eye is drawn to the exceptions in the presence of many comparisons, perhaps the trout's eye is also drawn to the one that stands out from the rest.

In situations when your fly is lost amid myriad natural insects, sometimes the addition of movement can make your fly stand out from the rest. A subtle twitch or pop to the fly can draw interest from the trout. Sometimes the exception is noticed rather than the norm.

Once such instance occurred to me amid a heavy spinnerfall during a night of Hex fishing. The water's surface was carpeted with dead insects after upstream egg laying. Trout were slurping and gulping all around, but with my fly as merely one among many, the chances were not good that it would get eaten in preference to the others. After a few rejections, I allowed the fly to skate a bit at the end of a drift and was surprised by a splashy, lightning-fast strike. The fly was noticed because its movement attracted the trout's attention.

A fly that is well presented and acts naturally will more closely match the trout's search image for the prey it mimics than a fly that is a perfect match but poorly presented. Fraudulence is easily spotted from afar if the fly does not behave naturally, whether it is a poorly executed dead drift or an unnatural animation.

If something's not working and you're not catching fish, change something—either the fly or the presentation. I change flies more readily than I used to. If I have presented the fly repeatedly over "fishy water" and I have added any animation appropriate to the prey species my fly imitates, I change the fly before I will change locations, either to a different size or a different fly altogether. If I strike out again, I move on to a different section.

We have to listen to the answers the trout give us. In his book, *What the Trout Said*, Datus Proper wrote about search image, although he might not have used that specific terminology. Every time we offer a fly to a trout, we ask the question, "Is this what you want?" or "Is this how you want it?" Sometimes the trout say yes and our efforts are rewarded. Sometimes the trout say no. When we stop listening to what the trout say, we stop growing as anglers.

chapter six

What a Trout Hears

Jo and I stood in a riffle section of Spring Creek between Milesburg and Bellefonte, Pennsylvania, last May. It looked like a fishy stretch of water, but evidently the fish didn't share that opinion. I tried several different flies in every type of water and in every layer of the water column and had only hooked one small brown. I was close enough to Jo to see that she hadn't caught much, either.

We were fishing in the hatchless, midday sunshine without a single rise in sight because a massive thunderstorm had blown us off of Penn's Creek the evening before, spoiling both the hatch and the fishing. Instead of catching fish after fish as we had planned, we spent the evening back at the local B&B laying our shirts out to dry and consoling ourselves that at least we had one more day.

We spent the final day on Spring Creek. Jo was downstream from me and we were separated by the deep run. I was prospecting for trout, seeking a snacking fish in an otherwise slumbering population, and focusing more on technique than on catching fish. I was trying subtle variations in casting and presentation angles. This is my frequent ploy when fish are scarce, so that when I'm asked about the fishing by another angler in the parking lot at the end of the day, I can respond that I really wasn't fishing, but experimenting with new techniques. It makes me sound scientific and justifies how I didn't actually catch any fish. There are usually just two reasons one angler asks another about the fishing: either he caught a bunch and wants to share this with you, or he struck out—misery loves company. On this day, I was totally absorbed in aiming a tuck cast at the head of the run, concentrating on the subtle pop of the rod at the end.

"Jason!" The use of my full name snapped me out of the zone. She only calls me "Jason" when she's mad at me. It's like when your mother used your middle name as a kid.

"What?" I asked. This is an automatic response my mouth makes to buy time for my mind to assess the situation and think of possible excuses for what I might have done wrong.

"I've been yelling at you," she snapped. "Are you deaf?"

"I didn't hear you," I offered, gesturing toward the rushing water of the run with my open hand. "It's pretty noisy."

"I'm quitting," she said flatly. "I need the keys."

"What, I'm supposed to just throw them to you?" Like I would just toss the car keys across the deep run? *I don't trust my throwing or your catching that well to bet our ride home on it*, I thought, a comment that I kept to myself. It dawned on me that it was time to quit anyway. I hoped there were no other fishermen in the parking lot.

My dad used to tell me to be quiet when he took me fishing. I thought it only applied to banging around inside the boat, which young boys are apt to do, but he told me it also applied to talking. It didn't seem to apply to the Cubs game on the radio, though I never thought to question it at the time. Maybe I just assumed the fish, like me, were all good Cubs fans. Like all fathers throughout the eons, I think he just wanted a reprieve from an eight-year-old's conversation. And a little peace and quiet.

If we can't hear over the rushing water, how do you suppose trout hear anything? Are they able to hear the sound of an active predator over the sound of rushing water? That would be like trying to hear a whisper at a rock concert. How do they filter out the background noise of the river? It's a pretty noisy place, especially underwater. Once we know a little more about their sense of hearing, though, we'll see these things are not as unlikely as they seem. Trout have a highly sophisticated sense of hearing well suited to the underwater environment.

A fish's sense of hearing is based on the perception of mechanical waves or vibrations in water. Trout use their sense of hearing for predator avoidance and prey detection, but it's also important in nearly every other aspect of their existence—from managing the current to habitat selection to obstacle avoidance and swimming. Their sense of hearing is really more than our idea of a sense of hearing. Their "hearing" also senses vibrations in the water—not only those associated with sound, but also those created by movement. This includes the movement of water in the form of current and the movement and activity of both the trout and other organisms.

Lacking the vocal capacity of animals that bark, moo, or meow, the trout's sense of hearing plays little role in direct communication; however, the lateral line, as an extension of their sense of hearing, does play a role in social interactions, especially in those fish that show schooling tendencies. The coordinated orchestration of schooling maneuvers is not possible without the ability to detect the movements of other fish.

As predators, trout are able to hear the splash of a grasshopper hitting the water or sense the water displacement or vibrations as a sculpin swims along the bottom. By using multiple auditory organs, the trout pinpoints the source of the sound, determines the direction of the sound, and can even estimate the distance to the source. The trout is then able to move in proximity to the source and close to the prey. Once in sight of the prey, the task of prey capture is accomplished visually. Even though trout are visually oriented in prey capture, their sense of hearing alerts them to feeding opportunities and helps locate the source of the sound. It offers information that can be obtained from a greater distance than it can through their sense of vision alone. Both the sense of hearing and the sense of smell are referred to as a long-range senses.

The use of sound for prey location is more important to larger, hypermature fish that use a mobile feeding strategy than it is to younger fish feeding from the drift of organisms in a pre-established feeding lie. Like hunters who stalk intersecting deer trails, the large, nocturnal trout cruise soft seam edges, pools, and flats to intercept the routes of prey fish moving to and from their feeding stations. The current is less in these areas, improving the effectiveness of the trout's hearing by reducing the background noise of the river. When marauding for prey, the roaming hypermature trout are more aware of and attracted to the sounds made by a potential prey meal because the river is quieter. They hear the sound of a swimming sculpin as it forages, a terrestrial mammal hitting the water, or a wounded baitfish. Whatever the source of sound, if it mimics a natural prey sound, it will attract the attention of trout lurking in the area. How many times have you hooked and played a small fish, only to have a large fish burst on the scene to try to eat it? Large fish can be attracted from well beyond their sight limits by the sound of a fish in distress—to them it means an easy meal. I have seen large fish waking to the scene from far away, attracted by the commotion.

Sound becomes part of the search image for nocturnal-foraging trout and therefore should also be an integral part of our fishing strategy when applicable. The importance of sound is an often overlooked aspect of night fishing for large trout. It may not be relevant to a Hex or Gray Drake spinner that drops soundlessly to the water during a nocturnal spinnerfall, but it certainly applies in cases when the natural prey that our fly and technique are supposed to imitate make noise.

At night I like fishing streamers that make noise; this can be done by including a noisemaker in their construction or by adding a plastic cone on the head of the fly. Many blunt-headed streamers make a ruckus by displacing water during the retrieve. Additionally, my night-fishing techniques include noisy animation during the presentation. When I am mousing, I add a bit more force to the forward cast than is normally needed, directing the angle downward toward the water's surface to slap the mouse fly onto the water. After the splash landing, I make an initial mend with a little more force than required to make the fly jump a little. I'll even add a twitch or two during the dead drift. At the end of the drift, I often allow the fly to wake a short distance once drag sets in.

Fishing at night is more of a handicap to the angler than feeding at night is for the trout. Not only are the fish visually adapted to low-light feeding, their acute sense of hearing facilitates nocturnal feeding. My initiation to night fishing is etched in my memory as a comedy of errors. My line was tangled most of the time, and I frequently stood on it, foreshortening my cast considerably. I never knew where my fly was or how much line I had out. I have since discovered fluorescent indicators, lines, and even posting material for dry flies.

Over a meal of overcooked meat, which is the way Lefty Kreh prefers his meat, he shared one of his night-fishing secrets with me: he uses a series of evenly spaced nail knots in his line every five feet as a means of determining the length of his cast. "At all these marks I secure a 10-turn nail knot with 10-pound test," Lefty explained. "Pulled down securely, nail knots neatly bury into the fly line but can easily be felt by the stripping finger on the retrieve."

If Lefty needs to cast 25 feet to the shore, he subtracts the length of the leader, counts the knots needed to reach the target, and holds it as slack coils in his line hand. His cast, when delivered, is right on target. His practical wisdom always astounds me, but there's one thing on which I disagree: I like my steak medium rare.

When fishing at night with streamers, don't forget to try your favorite sculpin pattern. Swinging sculpin streamers across logjams is often a good way to hook your trophy trout. Sculpins are nocturnally active and trout are often keyed into them as opposed to other species of prey fish that are nocturnally reclusive.

Sounds made by a prey source are less important to medium-sized and young adult fish whose main feeding method is to establish preset feeding lies. A fish waiting for drifting invertebrates to pass by its protected feeding lie, even if alerted by the sound of a potential meal nearby, is unlikely to abandon the feeding station, relying instead on the current to sweep food to its position. The trout's cost in exposing itself to current outweighs the potential reward. It is more cost effective for the trout to remain on station in the hopes that the current will deliver the food, allowing the trout to avoid unnecessary energy expenditures and minimizing its exposure to predation.

But the sense of hearing *is* important to drift-feeding trout in other ways. The sense of hearing, or more accurately the detection of mechanical waves, is important to drift-based feeding behavior for the role it plays in the evaluation and selection of potential feeding lies. Trout use their perception of mechanical waves to detect and evaluate currents, which is an integral part of their drift-based feeding behaviors. In this situation it is akin to the whiskers of a cat, which detect subtle changes in air movement. When feeding from the invertebrate drift, which is the natural occurrence of invertebrate prey organisms in the current, trout establish current-protected feeding lies from which they can survey the food particles passing in the milieu. The ability to detect nuances in current threads aids the fish in estimating the value of a feeding lie.

For drift-based feeding behaviors, a differential in current speed between the protected lie and the current delivering the food is vitally important in ranking one lie above another in desirability. The best lie offers the most food with the least expense. An angler must learn to "read" the water the way a trout "feels" the water. It is not enough to merely pick out potential feeding lies. An accomplished angler can pick the "alpha lie," the one occupied by the largest fish. Sometimes we get only one chance to catch that fish, and so the first cast should be directed toward the best lie.

Living as prey, especially during the early part of their lives, trout never lose their innate wariness. Their acute hearing also serves as a predator-alert system, an informational network they've learned to rely on to stay alive. Trout are always alert for the sound of an approaching predator. Even the stealthy heron, stalking quietly through the shallows, makes some noise in spite of its careful steps.

The same applies to our careful steps. The sound of our footfalls is easily transmitted from the solid ground where we walk on the bank to the water where the trout lies listening. Vibrations transmitted through the water travel far; since hearing is a trout's long-range early-detection system, the fish may have all fled by the time we arrive at the stream. In my early days, I used to wonder why I never saw as many fish as other anglers did. I soon realized that in my haste to get to the river, my heavy-footed, clumsy approach sent the trout rushing for cover. Now, with a careful approach, I mark a good many more trout than I used to.

Different soil types transmit sound differently as we approach the stream or lake. Because some soils are more compressible than others, they have different sound-propagation characteristics. The firmness of sand carries sound much differently than peat, where hollow footfalls seem to resonate. In the Upper Peninsula of Michigan, I like to fish a clear lake surrounded by a cranberry bog. The soft, spongy ground quickly gives way to a floating bog mat close to the shore. Walking on it is like walking on a mattress. My footsteps create visible ripples on the surface as I approach the water's edge. After my early fishless experiences on this lake, I borrowed the deer-stalking technique that I learned in my youth. I now take time in my approach and catch a good many more of the pike that dwell there.

Remember that even when ground appears solid, it still transmits sound. Just ask the boy with his ear to the railroad track about the ability of sound to travel through objects you might not otherwise expect it to.

SOUND

The basis of hearing is sound, which is transmitted as a series of mechanical waves through a medium that is compressible, such as air or water. Like a stone dropped into a pond that creates a series of ripples in the surface of the water, sound originates with a source that first creates the disturbance in the medium, be it air or water. The sound is then propagated through the medium by a traveling wave or series of waves transmitted in every direction from the point of origination. The propagation of the waves is like fans at a sports arena doing "the wave": it moves from one section to another as people rise, lift up their arms, and sit back down as the adjacent sections sequentially follow suit. A different way to think of it is as row upon row of dominoes, where each row falls into the next row—but then immediately springs back upright.

Sound has both amplitude and frequency. Amplitude is a measure of the power or loudness of sound and is directly related to the amount of change between the high and low extremes of the waves. It is measured in *decibels*. The number of individual waves per second determines the frequency of the sound. Frequency is the main determinant of pitch, a measure of sound quality. Frequency is measured in *hertz* (Hz). So think of amplitude as the "quantity" of sound (loudness) and frequency as the "quality" of sound (pitch).

The human range of hearing is different from that of trout. Based on the age of the person, most people can generally hear sounds between 20 and 15,000 Hz. Age attenuates high-frequency perception in older people, leading to a loss of hearing in the upper frequency range. Beyond the upper limit of normal hearing, the sound waves are not detectable to our ears. Ultrasound waves are beyond human hearing but are useful for many applications in the medical field. Likewise, if frequency is too low, it falls below the range of hearing. Frequencies below 20 Hz are felt rather than heard, if the amplitude is great enough. The sound is still transmitted, but without our awareness unless we feel the vibrations in the pit of our stomachs or the hollow of our chests, which is common at rock concerts.

Aquatic animals show tremendous variation in their range of hearing. Marine mammals that are capable of sound-based communication have a much broader range of hearing than most fish, especially in the higher-frequency range. Porpoises, sea lions, whales, and seals all have the capacity to hear sounds much higher in frequency than most species of fish and even humans. Even within the fish family, the range of sound frequencies that can be perceived varies tremendously between species; some, such as the shad, are able to detect ultrasonic frequencies. Most research, however, indicates that salmonids (including trout) have a much narrower range of hearing that is specifically oriented to low-frequency sounds, usually on the order of 100 to 2,000 Hz.

Unlike vision, which requires a direct, unobstructed line of sight to function, sound can bend around objects. For instance, you may not be able to see a person in another room, but you can often hear them talking because sound waves can bend around corners and around objects. Similarly, trout can hear the approach of a predator long before they might catch a glimpse of it. This gives them adequate time to hide or seek protection.

The ability of sound to bend around obstacles is called *diffraction*. The amount of diffraction is dependent on the wavelength of sound. Sounds

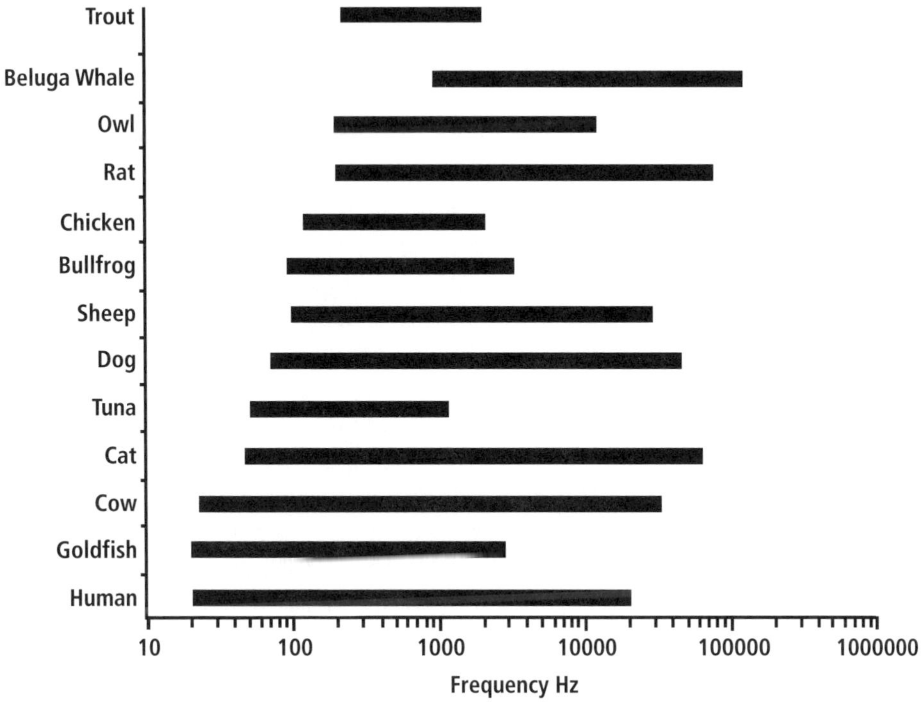

This chart shows a comparison of the hearing ranges of different animals.

with long wavelengths allow for the greatest diffraction. Short wavelengths have less diffraction, which is the reason a thunderclap sounds like a sharp crack of high-frequency (short wavelength) sound when you are close to it but has a low, bass rumble when heard from a distance. The long waves of bass sound transmit farther because they go around obstacles, while the shorter, high-frequency component of the sound is less able to bend and is attenuated by the obstacles. Long-wavelength sounds, such as those made by the water displacement of an approaching predator, bend more easily around objects than short-wavelength sounds and are apparent to trout concealed in protective lies.

That is the reason why our footfalls on shore alert trout of our approach long before our arrival. The low-frequency, long-wavelength aspect of the sound transmits far and wide, even following a bend in the river. Trout hear us long before they see us. While most anglers are aware of the trout's ability to see us on shore, they too often ignore the sensitivity of the fish's hearing. Merely crouching is not enough to effectively approach spooked trout; you also need to be conscious of your footsteps. Keep them soft and interrupt the cadence, pausing occasionally.

The same principles apply to fishing from a boat. Banging and clanging in a boat transmits easily to the fish below. Because the boat is immersed in the water, noise from heavy footsteps, dropped gear, or banging oars is carried through the hull of the boat, creating vibrations in the water. Since the boat is overhead and fairly close to the fish, these vibrations may be sufficient to frighten them. A frightened fish is more concerned with personal safety; it will stop feeding, at least momentarily, which is long enough for the boat to pass and with it, the opportunity to catch trout.

Talking while fishing does not often disturb the fish. The pressure waves our conversation creates in the air are poorly transmitted as vibrations in the water. While I certainly would not advocate shouting, the sounds from above penetrate minimally at the air-water interface and generally fall outside of the range of trout hearing. On the other hand, a radio that sits on the metal seat or the bottom of the boat, through direct contact with the hull and thus the water, probably does have more penetration into the water. You'd be better off placing a folded towel between it and the metal seat to dampen sound penetration.

AIR VERSUS WATER

Sound is acoustical energy with two distinct components: a pressure gradient and particle motion. In other words, the transmission of sound has characteristics of pressure waves. It has alternating high- and low-pressure pulses, but it also involves movement of the particles of the medium through which it passes; individual molecules of air or water are displaced by its passage. Which of the two components of sound energy predominates in its transmission depends on the medium through which it passes and, especially for underwater sound transmission, the distance the sound travels.

When sound travels through air, it does so primarily as cyclic waves of pressure. This is because of the compressible nature of air, which has large open spaces between molecules. Sound is transmitted through the air as gas molecules collide with each other and radiate outward in every direction from the source, but individual net-particle motion of air molecules is less evident. As a result, sound travels through air as a series of pressure waves with little net movement of the individual molecules. A change of pressure correlates with the passage of each wave—the pressure rises as the wave approaches and falls in the aftermath of its passage.

Terrestrial animals have adapted to the dominant feature of sound transmission in air by developing an eardrum that responds to pressure changes. The thin membrane is very sensitive to subtle changes in pressure, deflecting inwardly or outwardly as the wave passes, creating the sensation we perceive as sound. For example, human speech is generated by vibrations in the vocal chords that are transmitted into the air as our exhaled breath passes over them. The pressure waves are transmitted to the eardrum of the listener and are perceived as sound.

The behavior of sound in water is similar to that in air, but with some significant differences. Water is vastly less compressible than air, which means that the individual water molecules are much closer together than are the molecules of air. In other words, there is less space between them. That, and the difference in the elasticity of the two mediums allows sound to travel much faster in water, with a speed that is that is nearly five times the speed of sound in air. Think of a fast-action rod that deflects and responds quickly; once it is loaded, it unloads fast. On the other hand, a rod that is soft and subtle is a slow-action rod and requires more time to complete the stroke. The stiffness of the fast-action rod makes it faster, which is analogous to the "stiffness" of water over that of air, making the transmission of sound faster underwater.

An underwater acoustic stimulus has features of both components of sound transmission: pressure waves and particle motion. Since water is much less compressible than air, the pressure changes associated with the underwater transmission of sound are not as dramatic but are still present. Although fainter, the pressure waves associated with underwater sound can be detected from farther away and give the trout "far field" sound detection. Particle motion is more pronounced in underwater sound transmission, but it is limited in range. The particle motion aspect of sound drops off quickly. It is more akin to vibrations rather than pressure waves; this accounts for "near field" sound detection. To get the full impact of acoustic information, fish have developed the ability to detect both the subtle underwater pressure changes from more distant sources and particle motion from sound sources closer to the fish. Both features of sound transmission provide useful information to the trout.

The perception of sound underwater happens like this: Sound originates from a stimulus such as a mechanical disturbance in the water. This is transmitted by the reciprocating collision of individual molecules of water in a "to-and-fro" manner, yielding greater net movement of individual molecules. Pressure waves are caused by alternating compression and decompression. The result is a series of physical waves, which carry both pressure changes and vibrations through the water. The waves are transmitted to the fish, which detect each component of sound in a unique manner. The trout uses a different mechanism to detect each characteristic of sound; since the two features of sound have different ranges of transmissibility, they can be subdivided into near- and far-field sound perception.

The hearing mechanism of fish is oriented to detecting both aspects of underwater sound—they sense both vibrations and pressure changes. Though they lack a pressure-sensitive eardrum, they have turned the swim bladder into the aquatic equivalent of a resonating chamber capable of sensing pressure changes. They also rely on vibrating *otoliths*—dense crystals, analogous to the crystals of old radios, that sense the vibrations of underwater particle motion. While our ears are well adapted to detecting the pressure changes that are the predominant feature of air-transmitted sound, fish have adapted hearing mechanisms that can detect the multiform aspects of underwater sound.

THE ACUSTICO-LATERALIS SYSTEM

The human sense of hearing is concentrated in a single organ—our ears. For trout, it is not as simple. Their *acustico-lateralis system* includes the sound-receptive apparatus and equilibrium center of the ear as well as the superficial receptors of the lateral line and single, isolated receptors randomly located on the surface of the trout's body, mostly concentrated in the head and face.

In addition to detecting waterborne sound waves, the acustico-lateralis system also provides the trout information about gravity, angular acceleration, water flow, and equilibrium. Three main organs play a role in the acustico-lateralis system: the inner ear, the lateral line (in conjunction with other superficial "motion detectors"), and the swim bladder. Even though fish smoothly integrate information from all receptive sources, it is helpful for the sake of simplicity to consider them separately.

The Inner Ear

Lacking an eardrum, trout have no need for the external part of the ear most vertebrates rely on to collect sound waves or an ear canal to funnel those waves toward the eardrum. For animals such as deer and cats, the large pinna is the most visible part of the ear external to the skull. It stands erect and ready to gather sound waves, amplifying and directing them to the eardrum. The hearing mechanism is much different for fish—trout don't even have an external opening for the ear, much less a pinna!

The trout's inner ear is embedded in the skull of the fish, close to the brain on either side of the head. The upper part of the inner ear has three fluid-filled canals arranged along each of the three dimensional planes, x, y, and z. Analogous to a gyroscope, hairlike receptors at the base of each canal detect angular accelerations and decelerations of the fluid within the canals as the fish turns.

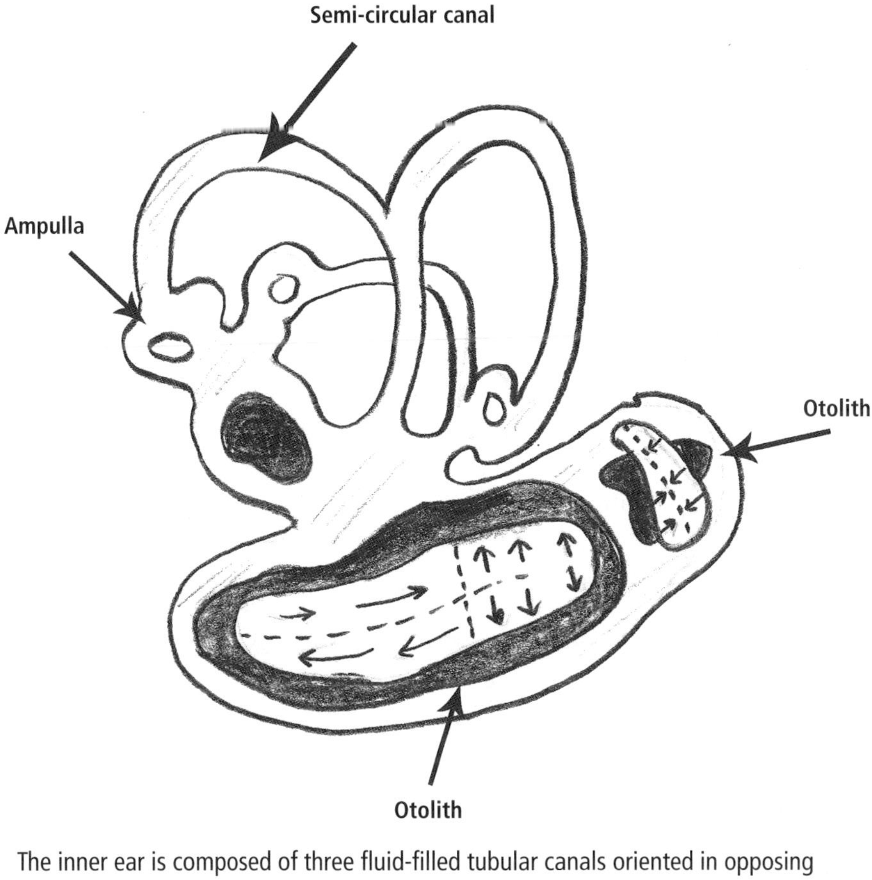

The inner ear is composed of three fluid-filled tubular canals oriented in opposing dimensional directions that act as a miniature gyroscope. Otoliths, sensitive to vibrations, rest on the tips of cilia that extend from the neuromasts lining the chamber in the lower part of the inner ear.

The lower portion of the inner ear contains stonelike calcifications called otoliths. Some fish species have two otoliths in each inner ear, but most have three. With two inner ears, therefore, most fish have six otoliths. Like the canals in the upper portion of the inner ear, the slightly oblong otoliths are oriented at right angles to each other, roughly corresponding to the three dimensional planes. Each otolith is suspended in a fluid-filled chamber lined with sound receptor cells called *neuromasts*.

The neuromast is the receptor cell of the fish's sense of hearing, serving both the inner ear and the lateral line. At the base of each neuromast, nerves originate to connect the cell to the brain. At the top of each nerve, tiny hairlike extensions called *cilia* project upward from the cell. Surrounded by neuromasts, the otolith rests on the tips of the cilia. Like miniature antennae, the cilia are sensitive to any deflection associated with sound.

Early crystal radios used the same principle in detecting radio waves. A crystalline mineral, often lead sulfite, resonates in a sound field, which can be detected by lightly touching a fine wire to the mineral's surface. If amplified, the sound can be heard through headphones. In the early years of broadcast radio, simple crystal sets were effective for receiving local signals but became obsolete with improved technology. In the case of trout, the otolith is analogous to the crystal and the neuromast is the equivalent of the fine wire that contacts it. In both cases, near-field sound vibrations are heard.

Vibrations within the water transmit easily and essentially unchanged through the trout's body, which is also mostly water, and are conducted to the inner ear. When the trout is within a sound field, the movement of the heavier otolith suspended in liquid of the chamber lags behind that of the surrounding tissue in response to the sound vibrations. The difference in movement between the otolith suspended in fluid and the neuromasts that surround it deflects the cilia on the neuromast receptor cells, sending impulses to the brain that are registered as sound.

The disproportionate movement and vibration of the otolith allows the neuromasts of the inner ear to detect low-frequency vibrations associated with the particle motion of underwater sound transmission. These vibrations are not transmitted very far in water and fade out quickly. They originate from a source close to the fish and provide near-field sound perception, which is sound generated by sources close to the fish's position.

Rather than projecting straight upward, the cilia of the neuromasts that are in contact with the otoliths are angled in such a way that the cilia

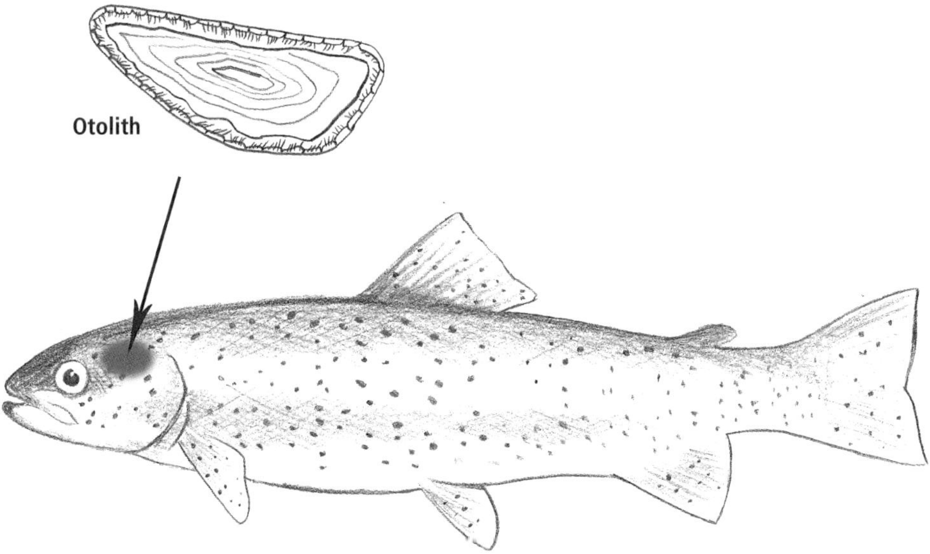

The otoliths, suspended in fluid, rest on the tips of the cilia projecting upward from the neuromasts that line the chamber. Nerves collect information from neuromasts to form the auditory nerve, which sends information to the brain.

of adjacent receptors are oriented in opposing directions. The directional alignment of cilia in conjunction with the overall orientation of the otoliths gives directional and distance information to the trout. By interpreting the movement of the otolith by the specific receptors it activates, the trout knows the direction of the sound source as well as the approximate distance to it. For instance, a sound originating from the left side of the fish triggers a pattern of movement in the otoliths, engaging specific neuromasts by deflecting the cilia. The trout then recognizes this as originating from a left-side sound source.

Our hearing system triangulates the source of a sound by comparing the sound intensity in each ear, which gives a rough idea as to direction and distance. The trout's hearing system of vibrating otoliths, especially combined with information gathered from the lateral line, allows a more precise determination of direction and distance. So accurate, in fact, that it can augment the trout's vision-based feeding mechanism, with hearing used to detect and approximate long-range feeding opportunities.

The otolith in the inner ear responds not only to sound, but also to linear acceleration and gravity. This is possible because the otolith, which is denser than the tissues that surround it, reacts to the forces of movement.

Working in combination with the semicircular canals in the upper portion of the inner ear, it provides the trout balance and equilibrium. Trout are aware of up or down, side-to-side, and forward and backward movements of their bodies. Information from these receptors not only provides a sense of equilibrium to the trout, but also aids in spatial orientation in a three-dimensional world. For instance, the force of gravity is detected, allowing the trout to remain upright in the water.

The same apparatus in your inner ear detects the movement of your body even when your eyes are closed. In fact, motion sickness is caused by a mismatch between the movements your inner ear senses and the lack of movement in the visual image your eyes are seeing. If you are fishing on the open water on a rough day and feel a little nauseous, the worst place to be is inside the cabin where your eyes don't register the boat's movement. Instead, go outside and look at the horizon. Then, relative to the horizon, your eyes will perceive the motion your ears already detect and the mismatch is eliminated, which lessens the effect of the motion sickness.

Otoliths are formed gradually over the lifetime of the fish. They are largely made of calcium carbonate but also contain trace elements from the water in which the fish lives. Since the rate of deposition of calcium in the otolith varies with the growth of the trout—it's slower in the winter and more rapid in the spring—the uneven accumulation of minerals results in ringlike layers in the otolith. The pattern of rings are analogous to the rings of a tree and can be used to age the fish.

The composition of the otolith offers forensic insight into the character of the water the fish inhabits. Usually, trace minerals from resident waters are deposited in the otolith, providing a useful reflection of water quality and character. For migratory species, examining sequential layer analysis of the otoliths allows biologists to tell how old the fish was when it traveled through different water systems.

The Swim Bladder

The swim bladder accounts for up to 7 percent of the total body volume in most fish. It lies below the dense vertebral spine, which for most fish is the approximate center of gravity. The resulting mismatch between the center of buoyancy and the center of mass creates hydrodynamic instability, rather than adding stability as was once thought. The result, however, is a fish capable of quick movements and fast turns, ducking and weaving like a jet plane in a dogfight. Like a modern jet fighter with aerodynamic instability built into the design, hydrodynamic stability in the fish is sacrificed to increase maneuverability, which improves prey-capture success and evasiveness from predators.

The trout must make constant corrective "trim" movements to offset its inherent instability; the flick of a fin or a swish of the tail adjusts for pitch, roll, and yaw, which are three dimensions of deviation associated with hydrodynamic (and aerodynamic) instability. Fish are always fighting the tendency to roll belly-up, which dead fish do immediately upon their demise because of the low center of buoyancy relative to the center of mass.

The primary role of the fish's swim bladder is buoyancy regulation. The bladder is an air-filled sac to which air can be added or removed according to the depth of the fish. Achieving *neutral buoyancy* allows the fish to maintain a constant depth in the water without actively swimming. In biological terms, the swim bladder provides static lift, as opposed to the active lift that occurs through active swimming movements. Not all fish have swim bladders, but most boney fish with rays in their fins do, including trout. The exceptions are some of the bottom-dwelling species such as sculpin and the cartilaginous fish such as sharks, skates, and rays. Lacking a swim bladder, these fish must actively swim to avoid sinking since their bodies are denser than the water in which they swim. Swimming stingrays seem to mimic a bird in flight with the graceful movements of their wings. When they stop swimming, however, they settle to the bottom and conceal

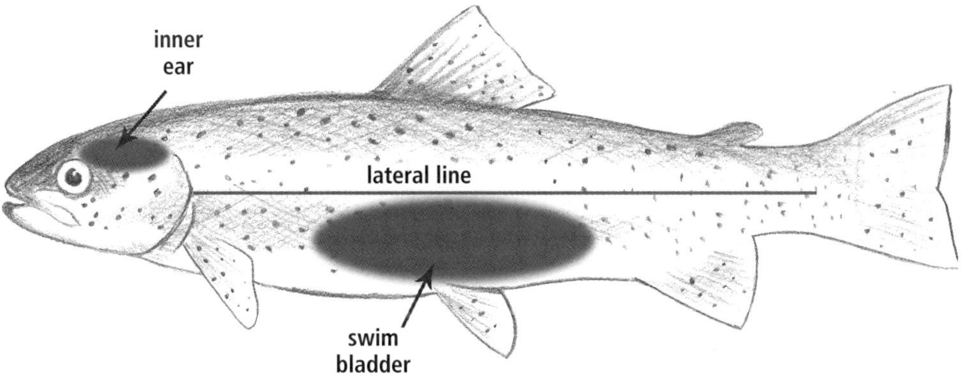

The acustico-lateralis system of fish encompasses all their mechanical receptors and hearing organs, including the inner ear, swim bladder, and superficial receptors in the lateral line and facial branches.

themselves under the sand where they are a risk to people wading along the shallow beaches. If you are shore fishing or wading along the flats in the tropics, water sandals are an important safety precaution. Most human injuries from rays occur when a person inadvertently steps on one.

The energy saved by a swim bladder is substantial to cost-conscious trout, which already spend a great deal of energy fighting the current. If they also had to constantly provide active lift, they would quickly tire. When Jo and I fished near Bellefonte, Pennsylvania, we fed the trout from the city park bridge—a quarter buys you a handful of pellets from the curbside dispenser. Situated in their current-protected lies, it was interesting to see just how little effort was needed for the trout to hold their positions. They were not actively swimming to remain in place; instead they used small flicks of their fins and tails to adjust to the current. Neither did they rise or sink in the water column thanks to their swim bladders, which provided the appropriate amount of floatation for the depth of the water.

Many species of fish, including trout, have a connection between the swim bladder and the esophagus at the back of the mouth. Air can be introduced into the swim bladder by gulping and air can be released from the swim bladder by belching or burping it back out. When fish blow bubbles, this often represents air that has been released from the swim bladder. The connection allows rapid decompression of the air sac if the fish undergoes rapid changes in depth. A lake trout caught from deep water and reeled to the surface by an angler can safely be released without damage from the decompression caused by the rapid ascent. The trout's swim bladder spontaneously decompresses by belching air as the fish rises to the surface.

This is not the case for all deepwater species of fish. We once caught several rockfish while fishing among the islands of Alaska's Inside Passage. Raised from a depth of more than 100 feet, the swim bladders of these fish often protruded from their open mouths by the time we reeled them to the boat. Lacking a connection between the swim bladder and the esophagus, rockfish and many other fish rely on a small organ called the gas gland to add air to the chamber to increase buoyancy. Likewise, air must be reabsorbed to reduce buoyancy. This process takes longer and buoyancy adjustments are slower for these fish. When these fish are reeled in from deep water, the air sac cannot compensate for the rapidly changing pressures associated with the change of depth, and the swim bladder often prolapses through the fish's mouth during the rapid ascent. This is very harmful to the fish and often leads to its demise.

The swim bladder is also involved in sound production in those species that vocalize or make sounds through the action of sonic muscles. The rapid contractions of these muscles interact with the swim bladder they lie against, creating grunts and drumming noises. Most trout lack vocal capacity, but the speckled seatrout (also called the spotted seatrout) makes grunting sounds during spawning activities. This "trout" is not actually a member of the trout family—it is instead part of the drum family.

The swim bladder also facilitates the fish's sense of hearing. In this respect, it acts as a resonating chamber, improving the fish's hearing in two ways: first, it broadens the range of sound perception by raising the upper limit of frequency detection; and secondly, it amplifies the pressure-wave component of far-field sound detection, thus improving the sensitivity of sound detection.

Like an amplifier, the swim bladder raises the fish's upper-frequency range of sound perception, allowing fish to hear higher frequencies than would otherwise be possible. The swim bladder is a fibrous membrane with a large surface area that vibrates in response to sound. Because of the close proximity of the forward aspect of the swim bladder to the inner ear, the vibrations of the swim bladder are easily transmitted to the inner ear, where they are detected as sound. A swim bladder is like having a second receiver, one that is selectively tuned for high-frequency sound.

The upward shift in frequency detection is an adaptation postulated to help fish filter out the predominantly low-frequency background noise of the river. This allows them to concentrate on those sounds more relative to prey detection and predator avoidance, which are of a higher frequency. It acts as a signal booster, accentuating relevant sounds while muffling the distracting ambient sounds. Perhaps for fish, it is possible to hear a whisper at a rock concert.

Additionally, the overall sensitivity of a trout's hearing is enhanced by the swim bladder. The pressure waves associated with far-field sound are easily transferred from the swim bladder to the skull as vibrations and hence to the sound receptors in the inner ear. This not only broadens the scope of detectable frequencies, but also magnifies the sensitivity of the trout's hearing. Similar to a satellite dish that gathers faint sound from long ranges, the swim bladder facilitates hearing by amplifying sound intensity, which is essential for far-field sound detection. Like our vibrating eardrum, the swim bladder translates the pressure waves associated with far-field sound into vibrations detectable by the otoliths.

In many species of fish including minnows, catfish, and carp, the swim bladder is connected directly to the inner ear by a series of ossicles analogous to the hammer, stirrup, and anvil that connect our eardrum to the inner ear, literally turning the swim bladder into a giant eardrum. Because of this direct connection, carp and catfish are able to hear better than trout!

The Lateral Line

Often misunderstood, the lateral line has been described in many different ways—sometimes as an antenna that improves hearing, other times as a remote sense of touch. Neither of these analogies is completely correct, but neither of them is entirely wrong, either. The lateral line is actually an organ that detects mechanical waves in the water, whether they originate from sound or from movement. The lateral line contains neuromasts, the same receptor cells as found in the inner ear, which respond to the same stimuli of vibrations in the water.

Thousands of individual neuromasts cover the bodies of most fish. Many are concentrated in a linear canal called the lateral line that extends from the head of the trout to its tail. Most fish also have interconnecting, linear branches on the head that extend the lateral line forward to encircle the fish's eyes and lower jaw. Additionally, many free neuromasts—receptor cells that are not organized in lines or channels—also cover the body of the fish, especially the head. Like a cat's whiskers, the lateral line and free neuromasts enhance the trout's ability to detect auditory nuances and water displacement.

The superficial neuromasts on the trout's body have a similar cellular structure as those in the inner ear; cilia projects from their surface, but the cilia of the lateral line neuromasts are protected by a gel-like "cap." By deflecting the cilia, the neuromast registers sound waves and water movements. The cilia are highly sensitive, detecting miniscule displacements. The information is sent through nerves to the brain, where the impulse is perceived and integrated with the information from other sources. The nerves carrying information to the brain are different from those that innervate the inner ear. Since they detect mechanical waves in water, the superficial network of sensors plays an important role in sound detection, localization, and recognition. But since mechanical waves also arise from water flow related to current, movement of other fish within the water, and movement of the fish itself, these stimuli are also detected with the lateral line and other superficial receptor cells.

In addition to receiving information from the receptors, nerves also carry information in the opposite direction—from the brain to the neuromasts. These signals adjust or fine-tune the function of the receptor cell. Through this adjustment, the receptors are sensitized to relevant frequencies related to prey capture and predator avoidance while at the same time dampening the ambient noise of the river or current.

The linear arrangement of the lateral line allows the fish to perceive mechanical waves along the entire length of its body. The neuromasts in the lateral line are often aligned with the hairlike sensors oriented in opposing directions in order to obtain the maximum information from each stimulus. By comparing the information gathered by the receptors from one end to the other, the trout is able to distinguish the approach of a predator from a potential prey meal and even recognize its own movements and the movement of water. The comparison also allows a directional indication of the sound source.

The wealth of information provided by the lateral line is difficult to overestimate. Lacking an analogous structure, we can only conjecture about other uses of the lateral line. It plays a role in every aspect of a trout's life. Information derived from the lateral line has several applications, all arising from the detection of mechanical waves in water. This includes prey capture, predator avoidance, obstacle avoidance, habitat selection, and schooling activities in those species that show schooling tendencies.

For prey capture, the lateral line detects and localizes the sound of potential prey meals. While it is true that trout are visual hunters, their vision is limited by water turbidity and clarity. Even in the clearest water, the resolution of trout visual acuity means their vision is not sufficient for long-distance prey identification. The lateral line, in conjunction with the other organs of hearing, provides long-range prey detection.

Subsurface feeding is facilitated by information from the lateral line, providing a means of prey detection and evaluation. A swimming fish sends cyclic vibrations through the water, the magnitude and frequency of which offer clues as to its size. I am reminded of a scene from the movie *The Hunt for Red October* in which the sonar man determines the type of enemy submarine by listening to its acoustic signature through his headphones. Each vessel can be categorized by auditory information from water displacement and the cavitation of the propeller. In the same manner, a large fish makes a different sound and pattern of water displacement than does a small fish. By analyzing the disturbance caused in the water, a predatory fish can estimate the size and probability of success of a prey encounter before visual contact is made. Since predatory fish usually target prey fish that are approximately one-fifth their own body length or less, a predetermined estimation of the size is important; it gives the predator a clue as to the expected outcome. If the other fish is too big, the predator decides to abort the prey encounter instead of wasting energy in a futile effort.

As determined in a study by Horst Bleckmann, surface-feeding fish are alerted to the presence of a potential prey opportunity when a terrestrial insect falls in the water by means of minute surface waves caused by the struggling insect. By using the lateral line, the trout is able to detect and locate the direction of the sound's source and estimate its distance to the prey. This is demonstrated in a summer scenario familiar to anglers: a grasshopper lands with a splat on the water and the insect vigorously struggles by thrusting its powerful rear legs in a vain attempt to swim. If the distance to shore is short, sometimes the grasshopper's plight ends well (at least for the hopper!). But often a trout, as if following a laser tracking beam, pinpoints the area. Initially attracted by the splash landing, trout can also hear the flailing insect. With neuromasts that are fine-tuned to the sound frequency of the struggling insect, the trout are able to distinguish the noises made by the prey in spite of the ambient river noise. For prey detection, the lateral line serves as a proximity detector, much like a cat's whiskers, except these "whiskers" can be fine-tuned to the specific sounds of prey.

While bass fishing in a friend's pond in early June, I caught several small bluegill that barely bent the rod. The exception was one tenacious little fish that when hooked scurried toward a cluster of lily pads only to dodge toward deeper water at the last moment because a large bass crashed through the lilies. The bass heard the struggling fish from a distance of four or five yards and cut a wake as it approached. Even though the turbid water and dense vegetation prohibited the bass from visually identifying the hooked fish, its struggles served as a homing beacon. The bluegill, however, had already begun to flee before the bass became visible, having been alerted by the bow wave created by the approaching predator. Neither fish could have seen the other through the dense vegetation that separated them, but both knew of the other's presence.

Likewise, trout can also hear the sounds of approaching predators. Mechanical waves arise not only from sound but also from water displacement created by movement. A fish moving through the water generates

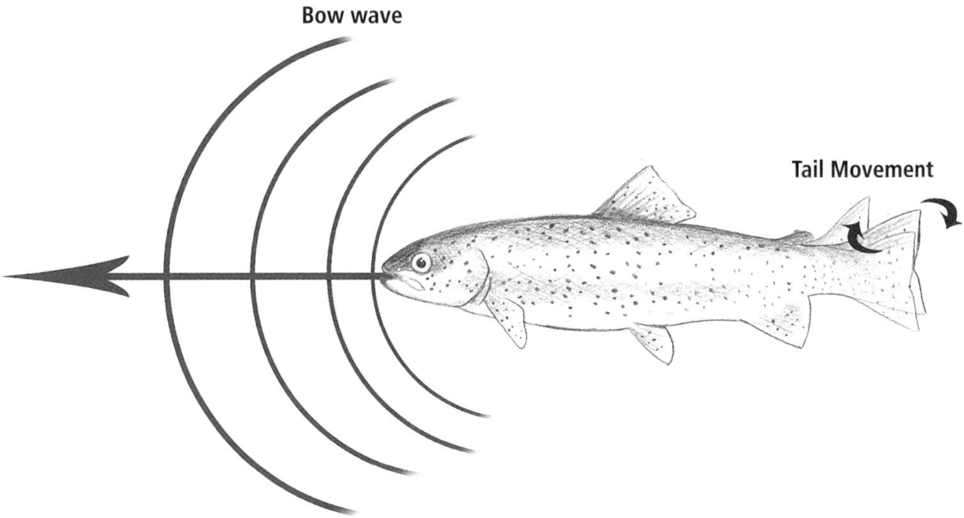

Both the tail vibrations and bow wake created by the movement of a fish betray its presence to other fish in the vicinity, alerting the smaller fish to a potential predator.

a strong bow wave ahead of it and series of eddies and vortices behind it. The water displacement from the bow wave heralds the fish's approach while water disturbances in its wake testify to its passing. Both are detectable to the neuromasts on the surface of a trout's body. If a large predatory fish is cruising through the territory, smaller fish are aware of its presence, even without seeing it.

Piscivorous fish can actually track the wake of a prey fish by following the turbulence in the water made by the recent disturbance. Recent studies show that catfish follow prey wakes for up to ten seconds after the prey fish has passed using only the lateral line, accurately tracking the three-dimensional swim path of the prey for a distance of more than fifty-five times their body length before overtaking the prey. This experiment was done without visual input to the catfish and underscores the importance of the lateral line to feeding strategies. Tracking a prey wake would obviously be impaired by current, with stronger current erasing the signature faster than slow current.

Trout also use the lateral line while swimming to avoid hitting obstacles. In a process known to researchers as *hydrodynamic imaging*, fish are able to detect the presence of obstacles, other fish, and prey using only the lateral line. Sensing the disruption to the flow field of water, which is the water-filled space around their bodies, trout are able to discern an accurate map of objects within their immediate surroundings. Many of the studies on the lateral line involve Mexican blind cavefish since those fish lack visual input. Relying exclusively on the lateral line, the cavefish sense the presence of obstacles and objects close to them by recognizing changes in the flow of water around their bodies, forming a hydrodynamic image. Using the entire length of the lateral line, they detect minute disturbances in the flow of water caused by objects in it. For instance, they can swim rapidly and unknowingly toward the wall of the cave, but will slow as they approach it and glide past without hitting it, even though they are blind. The wall rebounds minute shock waves from the bow wave created by the fish, which are detected by the fish as it nears the wall. In experimental conditions, the fish use flow-field distortions caused by proximate obstacles to sense their surroundings and move with confidence through elaborate grids designed by researchers.

The lateral line also enables habitat selection, including the choice of feeding lies. Based on information provided by the lateral line through sensitivity to water flow and turbulence, trout evaluate and select an appropriate feeding lie. Choosing the best feeding lie is vital to trout survivability. The lies are allocated based on dominance, with each trout occupying the best feeding position it can actively defend against challengers. An optimum feeding lie is one that offers a current differential—in other words, a current-protected position from which to survey passing food items in the current. The best feeding lies offer the most food with the least effort in procuring it. Since the current differential cannot always be seen—it would be analogous to "seeing" wind—it must be detected through other means. Comparing information from the lateral line on each side of the body, trout are able to optimize the current differential.

In one study, brook trout were able to hold in an ideal lie without visual input. If the lateral line was impaired by the researchers, the brook trout lost the ability to hold in current. They lost the ability to make the tiny corrections needed to maintain their precarious position along the very edge of fast water and were swept away. They were no longer able to detect the seam that lies between the fast current and the soft-pocket holding position. Trout are able to hold in current-protected lies through the use of the lateral line without visual input, but they cannot hold in the same lie using only visual input without the use of the lateral line.

The trout's ability to discern current enables it to move efficiently through the stream and avoid wasting energy fighting the strength of the

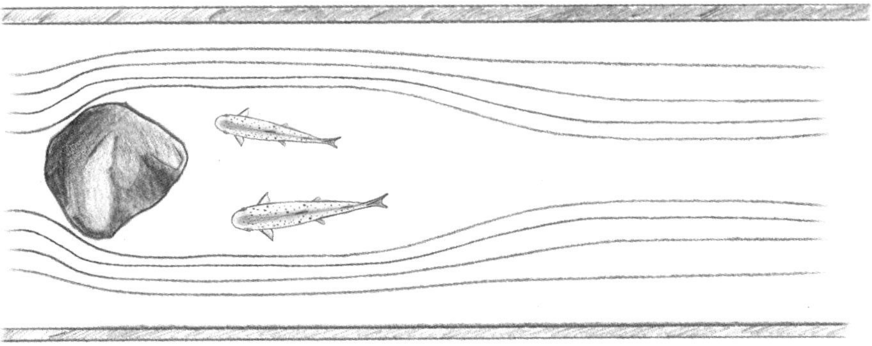

Using the lateral line, trout are able to maintain positions in feeding lies on the very edge of current—saving energy on the soft-water side of the current seam while the food passes by in the main flow, often at a speed many times the strength of their lie.

current. Since tremendous variation in flow speed is a feature of moving water, fish are able to select pathways that offer less resistance to movement. Observe how trout move; they don't usually swim in the midcurrent section of the vertical water column, for it is there that the strongest current is found. Near the bottom, friction between the water and the streambed causes the strength of the current to be a fraction of the fastest current. When trout swim upstream, they slide along the bottom, hugging the streambed as closely as possible.

The lateral line is also important for schooling behavior in those species that school. Observing the manner in which a school of fish seems to move as one is an impressive sight. The amazing synchrony of movement and responsiveness of large numbers of fish is remarkable, not only in respect to uniform speed of swimming and individual spacing, but also in the execution of complicated defensive maneuvers that require each individual to instantly react to changes in speed and direction simultaneously.

Schooling fish use the lateral line as well as visual input to maintain the integrity of their formation. Visually impaired fish are still able to swim in schools, holding a uniform position relative to their neighbors; without the lateral line, they seemed to lose their bearings. School structure and dynamics depend upon the sense of sight and the lateral line. Vision is important for maintaining the position and the angle between fish. Sensory input from the lateral line is primarily important for monitoring the swimming speed and direction of travel.

WHAT A TROUT "HEARS"

When considering what trout hear, it is important to remember that their sense of hearing is much different from ours. In fact, biologists no longer describe their hearing as that, referring to it instead as *mechanoreception*, which more accurately describes the perception of mechanical waves. Since mechanical waves arise from any disturbance in the water, mechanoreception combines the sense of hearing with the ability to perceive water displacement through the lateral line and individual receptors scattered over the surface of the trout's bodies. So, it is difficult to separate what is heard with the ears and what is "heard" with the lateral line and superficial individual receptors.

There has always been concern among biologists about the redundancy or functional overlap between the inner ear and the lateral line. Usually, given the efficiency of evolution, only one mechanism develops for each sensory modality in each species. Because of the inefficiency of functional overlap, dual mechanisms are rare. But most modern researchers agree that the lateral line facilitates different behavioral functions than those facilitated by the inner ear. The length of the lateral line and the concentration of neuromasts on the head and face allow the trout very precise localization of sound, much more than is solely provided by the inner ear. This improves feeding efficiency and survival rates.

Given the inadequacy of our hearing for underwater use, we tend to overlook the amount of mechanical wave-borne information that is available to trout. Because we can't hear the subtle disturbances made by a struggling insect, we downplay their importance in feeding behaviors of fish.

More than forty years ago, Marinaro wrote of the leisurely rise of a trout swimming just beneath a floating insect, as if the trout were making a final inspection. Could it be that the trout was actually listening for subtle sounds of the insect? Was it waiting for the last piece of the search-image puzzle? With its neuromasts tuned to near-field sound, the trout could be listening for final evidence before committing. Perhaps we should broaden the concept of search image to include the sound signature of prey, at least for trout.

The prey trout feed on are alive and make noise. And trout, it turns out, are exquisitely designed to detect prey-related noise. Except for the earliest stage of the trout's life cycle—when they feed on plankton—their food is animated and mobile. Whether it is the vibration of a swimming fish, the scrape of the crawfish's shell over the rocks, or the waves made by an insect struggling to break through the surface film, the prey trout eat make noise as they move about and interact with their environment.

Adding noise to presentation is not a new concept to fishing. I remember sorting through my father's tackle box as young boy, impressed with the wide array of plugs. He told me the names of each as I held them up and questioned him in the persistent, unrelenting way of young boys. One particular thin-body plug that looked like a fish had a loose bead inside that rattled if you shook it. He told me it worked by imitating the sound of a swimming fish, but it didn't sound convincing to me as I shook it next to my ear.

Adding sound features to fly design has become more common. New flies that vibrate, shake, rattle, and roll at the right pitch will attract trout by mimicking the sounds of a baitfish moving through the water. The water displacement aspect of swimming prey fish has been added through soft plastic cones and changes in the head shape of streamers. With the number of innovative fly tiers, they may someday find a way to imitate the scrape of the crayfish over the rocks or the fine vibrations of the flailing legs of the hapless grasshopper.

Trout also hear us, not only our footsteps on the bank, but also those made in the water, not to mention the splashing sounds made during wading. If a fish can detect the scraping of a crustacean scuttling along the rocks, it surely must also hear our boots crunching the gravel and rocks as well as the drift boat scraping across the gravel.

The trout's sense of hearing is uniquely adapted to the underwater world in which they live. It is also highly attuned to the relevant sounds they need to discern in order to survive.

If a tree falls in the forest and no one is around to hear it, does it make a sound? It's an interesting philosophical question relating to perception and reality, but one that can never be proven. Even with a listening device or video camera, you are still "there" even if only remotely. If an insect swims to the surface of the stream and struggles to break out of its shell and through the surface film, does it still make noise even though we can't hear it? Evidently the trout think so.

chapter seven

Chemoreception: Smell and Taste

Amid the waning evening light, three couples sat in the long, wooden river boats that are unique to Michigan's Au Sable River. Al and Sue Ott were in one boat, followed by Dan Pesavento and Denise Andresen in another. Jo and I were in the third boat along with guide Alex Lafkas. We had just finished a fine riverside steak diner in the small picnic area downriver from the Holy Waters and were paddling out to our first "stakeout" of the night to wait for the Hex, a giant nocturnal mayfly common to Michigan on midsummer evenings. We pulled up along a shallow grassy bank and watched the sun set over the river.

It was Jo's first "Night of the Hex," to paraphrase the title of the old Richard Burton movie that stirs visions of long, sultry summer nights. Fishing the Hex hatch is the equivalent to "stakeout angling." It combines the skills of fly fishing with the requisite patience of deer hunting; there are long periods of waiting interrupted by heart-pounding thrills. Maybe we should call it "stealth fishing."

We settled in for the wait, hoping the excitement would come later. The first indication of the thrills to come was the appearance of a swarm of bugs, in a column 25 feet high and coursing upstream, turning the night sky above the stream into an entomological thoroughfare. We heard a faint humming overhead, and shining the flashlight upward revealed a horde of bugs that would do Moses proud; they were not locusts, but mayflies heading upstream to lay eggs. Their upstream flight would be halted at the long riffle section we had so recently floated through. There they would lay a mass of eggs in the water just before their bodies, spent in the effort of procreation, would fall dying onto the very water that had given them birth.

And if we figured it right, the trout would gobble up the dead insects voraciously and we could pass off our spent-wing spinners on a few of them.

As the upstream exodus built in numbers, a fecund smell filled the windless night air—a rich, "after the rain" kind of fertile soil smell, reminiscent of the black earth that filled the plastic bait tub of nightcrawlers I used in my crappie-fishing days. It also reminded me of another smell from the bait store, that of the cricket box. The obvious odor wafted down from the treetops.

"The Hex have arrived," Alex informed us.

"Now we wait for the trout," I added in a whisper.

And wait we did. Even the normally verbose Alex was silent. (This was the new and improved Alex though, without caffeine and nicotine. The old Alex would have had a harder time sitting still.) Fortunately, we didn't have to wait long. The baritone sucking sound of a big fish broke the still night. Alex deftly slid us into position with his push pole and Jo unleashed a cast toward the feeding trout.

"Set the hook!" Alex shouted a fraction of a second after the slurp of the trout.

"That's not my fly!" Jo insisted, but she reflexively set the hook anyway. It turned out that Alex was right—it was her fly. He expertly netted a very worthy brown trout a few minutes later.

It was a memorable night—Jo joined the "Over Twenty Club," a term our group coined to describe those anglers lucky enough to have caught a 20-plus-inch fish. Hers, at 22 inches, made her the toast of the nightcap.

We've coined a few other phrases while chasing the Hex. "When in doubt, set the hook," is one that is usually followed by the response, "Yeah, hooksets are free." Some of these sayings have come from lessons learned the hard way. Jo got her fish that night, but it underscored how easy it is to lose track of your fly at night and mistake its position. So remember: when in doubt, set the hook—hooksets are free.

The night was memorable for other reasons as well; it impressed upon me the odor given off by insects. Never had I noticed it so strongly. With my typically human weak sense of smell, maybe it just took overwhelming numbers of insects for it to finally be apparent, but this night it was obvious. It smelled "buggy," for want of a better term. With a better sense of smell than ours, it must be even more apparent to trout.

If you've ever watched a hunting dog quarter a field, you know how weak our own sense of smell is compared with other animals. In fact, our sense of smell rates near the bottom of olfactory sensitivity among animals.

When you think of a salmon following the scent of its natal river from among thousands of other scents in the ocean, our shortcomings are even more apparent. Think of how diluted the scent trail must be in a body of water the size of the ocean, yet the salmon still manage to find their way home. Using scent trails, they follow the smell to the source—but what exactly is a scent trail, or an odor? Deer hunters know; most have spooked deer when they weren't careful about wind direction in selecting a deer stand.

Odors are created by the release of molecules into the medium that surrounds the substance of origin. For terrestrial animals, odors arise from the release of molecules into the air. You smell the wine in the glass because of the aromatic chemicals emanating from it, wafting through the air to your nose. Volatile chemicals, often esters and alcohol, are released as the wine is agitated, adding to the pleasing aroma. Wines, especially reds, are often swirled in the glass before drinking to enhance the release of these aromatic flavor enhancers. Because of the interrelationship between smell and taste, wine goblets have a large globe but a narrow mouth, which concentrates the aroma into the nose as the wine is sipped, thus improving the flavor.

That juicy steak smells better than it did before it was cooked because the process of cooking excites the food molecules and vaporizes some of the moisture in the food, which releases more particles into the air to excite your senses and incite your hunger. For fish, odors are carried in the water by any substance that dissolves or solubilizes in water. In the air, volatility of a substance increases its odor while in the water, solubility increases the strength of the smell.

Chemoreception is the detection of those chemicals transported through water or air. It combines *olfaction*, or the sense of smell, and the sense of taste, which is called *gustation*. In the simplest terms, chemoreception is the detection of chemicals, either arising from odors with receptors in the olfactory organ, which for us is our nose, or in the mouth from interaction with food. Because of the functional overlap between the senses of smell and taste, biologists frequently combine the two senses together under the larger category of chemoreception. The receptor, whether it is a taste bud in your mouth or an olfactory receptor in your nose, provides the same function in each case, detecting the same stimuli—chemicals.

In terrestrial animals including humans, the separation between taste and smell is a bit more obvious. It is easier to see them as entirely different senses because of the differences in the physical environments in which they operate: airborne molecules excite our sense of smell and water-soluble molecules delivered to our taste buds in our saliva elicit the sense of taste. Ergo, they operate in different mediums, air and water. But even in humans, the distinction between these two senses is a little blurry. Think how hard it is to taste food when you are stuffed up with a cold. The congestion that fills your sinuses does nothing to interfere with your taste buds, but food doesn't taste as good because of the lack of olfactory input—in other words, because you can't smell it. Back in elementary school, an innovative sixth-grade science teacher instructed us to close our eyes and pinch our nostrils in a simple example illustrating the contribution made by the sense of smell to the perception of taste. Most of us were unable to distinguish one food from another without the olfactory input. Because fish inhabit an aquatic environment, their senses of smell and taste overlap even more.

Despite the overlap, distinctions between these two senses are relevant. Biologists separate olfaction from gustation by anatomical organization; input from olfactory is mediated by the olfactory nerve while gustatory sensation travels through an entirely different nerve network. This is true for fish and land-based animals alike. The receptor for each sense is also slightly different.

In trout, another way of separating smell from taste is by recognizing differences in the type of information they each convey to the brain. Taste mediates consummatory activities related to feeding, such as the pickup of food material and the subsequent biting, chomping, and swallowing. The sense of smell relates to more complex behaviors, with information conveyed through chemical messengers between one fish and another influencing behaviors such as courting, spawning, and long-range prey or predator detection.

For fish, chemoreception is not limited to the mouth and olfactory organ as it is for humans. In fact, fish have four distinct chemosensory systems. Olfaction and gustation are only the most obvious ones and most analogous to our human senses of smell and taste. But many fish have two other chemoreceptive mechanisms: solitary chemoreceptor cells (SCC), which are the equivalent of random, isolated taste buds on the face and forward edge of fins; and a common chemical sense, which is a poorly understood system of free nerve endings that have a weak chemosensory capacity. The solitary chemoreceptor cells and common chemical sense are most highly developed in catfish and other bottom dwellers. For trout, however, these secondary systems are not highly developed; SCC receptors are limited to the external surface of the lips, and perhaps to some extent on the face.

Barbels, which are long, slender whiskerlike organs on the faces of catfish and somewhat smaller organs on other species such as koi, are extensions of the sense of chemoreception. Heavily populated with SCC receptors, they aid the fish in feeding in murky water where vision is limited. Some species, such as the mullet, actively wriggle their barbels into the mucky bottom, while in other species such as bullheads, the barbels assist in nocturnal feeding. They are like antennae loaded with taste buds, constantly alert for any potential food material.

As a solvent, water has the capacity to solubilize a wide range of organic and inorganic compounds. In fact, water is often referred to as the universal solvent. These compounds may be generated by resident organisms over the course of their everyday activities and include saliva, mucus, waste, and excrement. Solubilized material can be from sources within the river or terrestrial material from the watershed served by the river. A lot of

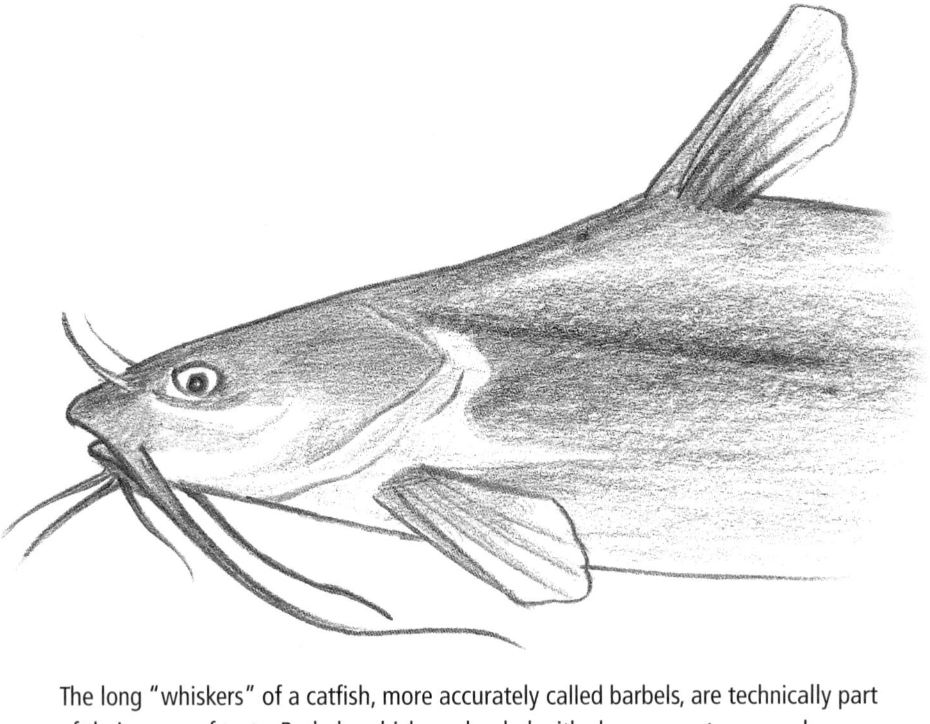

The long "whiskers" of a catfish, more accurately called barbels, are technically part of their sense of taste. Barbels, which are loaded with chemoreceptors, are also present on carp, koi, sturgeon, hagfish, and even some species of sharks.

decomposed material from the ecosystem and the watershed ends up in the water, creating a background of olfactory sensation.

In trout, the senses of smell and taste work together in food selection and acceptance. Living in a world rich in dissolved substances, fish must sort out the meaningful information from the milieu of background substances. The ability to detect the important information is an essential function for trout, impacting nearly every aspect of their lives. It's important for prey detection and recognition, aiding in food selection and feeding behaviors. The trout's receptors are highly sensitized to chemicals related to food opportunities.

Chemoreception is also important in predator avoidance, especially as a long-range warning system. An actively foraging predator is an immediate danger to trout, especially younger fish. The predator releases chemicals into the water during the process of feeding and eating. These chemicals serve as alarm cues to other fish that an actively feeding predator is in the area, alerting them of the potential threat. These cues are chemical compounds that arise from predator activity and serve to alert other fish. Although the cues lack directionality, especially in rivers and streams with current, fish located downstream of the threat will be alerted. Of course, this does little to alert trout that are upstream from the predatory fish.

Chemoreceptors in fish also play a large role in reproduction and sexual behaviors. During the spawn, the streams are full of steroid pheromones and other compounds associated with sexual activity, which are important for courtship and mate selection. *Pheromones* are chemical messengers that carry information from one fish to another, generally of the same species, which is detected by the second individual and elicits a social response or behavioral change. Pheromones act outside the body of the animal from which they originate.

Pheromones come in many forms and arise from different tissues in the trout's body, with skin and sexually active tissues being the most common. They also arise from other resident species in the river. For instance, pheromones regulate aggregation activity and are probably involved in the synchronization of mass events such as insect emergences, in which tens of thousands of individuals simultaneously release from the streambed and rise to the surface. Terrestrially, pheromones are used as trailing markers that allow ants and other social insects to return to the nest with food. For fish, the most common pheromones are those chemical messengers involved in reproduction and mating, but they also include those associated with alarm signals warning other fish of predatory threats.

Sexually active tissues in the fish manufacture and release sexual pheromones into the water as the spawning time approaches, reaching a peak as the eggs ripen in the female. Females send messages through pheromones, indicating receptivity to sexual advances, arousing the interest of the males. Competition for females begins, which triggers male aggressiveness during mating. Chemoreception is also responsible for parental guarding of the redd after the spawn, at least for those species of fish that guard their nests. The female of many species guards her redd after spawning, identifying it from others by her sense of smell.

Without chemoreception, migration activity in *anadromous* species would be impossible. Anadromous fish leave their natal rivers or streams (where they hatched and spent the first few months of life) and migrate to the ocean where they spend the majority of their lives, returning only to mate and spawn. Salmon, smelt, sturgeon, steelhead, and striped bass are just a few examples of anadromous fish. The smells of home help guide them back to their natal river. *Catadromous* is the opposite of anadromous. Catadromous eels, including the American eel and European eel, are born in the ocean, migrate to freshwater as juveniles to grow into adults, and then return to the ocean to spawn. Many marine inhabitants also move considerable distances from feeding waters to breeding waters, including whales, loggerhead turtles, and many species of fish. They are not considered anadromous because they don't leave the ocean.

THE CHEMORECEPTOR

Chemoreceptors are tasked with the detection of chemical substances, either waterborne substances sensed through the olfactory organ or in the mouth and pharynx through gustation receptors once the food item is ingested. Surface chemoreceptors (SCC) are also present externally and are concentrated in the lips, parts of the face near the lips, and in the gill rakers. A few species of fish have clusters of SCC along the fins but these have not been verified in trout.

The chemoreceptor for olfaction is the olfactory sensory neuron (OSN). It is embedded in the lining of the olfactory organ. A tiny projection extends upward from the OSN through the surface lining and is exposed to the water circulating through the olfactory organ. As the water passes through the olfactory organ, these microscopic sensors react to relevant chemical substances. A chemical is detected when it binds to the receptor, which then sends a signal coded with information through the olfactory nerve to the brain where the information is registered and integrated with other sensory input. By the nature of the signal, information is provided as to the odor type and intensity.

The gustatory receptor is different; receptors are organized in clusters called taste buds, which are combined with supporting cells. There appear to be several different cells in the taste bud, but the exact functions of the individual cells are still unclear. Nerve conductance to the brain is through several different cranial nerves; which nerve depends on the location of the taste bud.

Trout chemoreceptors are able to detect four major classes of chemicals: amino acids, bile acids, sex steroids, and prostaglandins. Amino acids and bile acids are most useful as biological markers to indicate feeding opportunities and the presence or identification of other fish, whereas sexual steroids in the form of pheromones and prostaglandins are part of the chemical signaling system of fishes, serving as chemical messengers between fish.

Amino acids, the building blocks of proteins, are key components of food and are used as markers for prey identification. Within the trout's predatory diet, protein is a major component of nutrition. The fish's ability to detect protein gives it a reliable indicator of feeding opportunities.

Bile acids are products given off by the digestive activity of all fish. Bile acids, manufactured and released into the gut of fish, aid in digestion and absorption of the food. Bile acids are reabsorbed by the gut of trout but some of the bile acids are lost in the feces and are detectable to other fish. Just like dogs that sniff each other or the stools of other dogs, fish can identify other trout of the same species and even recognize kin. Both amino acids and bile acids appear inadvertently in the water as byproducts of digestion, feeding, or biological activity.

Steroid hormones (pheromones) and prostaglandins serve as chemical messengers, carrying signals from one fish to another. They not only mediate individual information such as the receptivity of a female to male advances, but also aid in synchronizing large-scale activities. Pheromones are sexually active compounds that mediate reproductive urges and spawning behavior and are detected by the chemoreceptors of other fish of the same species. Prostaglandins, organic compounds that are in the tissues of fish, also circulate through the bloodstream to initiate spawning activity. When they appear in the water, they are detected by other fish and synchronize mating activity. This is part of the chemical signaling system, a communication network that transmits information from one fish to another.

SMELL

Land-based animals recognize odors or smells that are caused by the release of volatized chemicals into the air by the source of the odor. You can smell coffee in the morning because of the vaporization of aromatic and volatile chemicals released in the brewing process.

Chemicals are released into the water in the same manner. In fact, the river is alive with smells and odors, but we fail to notice these since it is outside of our ability to detect them. A predator feeding upstream loses bits of his meal into the water, thus advertising its presence in the process. A female nearing the spawn releases prostaglandins and pheromones as her eggs ripen. Insects bursting through the pupal case in the act of emergence also leave perceptible traces. Even waste products from fish and other organisms not only carry trace markers that are identifiable to other fish, but also attract the attention of detritivores, those organisms who break down waste into reusable compounds as part of Mother Nature's recycling program. Chemicals are continually released into the water from a variety of sources.

The sense of smell in trout is concentrated in paired olfactory organs, one located on each side of the fish's head between the eyes and the mouth. Two nostril openings serve each olfactory organ. The anterior or forward nostril is for incurrent water and is separated by a fold of tissue from the posterior or excurrent nostril. The tissue fold deflects water into the anterior nostril, after which it enters the olfactory chamber. Water exits the olfactory chamber through the posterior or excurrent nostril.

The nostrils have no role in breathing as they do in land-based animals; trout can't breathe through their nostrils. Water that enters the anterior nostril only exits through the posterior nostril. It doesn't pass over the gills because the trout's nostrils don't communicate with the oral cavity in the back of the mouth as they do in humans.

The olfactory chamber is lined with mucosa, an epithelial membrane similar to that found in human nasal passages. Millions of OSN chemoreceptor cells populate the mucosa's surface, which is raised in a series of complex folds and convolutions called a *rosette*, because in salmonids, it looks like a flower. The structure of the rosette increases the surface area of the chamber and thus the numbers of receptors, thereby greatly improving the trout's acuity of chemical detection. Impulses from the OSN receptors collect into the olfactory nerve that sends messages to the olfactory bulb of the brain where the information is decoded and classified.

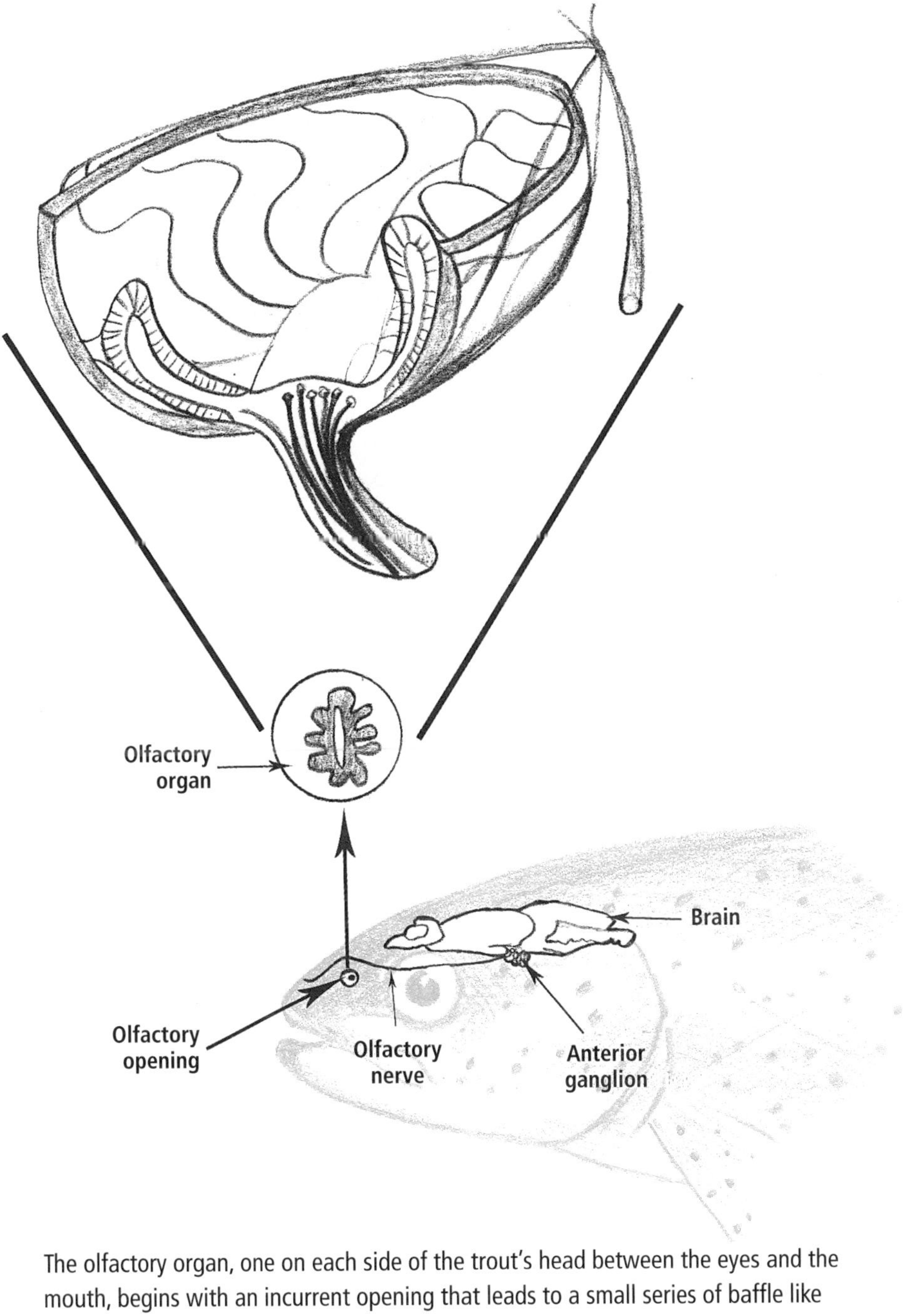

The olfactory organ, one on each side of the trout's head between the eyes and the mouth, begins with an incurrent opening that leads to a small series of baffle like folds that are lined with thousands of tiny receptors.

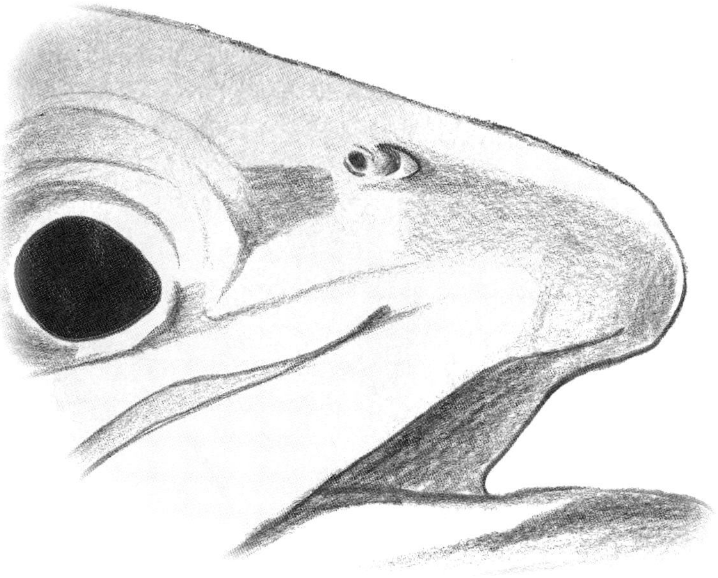

People inhale and exhale through both of our two nostrils, but on each side of their head, trout have a separate opening to draw water into the olfactory organ and one for water to flow out of it.

Water enters the incurrent nostril passively when the trout faces upstream in the current. The water carries with it the scent from upstream sources. Inflow is increased actively when the trout swims or through respiratory movements, such as when it flares its gills to draw water. A trout's chemoreceptors are able to detect miniscule amounts of chemicals in the water. Trout can detect testosterone and bile acids at concentrations of one molecule to ten billion molecules of water!

Trout olfaction also has the acuity to discriminate two or more odors in the mix at a time, which is hard for most people. Usually one smell predominates for us and the other is overshadowed. I've noticed that food seems to taste better in restaurants now that smoke-free policies are more universal. The smell of smoke always seemed to overpower the aroma of food. Trout don't seem to have the same problem, though. They are able to detect subtle mixtures of chemicals, even if one is in a higher concentration than the other.

Even though the trout's sense of smell is highly sensitive, it is nondirectional. Unlike sound, which is accurately located by trout as to direction

The incurrent nostril is separated from the excurrent nostril by a flap, clearly seen just forward to the eyes.

and distance, smell offers fewer clues as to its location. The source can be tracked, however, by the relative strength of the scent. Closer to the source, the scent is stronger. In still waters such as lakes and ponds, the chemicals radiate in every direction from the source. In rivers and streams, the odor is carried downstream. A concentration gradient still allows the scent to be tracked, but the recipient must be downstream of the source. Typical of a hunting dog that casts back and forth across a scent trail, following the odor-concentration gradient to the hiding game bird, fish also follow the strength of the chemicals to the source. In one experiment, an eel was able to track a scent using only its sense of smell. Swimming back and forth through the scent trail, the eel was able to locate the source. The sensitivity of the chemoreceptors makes the fish's sense of smell its long-range organ of chemoreception.

GUSTATION

I don't know what midges taste like, but I should given the numerous times they've inadvertently found their way into my mouth. I must have either blocked their flavor from my memory or spit them out before the taste registered. If you have ever experienced a heavy hatch, I'm sure you know what I mean.

Late last winter northern Arkansas' Norfork Dam was turned off, creating a slack-water paradise on the Norfork River for midges in the afternoon sun. One particular morning was cold but the sun had warmed the water late in the day, causing the midges to bloom like mosquitos on a summer's eve. Clouds of insects swirled above the water's surface and dead bodies collected in backeddy foam. We trailed zebra midges of various colors and midge emergers behind a tiny foam indicator and caught cutthroat eager for a midwinter snack. I was just as grateful that day for my shore lunch as the trout were for the midges. To each his own, I guess.

When we think of gustatory sensations, we think of the taste of our favorite foods tickling our taste buds. Perhaps this is a seared steak and a fine glass of wine made more pleasing by its rich aroma. Our family tradition includes a birthday dinner for the celebrating family member and this is as much a favorite among our clan as any gift. Food is also a centerpiece on every holiday.

Taste is just as important to trout—it plays a large role in prey recognition and acceptance. Just as we can tell one food item from another, trout are able to identify and respond to the chemical cues offered by prey species through their taste buds.

Taste buds are intolerant of dry conditions and function only in an aqueous environment, one that has abundant moisture. As such, their location is limited to the mouths of terrestrial animals since the abundant saliva ensures adequate hydration. But in the watery world of fish, taste buds are not limited to the oral cavity. They appear on the lips, the gills, and even over the surface of the body in some species. Scientists deem these surface receptors part of the gustatory system rather than the olfactory system because the nerves carry the impulses from these receptors to the primary gustatory nucleus of the medulla, the part of the brain where taste information is processed. The receptors are also consistent in structure with those in the mouth. Many types of fish can actually taste food through surface receptors long before the food enters the mouth! As stated earlier, the separation between the senses of taste and smell is blurry in fish.

In scaleless, bottom-dwelling fish such as catfish, solitary chemosensory cells are scattered across the surface of the body. They are not limited to the mouth and barbels. These aid in food location and capture in the normally turbid waters where catfish forage. With the limited vision available in murky water, solitary surface chemosensory cells have developed to augment feeding success.

Ironically, the one location where the taste buds are usually absent in fish is the tongue. In humans, the taste buds in the tongue were once elaborately mapped according to taste sensation. Newer research, however, shows that the location and organization of human taste buds is less rigid than originally thought and that all taste buds have the ability to discriminate flavors to some extent, although some individual preferences may be present.

In fish, each taste bud may have as few as five receptor cells or as many as sixty depending on the species. Receptor cells respond to nutritionally relevant substances, which are often in the form of amino acids. A small pore communicates from the bud to the surface and allows the sensitive chemoreceptor access to the stimuli. When chemicals are detected, nerve fibers that synapse with the receptor cells send the information to the brain.

For most animals, the gustatory receptors seem to be oriented toward feeding activity and recognition of feeding cues, whereas the olfactory sensory system responds to a broader range of stimuli including chemical messengers such as pheromones. This separation is less distinct in fish, but as a whole, olfaction senses more remote chemical stimulants, providing a long-range capability, whereas gustation is more for contact reception. The exceptions are the solitary chemosensory cells scattered on the fishes' bodies; they offer long-range taste perception, responding to distant stimuli.

CHEMORECEPTORS AND FEEDING

Feeding behavior is divided into appetitive and consummatory phases. During the appetitive stage, the fish's interest is piqued and an appetite builds. The appetitive stage is mediated by the sense of smell, in the same way as it is for people. The smell of bacon in the morning makes your mouth water and stomach rumble in agreement. You may not have even perceived hunger until the smell of the food brought it to your attention. As the fish's long-range sense of chemoreception, olfaction offers the first clues of a potential feeding opportunity. Using its sense of smell, the fish begins to seek out the food source. In one study, trout reacted to a mixture of amino acids that mimicked naturally occurring prey with an increase in activity normally associated with foraging behavior, including swimming and even snapping of the jaws, which demonstrated an awareness of the food. In other words, once the trout got a whiff of a meal, they began to actively seek it out. For salmonids, the olfactory system is thought to be necessary for the appetite phase, while it seems less essential to species such as catfish and other bottom dwellers with extensive external taste receptors.

The consummatory phase begins with the actual ingestion of food. Once the food enters the trout's mouth, olfaction no longer plays a role in whether the food is accepted; there is no communication between the olfactory organ and the mouth as there is in humans and other terrestrial animals. The taste buds regulate the feeding behavior from that point on. Olfaction regulates the feeding intention of trout through the pickup stage, which is the point when the trout actually takes the food item into its mouth. After that, the gustatory sense determines whether the trout will shallow the item or expel it. Even in visually oriented predators such as trout, a meal may be rejected based on taste once it is in the mouth.

Since the food may either be swallowed or rejected, even once a potential meal is in the mouth, the trout is not fully committed and can change its mind. Younger fish with less experience will experiment with objects by taking them into the mouth only to immediately expel them. Like human infants who seem to put everything into their mouths, young trout learn about potential food material in the same way. The mouth becomes more or less a tactile organ used to check out things. Older and wiser trout are less likely to do this, having previously discerned the edible from inedible through repeated prey encounters.

During underwater filming, I have seen trout expel items faster than you can blink. Conversely, I have also seen a fair-sized rainbow trout literally attack a yarn egg pattern, shaking it and swimming sideways before finally releasing it. Why the difference? Could taste and mouthfeel account for the variation? The actual time the trout held some of the objects in their mouths was less than a second, which would make a hookset impossible even if the strike detection was immediate. Do trout hold flies made of hard plastic or metal for a shorter time than they might something softer and made of natural materials? I have never seen a study directed to that question and I certainly don't have enough data to draw a conclusion, but the logical assumption would be that a softer fly made of natural materials might be held longer before it is rejected than one made of hard materials that taste like plastic or metal. Perhaps our deception in the case of softer, sweeter-tasting flies is not as immediately obvious to the trout.

Even though trout are visual predators, chemoreception assumes a larger role when vision is limited. Chemoreceptors still function in turbid water when vision is poor. In all but the murkiest water, even in a heavy sedimentary load, the chemoreceptors still function unaffected by the water conditions.

Large piscivorous trout with a mobile feeding strategy draw more water through the olfactory organ in the course of their movements and hence more olfactory stimuli engage their perception. They often like to cruise upstream when actively foraging to maximize their olfactory input. With this equivalent of olfactory radar, they allow the water passing through their nostrils to notify them of upstream feeding opportunities. Like a bird dog that likes to hunt into the wind, the big trout like to stack the deck in their favor. In fact, the first territory they usually visit at the onset of their dusk feeding activity is the initial feeding range just upstream of their home site. As dusk settles on the river, an angler should identify potential home sites and target the first 20 yards upstream of them with a streamer, especially soft seam edges.

Fish are able to approximate the location of potential prey through olfactory stimuli. By following a concentration gradient, fish are able to track a smell to the general location of its source. If a feeding opportunity is available, prey capture is visually mediated once the prey appears in the fish's effective range of vision. By comparing the strength of stimuli between the two olfactory organs, fish are able to roughly orient toward the source. In one study, eels were able to track a scent to which they were previously conditioned, moving back and forth through the scent trail like a bird dog quartering into the wind.

Obviously, the flow of water will influence the fish's ability to locate prey from scent trails. In extremely turbulent water, following a scent trail may be impossible due to the agitation and mixing effect. Like a bird dog hunting downwind, a large trout foraging downstream will have to pass by the source and turn back upstream once a scent is detected.

The sense of taste and the inherent satiation as a result of feeding contribute to operant conditioning, often leading to food exclusivity or *selective feeding*, when trout accept only a narrow range of potential food items. Selective feeding arises from repeated successful prey encounters when, via food consumption, the stimulation of the taste buds reinforces the continuation of feeding. This eventually satiates the trout's appetite to the point that other food materials may be refused. Selective feeding often occurs during insect activities when an abundance of food is available but often limited to a single species or stage. The opposite of selective feeding is *opportunistic feeding*, which is more likely to occur when multiple prey species are available but the overall availability of food is limited.

In considering the sensitivity of the trout's chemoreceptors, you can think of the sense of smell as a long-range version of chemoreception that initiates the feeding desire. The sense of taste is the more intimate version of chemoreception, more up close and personal, since the fish actually has to have something in its mouth to taste it.

ALARM CUES

The ability to recognize danger and avoid it is an obvious asset to all animals. Predator awareness improves the odds of survival for trout of all ages, but it is especially important at the early stages of life when they are the most vulnerable to predation. Like young children who are told never to take candy from strangers, young trout must learn the hazards of the river; they learn their lessons early in life or pay the price. Detecting the presence of a predator while there is still time to react offers the best odds of survival to the potential prey species, which raises the value of a long-range warning mechanism. The earlier the predatory threat is detected, the more effective the countermeasures the young trout can initiate.

One of their most effective predator alert systems is their sense of smell, which is sensitive to scents far distant from the source. Prey fish detect the presence of predatory activity in two ways: through the chemicals given off directly from the predator, meaning they literally smell the predator; and via alarm cues created by the predator's feeding activity.

Predator odors arise from the secretions of their bodies—mostly from the surface film and saliva, but also through waste products and feces. Predators effectively advertise their presence through the release of chemical markers, all of which are perceptible to other fish. The prey species use the information to initiate predator avoidance behaviors; alerted to the potential danger, they cease feeding and movements or seek a safe refuge to hide.

Alarm cues are byproducts of predator activity and serve to alert other prey fish of an urgent nearby threat. Alarm cues have a more profound impact on prey species than do predator chemical markers. It's akin to the difference between a tornado watch and a tornado warning—alarm cues elicit an immediate and dramatic response in prey fish, sending them fleeing for cover to minimize the likelihood that they will be the next victim. So, what compounds are potential alarm cues? One of the most potent is a substance found in the skin of prey fish. Minnows have specialized cells in the skin that contain an alarm pheromone, released only when the skin is damaged. When it is released into the water, its presence alerts other prey fish that there is an actively feeding predator and that he has just eaten one of their own, so to speak. Recall that a pheromone is a substance that is released by one individual and detected by another, carrying important information to the receiver. The presence of the alarm cue serves as a reliable warning of predatory risk to other prey fish.

In one study, flathead minnows exposed to an extract made from the mashed-up skins of other minnows of the same species detected the alarm substance. They reacted by displaying typical predator avoidance behavior and also showed a nervous and anxious demeanor.

Other compounds that potentially serve as alarm cues include disturbance pheromones, injury-released compounds from the ingestion of prey, and even saliva released by the predator through chomping, ingestion, or regurgitation of food material. These compounds alert prey fish to an actively feeding predator in the neighborhood.

In a recent study on alarm cues, predator-naïve, hatchery-raised brook trout quickly learned to identify predatory threats and respond accordingly. Using only their sense of chemoreception, these young trout learned to fear the predator without ever seeing the predator or feeling the effects of predation. The young brookies did not initially react to the chemical markers from the predator's body, but when simultaneously exposed to both the chemicals from the body of a predatory fish and the alarm cues associated with predatory feeding, young trout soon made the connection between the two. After the two chemical cues were paired together in repeated trials, the young trout quickly learned to exhibit appropriate anti-predator behavior, such as suspended feeding activity and decreased movement patterns, when exposed only to the chemical markers from the predator's body, even when the alarm cues were absent. They learned that when they smelled the predator, the alarm cues soon followed—that the presence of the predator meant the death of other prey fish.

Prey species can even discriminate the diet of the predator from telltale chemicals in the excrement. The alarm substance is resistant to digestion in the gut of the predator after the prey is ingested. It is passed into the feces where it serves to mark the territory of the predator, warning prey species against aggregating near the home sites and other frequented sites of predators. In a 1996 study by Chivers, Wisenden, and Smith, even damselfly larvae were able to assess a higher threat level from those predatory fish (in this case, pike) that had been feeding on damselflies from other pike that had previously fed on mealworms, solely from chemicals shed in the feces. The damselfly larvae associated a higher risk with the predators that had fed on their conspecifics (members of their own species), which elicited more immediate and effective protective countermeasures from the larvae. They responded by suspending feeding activity and decreasing movement. Similarly, brook trout identified and learned to avoid Atlantic salmon that had been fed other brook trout, merely from the scent of the salmon's feces.

If fish saliva, blood, scales, and bits of tissue have the ability to serve as potential alarm cues, we had better be careful with our flies and leaders after each fish we catch. After releasing the fish, carefully check your terminal tackle; clean off anything remaining on the hook or fly, whether it is tissue, blood, or a scale. Any residue on the fly may warn other fish and lower your chances for the next fish. Thoroughly rinse the flies in the river after every fish caught, using your fingers to dissolve any mucus or saliva trapped in the hair, feathers, or dubbing. Even the leader should be rinsed before casting to the next fish.

This idea also applies to washing our hands. Residual alarm substances may linger and potentially transfer to our flies, warning off other fish we might like to catch. I used to wet my hands in the river only before handling fish to be released, but now I also thoroughly wash them afterward. The benefit of this habit is twofold; first, prewetting my hands helps the fish, and second, washing afterwards might help me catch more of them. I believe that washing my hands thoroughly *after* each fish I catch, even rubbing my hands with sand from the streambed, removes any residual alarm cues from my hands and prevents such cues from transferring to my flies. Maybe this has become my superstitious habit, but I am not willing to risk it.

Wet hands are easier on the fish than dry hands, which are rough and more abrasive. This reduces the loss of the fish's surface slime layer, a mucous film that covers their entire bodies. Maintaining this layer is vital to the health of the fish since it serves as a shield against invading microbes and disease-producing bacteria. It lubricates the surface of the body to reduce friction and drag as the trout fights the current. It also aids in osmoregulation, which is the trout's ability to keep the internal environment in their bodies different from the water's osmotic concentration. Minimizing the handling of fish and wetting your hands prior to handling them improves the survivability of released fish.

Can the same compounds that serve to warn smaller fish of potential danger also attract larger piscivorous trout? Under experimental conditions, the answer is yes; alarm cues released by the consumption of prey, in addition to warning other prey fish, also attracted other predators to the site of feeding activity. Alarm cues, blood, tissue residue, and potentially saliva have the ability to stimulate other predators, drawing them to the area, eager to capitalize on a successful feeding opportunity. Sharks, for instance, are able to detect blood in the water in very low concentrations from distant sources and move swiftly to the opportunity.

Stress hormones can attract other predatory fish. These hormones are released in fish that are subjected to stressful events, including fighting on the end of a fly line. These compounds, when released by the stressed fish into the water, affect the behavior of other fish—not only those of the same species but also predators. Dr. Aaron Adams, a PhD of marine biology and a fly-fishing author, recently told me that lemon sharks "smell" the stress of recently caught and released bonefish and are attracted to the area in hopes of making an easy meal of the weakened fish. The sharks' long-range sense of smell attracts them from great distances. Adams's publications on handling fish and the survivability of released fish are enlightening.

Does this also happen to the trout we catch and release? Are we merely saving the trout temporarily, only for them to become an easy target for a predator? When asked about this phenomenon in trout, Dr. Steven Cooke, Canadian research chair in Fish Ecology and Conservation Physiology, said it probably occurs in all fish. He states, "Presumably all fish change their physiological signature left in the water (via excretion, skin, and gills) in response to a stressor. Moreover, when skin is physically damaged there are substances (usually alarm cues) given off that can alter the behavior of conspecifics [fish of the same species] and predators."

This raises concern for the survivability of caught and released trout. It suggests additional care and consideration is needed to ensure their safety and survivability. Not only should we take time to fully revive the trout we catch—which takes much longer in warm water than in cold—but perhaps we should also release them close to deeper water or structure where they can find shelter until their stress level subsides.

The alarm cues' ability to attract predatory fish is one of the main theories behind the development of fish attractants, which are supposed to attract larger fish. Usually a liquid or spray, these attractants are applied to the terminal tackle and are supposed to mimic the amino acid mixture associated with predatory feeding, thus attracting other predators. I have talked to bass fishermen who swear by them. Scent-impregnated worms and floating baits are more common than ever and are effective. Catfish anglers have been using stinkbaits for generations, concocting the foulest-smelling baits imaginable. Given the refinement and acuity of the catfish's sense of smell, it seems like overkill to me, but it seems to work for them. Maybe, like fly anglers, they are just trying to outdo each other.

Under actual trout-fishing conditions, I experienced results that left me in doubt about the efficacy of chemical attractants for fly anglers. Two years ago, I conducted my own experiment on the White River while streamer fishing for large trout. I wanted to determine if the smells associated with the consumption of prey fish would serve as an attractant for larger fish. Throwing large, gaudy articulated streamers for several days specifically for hypermature trout should be a good proving ground, or so I thought. If there was ever a time when an attractant effect would matter, that was the time.

The day before the trip, Dave Kranz, the owner of Dave's Bait and Tackle near my home, donated a dozen flathead minnows that I proceeded to skin on the kitchen counter, much to the chagrin of my wife. If you have ever tried to skin a small minnow, you already know the frustration involved. I have cleaned my share of fish, especially as a boy on Canadian fishing trips with my father. But this was something entirely different—more like microdissection. Obviously my standard fillet knife was too cumbersome, so I used a scalpel. Afterwards, I mashed the skins in a bowl to extract the amino acids and the alarm substance. I then siphoned off the fluid to make a turbid red slurry that I carefully labeled and placed in the cooler. I certainly didn't want to confuse it with the salsa!

With visions of catching one large trout after another and amazing my fishing buddies, I slept for a few hours before the long ride to the river. I couldn't wait for the chance to prove my theory.

The next day found us pounding the banks, rock piles, and deep pools in pursuit of our trophy. Tom Starmack fished from the front of the boat, using the same streamer I fished with from the back. I planned to compare the numbers of fish he caught to the results I got while using the slurry. A Minnesota meat fisherman in a prior life, Tom takes his fishing seriously and doesn't like to be outfished. Not wanting to add another element of competition, I tried to keep my experiment to myself. I thought the results might be more objective than would be the case if I announced from the very beginning that I was comparing the number of fish we caught. Not wanting to draw attention to my activities, I tried to surreptitiously dip my streamer in the slurry by turning my back, but Tom soon discovered my dirty little secret and even started to tease me about it, calling it my "secret sauce." He also, at least initially, claimed that I had an unfair advantage.

The fishing was great that trip, but the catching was not. Each of us averaged only two or three fish a day, with the largest barely over 20 inches—both measures far short of our hopes. I was disappointed in the results and ended up dumping the leftover secret sauce in the river. Since that trip, Tom and I have shared a good many laughs over my secret sauce.

Although one experiment doesn't conclusively substantiate or refute a theory, and this was clearly not a controlled experiment, the results did not show any attractant effect from the slurry of flathead minnow-skin extract. Over the three-day trip, I didn't catch any more fish than Tom did. All my experiment proved was the great lengths fishermen will go to in order to outfish their friends!

CHEMORECEPTORS IN SPECIES AND KIN RECOGNITION

Imagine what it might be like to identify another person using only their scent. With your eyes closed, you would be able to tell one person from another, friend from foe. Humans like the idea of individuality when it comes to scent, but lacking the ability to detect the olfactory nuances as other animals do, we have resorted to perfumes, colognes, deodorants, and the like. Just ask any woman; evidently there is quite a process in selecting the right scent to match her personality. The one my wife likes is pretty expensive and smells nice, but another bottle seems to show up every time I come home with a new fly rod. Along with a new dress. And shoes. But that's a small price to pay, I guess. (I probably shouldn't tell her about the rods in the garage, though; but then, I should probably check her closet from time to time, too.)

The ability to discriminate the scent of different individuals and those related to you is called *kin recognition*, and it is an important ecological and evolutionary tool used by many animal species. People also obviously recognize their kin, but through visual memory and voice familiarity, not our sense of smell. The ability to tell close relatives from the rest of the population is the basis of kin-biased behaviors, which are behaviors by an individual that favor others to whom they are closely related. Kin-biased behavior includes reduced aggressiveness toward each other and even food sharing among close relatives. These more complex social behaviors are common in higher animals. From an evolutionary standpoint, aiding your kin helps ensure each individual will have an increased contribution of genetic material to the next generation, either through themselves or via a close relative. Although trout are unlikely to share food with their "redd-mates," studies have shown reduced aggressiveness among familiar siblings and that kin recognition persists through the adult stage in trout.

Fish use chemoreception not only for kin recognition, but also to identify other individuals of the same species (conspecifics). Conspecific and kin recognition are vital to social relationships, mate selection, and social hierarchy.

Conspecific and kin recognition are possible in most animals through chemical traces in the feces (or from residue on the anus in land-based animals). Chemical recognition is mediated through the detection of amino acids, trace bile acids, and other individual markers in the feces and waste urine.

Dogs that sniff the anus of another dog are searching for traces of these chemicals and other individual chemical markers. Many species of fish use chemical detection in more or less the same manner. Not only is this helpful in identification, but in bullhead fish, a very communal species, dominant individuals are identified and social hierarchy is reinforced, which leads to a more stable social structure.

Chemical recognition is important to schooling fish. Fish school by species; the school is composed of the same species and therefore, recognition of conspecifics is essential. For schooling fish, there is safety in numbers—fish not in the school suffer a higher risk of predation. Additionally, chemical recognition is responsible for reschooling after dispersal.

When one dog sniffs another, it really is like a handshake. They are getting acquainted, associating the scent to the individual and establishing social dominance through pheromones.

CHEMORECEPTORS AND REPRODUCTION

Pheromones are getting a lot of attention lately, especially on the Internet where you can buy almost anything these days. Called "seduction in a bottle," they are supposed to enhance your attractiveness to the opposite sex and are added to some colognes and other fragrances. The role of pheromones in insect activity and behavior is well known, from bees and ants to emerging moths. In fact, pheromones are now used for insect control. Gardens often have insect traps for species such as Japanese beetles that are baited with pheromones.

For fish, detecting pheromones and other chemical messengers is solely the province of the sense of smell via the olfactory organ. Since the gustatory receptors are dedicated to consummatory feeding activity, they have little to do with the detection of chemical messengers from other fish. Olfactory receptors respond to a much wider range of stimuli than do the taste buds, including pheromones and other chemical messengers. Pheromones are responsible for spawning migration, mate selection, courtship, parental behavior (in those species that show it), and aggressive behaviors.

Pheromones are similar to hormones in some respects, but are different in one major way. Hormones are manufactured in the body of the fish and stay within the body of the animal that makes them, circulating in the bloodstream or in the tissues. They are secreted from one tissue in the body and travel through the bloodstream to a second tissue where they exert an effect. Essentially they are chemical messengers, but ones that stay within the same body. Pheromones are also chemical messengers, but they carry signals from one individual to another outside of the body. You might think of them as social hormones, communicating subtly but effectively on a large scale to multiple individuals. Many sexually active hormones are circulating in the body of the female in preparation for mating, and are later modified slightly and released into the water as pheromones to stimulate the mating interest of males.

To take an example from another animal, when a dog goes in heat, the changes in the hormones circulating in her bloodstream prepare her physically and mentally for breeding, conception, and subsequent pregnancy. In response to the changes of circulating hormones, her body begins to release pheromones, carried in her scent to male dogs and signaling her receptivity to male attention. The same is true of deer during the rut. In both cases, the chemical signals released from the females dramatically affect the males of the species.

Likewise, the female fish also releases pheromones into the water as the spawning season approaches. During the spawning season, the river is rife and rich with pheromones—a fertile chemical playground. For the autumn-spawning brown and brook trout, falling water temperature and a shortening photoperiod (hours of daylight) initiate the pre-spawn activity. For the rainbows and cutthroat species that spawn in late winter, the lengthening days and rising water temperatures trigger the process. In this regard, recall that the pineal gland, the photoreceptor gland in the head, senses the changes in photoperiod and acts as a hormonal "kick start" to the sexually active glands.

As the spawning season approaches, females begin to release *primer pheromones*, which initiate internal changes within the bodies of the trout in preparation for mating and courtship. These are followed by *releaser* compounds, which elicit behavioral responses in the fish. The changing pheromone levels shift the trout's focus from normal feeding activity to mating.

The pre-spawning period is a time of movement for all salmonids, including trout. Anadromous fish begin the long process of migration from oceans and large freshwater lakes where they have grown on the energy-rich menu back to their natal rivers and streams. River resident trout also move within the river. From their home ranges, they move upstream to regions of the river with suitable spawning conditions, which is determined by water temperature, flow, and substrate characteristics.

Rising levels of pheromones in the water, specifically prostaglandins, synchronize female ovulation. Not all pheromones released by fish are prostaglandins and steroid compounds, though. An amino acid has recently been identified in the urine of female fish that also serves to attract males.

Responding to the rising pheromones, the process of mate selection begins as males compete for breeding rights and females begin construction of the redd, which will be the repository for her fertilized eggs and the nest for her hatching offspring. The fertilization of the eggs by the male is based on the dominance hierarchy, but subordinate fish make a contribution by rushing into the proximity of the female to fertilize her eggs. Such males are called *sneaker fish*, and often the scent of their milt is somewhat disguised to avoid detection.

Other resident species in the river are stimulated by the pheromone slurry and are keen to capitalize on the opportunities it offers for feeding on the abundant, energy-laden eggs that spill from the redds during the spawn. It's like smelling your neighbor's barbecue—it makes you hungry. I have caught a lot of brown trout lurking downstream of spawning salmon.

After the spawn, nest-guarding behavior is common in some fish species and completely lacking in others. On one hand, goldfish females guard their nests after the spawn, with each fish using the sense of olfaction to differentiate her nest from all the others. On the other extreme, many salmonids die after spawning, leaving their offspring's hopes to providence.

I remember walking the banks of Alaska's Russian River late one August following the sockeye salmon spawn. It looked like a postapocalyptic, piscatorial battlefield, with the shores littered with the red carcasses of dead and dying fish. I found consolation in what would otherwise have been despair from the fact that these dying fish were the winners of life, having survived the gambit of ocean life and long travel to run the gauntlet of predators to ensure the next generation. Theirs was a noble death, and it benefited of the brown bears that roamed the river, fattening themselves on the energy-rich salmon ahead of their long winter's nap.

Not all salmonid members die after mating, though. When you see an enormous brown trout whose age may be in double-digit years, imagine how many spawning cycles it has survived. Imagine how many eggs she has laid or redds he has fertilized and the many generations of offspring he or she has surely produced. And then wish it farewell so it can contribute to the next.

MIGRATION

Hatchery work is often a slippery business, not from an ethical standpoint but in a purely physical kind of way. Standing on the floor of Klawock River Hatchery in Craig, Alaska, one of the Prince of Wales Hatchery Association's facilities, the floor was as slick as an ice rink as Jo and I sorted salmon with the hatchery workers, keeping some while allowing many others to return to the river. We stood in ankle-deep water covered with the slime of passing fish. The long raceway was full, mostly of silver salmon that were jumping and splashing before the flow of water carried them across the floor of the sorting room.

In a process called "salmon ranching," every summer the river's returning salmon are diverted through the hatchery. After workers count each species, most are returned to the river upstream of the diverting fence to continue their migration and spawn naturally as they have for genertions. Many are kept for food after workers have harvested the eggs and milt, which are incubated over the winter in the hatchery, yielding the millions of smolts (approximately one-year-old juveniles) to be released back into the river the following summer. Salmon ranching maintains a sustainable resource, satisfying the appetite of the world and the passion of anglers.

Watching salmon that had just recently arrived from the ocean, I realized many of them had likely been released from the hatchery as smolts several years prior. What experiences had they undergone in their long ocean voyage? How many miles they must have swum! What brought them so unerringly back to the very site where they first began life?

Anadromous behavior is a two way street. The first is the downstream migration of the smolts to begin a period of growth and maturation elsewhere, often in the ocean where the larger biomass supports a faster growth rate and size potential. The second migration is the return home, an upstream migration to return to the natal river to spawn.

Scientists have long wondered about the incredible feats of navigation required for salmon to return the exact stretch of the river they left when they were smolts. It has long been speculated that their sense of smell was at least partially responsible and new studies have verified its importance. Several theories are currently offered about the specific odor or mixture of odors that calls the salmon home. It is now thought to be a combination of smells the young fish indelibly etch in their memories through a process known as olfactory imprinting.

For most species, the young salmon remain in the river of their birth for the first year of life, imprinting on the chemical signature of their home river. The smells of home include the bile acids and fecal odors of their conspecifics and kin as well as the unique chemical fingerprint of the river, including the organic and inorganic composition of the water. Several years later as adults, the returning fish are guided home by the sense of smell and olfactory memory. In salmon with an experimentally impaired olfactory organ, homing ability is lost, leading to a high rate of straying. Fish that lose their sense of smell also lose their ability to return to their natal river.

Imprinting tendencies are strongest near the time of smoltification, which is the time of transformation in which the young freshwater fish prepare for the marine environment. One study suggests that sockeye salmon may be imprinted by one particular amino acid and imprinting occurs not only during parr-smolt transformation but also either just before or just after parr-smolt transformation. It seems that Mother Nature reinforces the olfactory memory of home just before the young fish depart for the open water.

Once in the open ocean, the Great Lakes, or some other destination ecosystem, the young smolts aggregate in schools, using their sense of smell to identify their conspecifics and kin. Coho and King (Chinook) salmon in Alaska follow the prevailing currents that carry their food—usually counterclockwise along the coast of Canada and Alaska. In the Great Lakes, salmon are attracted to the schools of baitfish that follow the rafts of zooplankton, which shift according to prevailing winds and waves.

After the period of growth and maturation, which for many species averages three years, the mature fish respond to changes in their bodies and the pheromones of other reproductively mature fish and follow the scent trail back home.

The odor of the salmon's conspecifics residing in their natal river contributes to the homing capabilities of returning salmon, amounting to a kind of long-range kin recognition. A recent study proved that salmon can tell the difference between water occupied by close relatives from water occupied by other fish and that the river water discharging into the ocean may contain these chemical messengers detected by returning salmon. Although diluted by the vast ocean, the sensitivity of salmon olfactory receptors allows for recognition. Additionally, the smell is magnified by the departure of the current generation of smolts as they exit the stream. Each year in the late spring or early summer, the newest generation of smolts is leaving the river for the ocean very near the time the mature population of the same species is returning. The fish in the river of origin are closely related to those fish returning, introducing the possibility of kin recognition and helping to guide the returning salmon home.

FISH ATTRACTANTS AND REPELLANTS

We were warned way back in Genesis 9:2 that fishing would be difficult: "for the fear of you and the dread of you shall be on every beast of the earth, on every bird of the air, on all that move on the Earth, and on all the fish of the sea." It seems that fish, and most other animals for that matter, are not overly fond of us humans, even going so far as to dislike the smell of us. If God so loved fishermen that he made disciples of several, why does fishing have to be so darn hard? I guess if it were easy, we might lose interest.

In the absence of scientific studies specifically designed for anglers as to which smells are most offensive to fish, much of what is now passed on as fact in this regard is actually anecdotal, based on personal experience or from the shared experience of others. Some of it is probably true, while some is probably just opinion and, as such, possibly incorrect. Every angler has his or her own thoughts on the subject and maybe even a few superstitions. But without hard, objective scientific data, I think I'll hang on to my own superstitions for now, at least until further evidence convinces me otherwise.

I'm not alone in having a personal bias. A lot of other fishermen also hang onto their phobias and superstitions. My friend Jamie Clous has a decal on his jet sled that forbids bananas, thinking the smell of them spoils the fishing. I know others who share his opinion, but he is particularly adamant. Not only can you not eat them on board his boat, but he also forbids them in your daypack or gear bag. Next he'll want an affidavit stating that you have abstained from bananas for the 24 hours prior to boarding! Some authors have proposed that fish are repelled by the potassium found in large quantities in bananas, but potassium is a natural inorganic compound in streams. If bananas actually have a repelling effect, it is more likely due to their strong smell rather than the potassium content.

Some anglers favor garlic or anise as an attractive scent for fish. But garlic has been believed to be a natural bug repellant, used to ward off everything from mosquitos to fleas in dogs. If it is that offensive to bugs, it wouldn't be a big stretch to think it also offensive to fish, which is the angling community's general opinion toward commercial insect repellants. At the same time, people who eat bananas during warm weather are thought attract mosquitos, making for a busier time swatting and scratching than those who do not. If the smell of bananas was as offensive to fish as is thought, wouldn't you think that insects would also be repelled by it rather than being attracted to it?

Many bass fishermen, nearly as superstitious as fly anglers, have for years sprayed their lures with WD-40, believing it to be a fish attractant. But since this a basically a petroleum product, doesn't that violate a rule about the repugnance of petroleum products to fish? I also know anglers who would rather endure sunburn than lose a fish, risking cancer rather than risking a slow day on the river. Or how about the angler who prefers to be eaten alive by mosquitos by avoiding insect repellant rather than getting outfished by his buddies?

The banned list for fishing success includes sunscreen, tobacco, petroleum-based products (such as gasoline and oil), bug spray, and deodorant. Perhaps we should also avoid perfumed soaps, shampoos, and other fragrant products. I was on a White River fishing trip one year when a novice angler came from the bathroom reeking of cheap cologne. Soon the whole room smelled like a bordello and no one wanted to fish near him! After the good-natured teasing he suffered, we never smelled it again—although he did continue to use his hair dryer daily. He didn't catch many fish on that trip, but was it because of his cologne or his inexperience? No one is willing to take the chance of it being the former, so no one in our group is allowed to wear aftershave anymore. It seems that one negative experience has established this guideline.

It has even been suggested that the body chemistry of certain individuals, especially those with fair complexions, offends fish. It seems that trout detect certain amino acids that are shed from our skin, and the smell repels them. L-serine has been identified as a culprit and is anecdotally reported to occur in higher levels in fair-skinned people than dark-skinned people. But in fact, L-serine is not unique to humans. L-serine is a relatively common, natural amino acid that may play a role in natal stream recognition.

Even our sweat contains amino acids and other chemical markers of our presence, so we can't drop sweat into the river for fear of offending the fish. Blood and other secretions are also no-nos.

Just how sensitive fish are to and repelled by these odorants is the subject of debate. Having inadvertently experienced the taste of bug spray first hand, I can attest that it is bitter and unpleasant. I wouldn't be surprised to find that the fish feel the same about it. Ditto for sunscreen. If the smell of bug spray repels mosquitos and other insects, it is not too big a stretch to assume that it is offensive to trout. I have fished with guides, however, who chew tobacco products and even spit into the river. You would think that would discourage the fishing. Though maybe that's why they recommended fishing upstream.

The idea of fish attractants opens a whole new can of worms, so to speak. Oils, amino acids, enzymes, and pheromones are common additives to fish attractants. These products are common in bass fishing, and there is nearly an entire aisle of scent-impregnated baits at the local outdoor store. I have used many of these to great success, but at the same time the dismal failure of my secret sauce—that homemade concoction of mashed-up flathead minnow skins—is still fresh in my mind.

All we can do is try to put it into some kind of perspective until objective data is available. The current research shows that fish smell a wide range of human-based odors, including the smell of latex or rubber gloves (which takes that idea off the table). We know that some smells encourage fish to feed, perhaps reassuring them during their final analysis of the food choice. Other smells warn fish of imminent danger and disrupt feeding activity.

Remember that since the sense of smell is inaccurate for locating the exact source of the odor, the fish actually has to be pretty close to the fly or lure to definitively determine it to be the source of the smell. It might be one of the last check-offs for the search image and perhaps an offensive smell could result in close refusals of the fly. A worst-case scenario would be if our flies were imbued with an alarm smell that disrupts the feeding activity of the very fish we are trying to catch.

For the present and foreseeable future, I will rely on common sense and try to avoid superstition. I think it makes sense to avoid smells that could put the fish off. Given the sensitivity of trout olfaction, it is best to avoid offensive odors rather than trying to remove them later. If I don't use cologne or heavily scented soaps and shampoos, it is one less thing to worry about later. And I'm careful with deodorants, applying them where needed but keeping them from contacting my hands. That way I avoid offending both my fishing partners and the fish. I also avoid scented lotions and hand creams. The fewer chemicals or odorants I get on my hands, the less I have to worry later about getting the scents off of my hands.

I am also careful to avoid getting bug spray on my hands. I use a spray that directs the product to specific areas as needed, but keeps my hands and fingers from direct contact. I fish wearing a broad-brimmed hat so that I need less sunscreen on my face, neck, and ears. I never spray the insect repellant or sunscreen onto my hands to wipe on my face. I close my eyes and spritz it directly onto my face and neck to avoid contact with my hands. After applying sunscreen, I grab some wet sand from the streambed and scrub my hands, just to be sure—it is important to reduce the possibility of transferring any artificial scents to the fly or tippet as I handle them.

Another habit applies to petroleum products: if you are using a power boat or a boat with a motor, fill up the gas tank and check the oil *after* each use rather than on the way to the river. That way you avoid handling fuel and oil products just before you fish and you still ensure that you'll not run out of gas!

We all have our proven rituals, habits, and even a few superstitions associated with fishing. It's important to develop good habits. There's no practical way to be certain we are free of fish-offensive odors, but we can eliminate most of them. The protein markers that identify us as humans, however, still linger on every object we touch.

chapter eight
More Sense

It was the third day of the first really hot week of the summer. The Fourth of July was still several days away but the afternoon temperatures were already climbing into the high nineties. We caught several nice fish on Montana's Ruby River early that morning, but once full sunlight overspread the river, the fishing slowed. Our shirts clung to our backs by the time we walked to the car, put our rods away, and opened the cooler. The trout were starting to feel the effect of the rising water temperature as well, so we limited our fishing to mornings only, partly out of respect for them and partly for our own comfort. It may be dry heat, as people like to say, but when its almost 100 degrees, it's still hot. Of course, the heat wave had to time *its* arrival in Montana to coincide with *our* arrival in Montana. We would have to make some changes to our all-day fishing plans—maybe by including an afternoon siesta. All the same, the cold beer tasted fantastic.

Jo and I were fishing that week with Lance Wilt and Mitch Rotz, transplanted central Pennsylvania fishing guides hanging out in Montana for the summer. To avoid the hot, humid dog days in Pennsylvania, they spent summers guiding in the Montana Rockies, home of dry heat. Someone had evidently given them some bad advice—it was probably fifteen degrees cooler back home.

We had used the early morning light for photos and video, analyzing a stretch of water for current characteristics, trout lies, and presentation angles. It was no surprise that the trout had selected a deep, choppy run behind a drop-off; with the rising water temperatures, the turbulent water, rich in oxygen, was like a fish magnet.

We bounced around different ideas for the next morning's fishing. We had begun the week on the lower Ruby River, but when the heat rolled in we needed to find cooler water. The soaring temperatures had changed everything. We considered fishing closer to the dam where the water temperature was lower, or perhaps heading to the upper Ruby, well above the reservoir where the water was also cooler. In the summer heat, rivers are often cooler near the headwaters. Fish also know this.

Understanding the trout's response to elevated water temperature is key to summer fishing success. Fish don't like hot conditions any more than we do. Sustained air temperatures that are uncomfortable for us usually produce water temperatures that are uncomfortable for them. Neither do trout favor extremely cold water. They have a narrow range of preferred water temperature. Just because trout are poikilothermic doesn't mean they are indifferent to the temperature of the water. They simply lack the internal mechanisms to do anything about it. Instead they rely on external mechanisms for thermoregulation, the understanding of which needs to be the basis of our summer and winter fishing strategies.

Identifying the locations where trout gather to relieve thermal stress is the difference between a hot fishless day and a day of hot fishing. Our Montana experience bears this out: the next day we drove a long ways upriver to find cooler water and were rewarded for our effort with catchable fish.

THERMORECEPTION

Inherent in the trout's ability to respond to thermal stress—a physiologic state induced when water conditions are outside the comfortable norm—is the ability to perceive the water temperature. To react, they have to detect.

Fish have receptors under the skin that detect fluctuations in water temperature. Nerve fibers then carry this information to the brain. The receptors are specialized nerve endings sensitive to changes in water temperature. Internal thermoreceptors located in the hypothalamus (a portion of the brain) also sense internal changes in body temperature. Both work together to initiate thermoregulation behaviors when the temperatures fluctuate outside of the range of comfort. The receptors are very sensitive, with the ability to sense changes as small as one degree Fahrenheit.

As noted in chapter 3, in addition to gaining heat from warm water (conduction) simply by being immersed in it, trout also gain heat through the absorption of solar radiation from the sun. This heat registers not only in the superficial or internal thermoreceptors, but also is recognized by the pineal gland in the form of light energy.

Brown trout prefer an average water temperature of 54 degrees Fahrenheit with a diurnal (daily cycle) range of 50 to 56 degrees. Different species of trout have different preferences for water temperature, but all are equally intolerant of extremes. The different trout species' preferences in water conditions, especially temperature, determine where along the course of the river each species is usually found.

If we follow a typical mountain stream from its headwaters to its termination into the ocean or another body of water, a distribution pattern is apparent. Arising from snowpack or ice melt, initially the water is cold, low in organic mass, and high in inorganic composition such as minerals from glacier melt. If the stream originates from underground sources in the form of springs or seeps, the headwaters are also cooler in the summer relative to the lower sections where water has gained heat from the hot surface climate. The first trout species to appear progressing downstream are the brook trout and cutthroat trout, which favor cooler water and can tolerate the lower biomass. As the stream descends into the verdant valley, the water temperature warms and the organic biomass increases. The next trout species to appear at that point is the rainbow, soon followed by the brown trout. In the lower river valley where the water warms further and the biomass continues to rise, the last trout species to disappear is the brown trout; after this, river conditions begin to favor warmwater species such as bass, catfish, and bullheads.

The trout's ability to detect water and internal temperatures that rise or fall outside the ideal range leads to thermoregulation, whereby the trout reacts to relieve the thermal distress thus created. Detection is only part of the equation. Understanding the way trout respond is the key to unlocking summer and winter fishing strategies.

THERMOREGULATION

How an animal responds to thermal variation in its environment, which is created when the temperature rises or falls outside an optimum range, is called *thermoregulation*. Using physiological thermoregulation, humans and other warm-blooded animals respond via internal mechanisms; we unconsciously adapt to thermal stress by undergoing changes within our bodies to either conserve or dissipate heat. The goal of thermoregulation is to maintain the body temperature within an optimum range.

When it is hot, we cool our bodies through the evaporation of sweat from our skin's surface. This doesn't always work for species with a dense hair coat, so for them, panting usually replaces sweating. Peripheral blood vessels dilate to increase blood flow to the extremities and skin, which facilitates the transfer of heat. We also use behavioral changes to stay cool as well. We shed clothing—especially dark colors—seek shade, jump in a pool, or pop the top on a bottle of beer.

When cold, our peripheral blood vessels constrict to keep the warm blood in the body core, which keeps the body heat concentrated around the vital organs. We also shiver to generate heat through intense muscle activity. Again, we behaviorally adapt as well, putting on extra layers of warm clothing or going inside by the fire.

Trout and most other fish are described as "cold-blooded" and thus can respond to thermal stress only through behavioral thermoregulation, which is also called external thermoregulation since it involves changes outside the trout's body. With very few exceptions, most fish species have no internal means for heat conservation or dissipation. It is important to keep in mind that simply because trout are cold-blooded doesn't mean that they are unaware of the temperature or unresponsive to changes. It merely means that their response involves avoidance measures—relieving thermal distress by seeking more comfortable conditions.

The main reason trout and many other aquatic species are *poikilothermic* is the cost of doing business in the water. The energy expense to maintain a temperature independent of the water temperature is too great because of the enormous heat capacity and rapid heat transfer in water, which is much greater than in air. In other words, warm-blooded animals lose heat rapidly in cold water and gain it just as fast in hot. For example, an air temperature of 50 degrees is a little chilly, but being immersed in 50-degree water can lead to your death within an hour from hypothermia. Cold water literally sucks the heat from your body.

Organisms living in water can't replace the heat fast enough in cold water or dissipate it effectively enough in hot water to make feasible the maintenance of a different internal temperature from that of the water. It simply costs too much energy, so they don't bother. Thus, their internal temperature follows that of the external temperature, which has profound physiological consequences to the fish. If a warm-blooded animal faced the heat loss of cold water, its metabolic rate would skyrocket from the effort required to keep the body temperature in its normal range. The opposite occurs for trout in cold water; their metabolic rate plummets as their internal body temperature falls. Extremely cold water induces a hibernationlike slowdown of metabolic activity, which actually conserves energy. Saving energy at a time when they are eating little is a considerable advantage.

The trout's metabolic rate falls with the water temperature because the rate of biochemical reactions is slower at cooler temperatures. My high school chemistry teacher taught me that adding heat to a chemical reaction accelerated the rate of reaction; at cold temperatures, the rate slowed. Since metabolism is the sum of all biochemical reactions within any living body, a lower water temperature for a fish reduces the fish's metabolic rate, meaning it is burning less fuel. The fish save energy during the winter, which is a good thing because feeding opportunities are fewer in the winter as well.

A great fallacy, often repeated, is that trout stop feeding in hot weather. This couldn't be further from the truth. Summer fish still need to feed. In fact, the body's elevated internal temperature pushes the trout's metabolic rate into overdrive, meaning they actually need to eat *more*. Warm water changes their feeding patterns dramatically. They need to feed during the late summer for another reason, as well: they need to eat more when food is abundant to store up energy reserves for the lean months of winter when it is scarce.

SUMMER AND WINTER FISHING

Finding fish is the key to catching trout in the temperature extremes of summer and winter. The most suitable water holds the highest number of fish. The basis of summer and winter fishing strategies is an understanding of the thermoregulation behavior of trout, which determines where the trout are found in the river—a prerequisite for catching them. The manner in which trout respond to thermal discomfort is consistent, which allows for predictability in our seasonal fishing strategies.

Trout respond to warm water by seeking to satisfy three goals: First, they seek locations in the river with a more comfortable temperature. Sometimes this includes moving to completely different sections of the river where desirable water temperatures can be found. Heat-stressed trout often move closer to the dam in tailwater fisheries because the water discharge is much cooler than the rest of the river.

For most tailwaters, the reservoir behind the dam is stratified provided it has sufficient depth. Stratification results in three distinct layers: a warmer upper layer called the *epilimnion*, which is separated by the thermocline from a deeper, colder layer called the *hypolimnion*. Since the water discharging into the river comes from the hypolimnion, its temperature is usually fairly constant, independent of the seasons. This introduces cold water into the warm summer river. In the summer heat, look for fish in stretches just downriver from the dam.

In freestone rivers, trout often find relief from warm water by moving upriver. The headwaters of mountain streams that are formed by ice, snow, or glacial melt are cooler than the streams' downstream stretches. Streams formed by groundwater seeps and springs are also colder near their headwaters since the water rising from underground sources is cooler than surface water. (A seep is defined as a groundwater discharge with multiple points of entry in close proximity to one another. A spring has a single point of discharge.) At any point where subsurface water discharges into a stream in the form of a seep or spring, summer trout will aggregate just downstream in the cooler water.

Seeps and springs can discharge along the streambed or the edges of the bank anywhere along the course of the stream. Examining nearby terrain features can often identify these discharge points. Look for dry gulches, gullies, and draws that intersect the riverbed. Even those that are dry on the surface may funnel subsurface water to the river, bubbling up as a spring below the bank. Also look for low marshy soil alongside the stream, especially where the ground is wet. Cattails in low-lying areas along the stream are also telltale signs of underground input. Trout will often aggregate downstream of these inputs.

Second, trout seeking heat relief avoid the sun. As noted in Chapter 3, trout often seek relief from the sun in deeper water where the light intensity is less. Don't overlook shady areas of the river, as well as undercut-banks. Trout will hold in any location where they can avoid the sun's heat.

The third goal for summer-stressed trout is locating stretches with high oxygen content. Warm water carries less oxygen than colder water due to the saturation differences based on water temperature. Warm water also carries oxygen for a shorter time than colder water. In other words, the oxygen dissipates faster, which means that trout will locate closer to oxygen sources in the summer. Whitewater, riffles, and areas of turbulence introduce oxygen into the water through the admixture of air. As a result, trout in warm water are often positioned just downstream from the sites of high oxygen content. Look for "hot trout" in deep, shady pools or runs immediately after rough-water runs and riffles.

Even though the trout's demand for food is higher in warm water, the natural rhythm of food availability in the stream is highest in the late spring and summer, so food is a secondary factor. Trout often shift their feeding behaviors in the summer to times when the sun is gone and the heat is less. This synchronizes conveniently with the natural daily cycle of aquatic food availability, which peaks at dusk and dawn.

Winter fish also seek to satisfy three goals, albeit different ones from those of summer. First, they need to find warmer water. Fish often move upriver in the winter, away from their summer feeding grounds. Browns and brookies, already upstream after the spawn, often linger in the warmer water through much of the winter and are slow to return to the colder water downriver. The late-winter-spawning 'bows and cutties are often headed upriver by midwinter as well in anticipation of their spawn. Trout often don't appear in the normal feeding ranges until late winter or early spring.

In the winter, anglers should once again look for springs and seeps, whose nearly constant temperature, regardless of seasonal influences, now offers the warmest water in the river. Winter trout often lie in the downstream trailing threads of warmwater inputs, often revealed to the angler by wisps of fog clinging to the warmer water surface in the cold air.

The sun, shunned by trout in the summer, is a winter friend of trout. You may find trout basking in the sun to gain heat. They still seek lies offering security from predatory threat, but they like the sun's warmth. Concentrate your attention on the sunny bank of the river.

The second concern for winter trout is energy conservation. Winter trout are very cost conscious, especially in regards to feeding efficiency. They won't often chase food with a low probability of success and won't fight strong current without good reason. Look for trout in sections where they can avoid strong current but still have a steady flow to deliver any food to them. Trout often aggregate in sections of the river that are vacant in the summer but satisfy the needs of winter. Once you find one trout, others are likely nearby.

The third consideration under winter conditions is food. Food availability is at its lowest point of the season and so trout need to capitalize on feeding opportunities. Even with a lower metabolic rate induced by the cold water, winter fish still need to feed—energy equals survival amid the harsh demands of winter. Trout feed more opportunistically in the winter than during the summer invertebrate events and emergences, so anglers

Seeps and springs introduce cooler water into the summer river and warmer water into the winter river, and so trout often cluster in the more comfortable sections just downstream from their discharge. These points can often be determined through a close examination of terrain features.

should try an array of different offerings. Skew fly selection toward the invertebrates common in the winter river, such as scuds and midges. Try to time your fishing to occur during times of peak food availability, such as the hatch of a winter generation of Blue-Winged Olives.

MAGNETIC RECEPTION

If it were not for the Earth's magnetic field, which deflects the charged particles associated with solar wind from the sun, the Earth's protective ozone layer would have disappeared long ago, leaving our planet fully exposed to the harmful effects of UV light and radiation. In fact, scientists conjecture that it was the loss of the magnetic field on the planet Mars that potentially condemned the planet, causing the nearly complete loss of the planet's atmosphere and rendering it inhospitable. Without its magnetic shield, its atmosphere was stripped away. NASA hopes to confirm these theories with the Mars Atmosphere and Volatile EvolutioN (MAVEN) satellite.

The Earth's magnetic field offers additional benefits. Although the earliest navigators used the sun and stars, the compass came into use in China around 200 BC. The first compasses were magnetic lodestones that when swung freely always pointed in the same direction. Rather than navigation, these were used in divination and geomancy. Today, the most common compasses contain a magnetized pointer that aligns with Earth's geomagnetic field to point at the magnetic pole.

I often take a compass with me when I am backpacking but seldom when I am fly fishing. I probably should put one in my vest just in case. They certainly don't weigh much or take up much room, but maybe I figure I don't need one. It's not that I never get lost, but as long as I follow the river, it should take me back to where I parked the car, right? I guess *that* theory only applies if I remember whether I need to walk upstream or downstream to get back. Some people claim to have an internal compass, but no magnetized particles have ever been found in people. Most experienced outdoorsmen and women can approximate a northerly direction using the sun or stars, but this approach doesn't work well with cloudy skies.

Scientists have long suspected that anadromous salmonids have some sort of internal compass since they are capable of orienting themselves when no other reference is available. Previous studies have shown that visually isolated salmon position themselves in accordance with the magnetic field of the Earth. Recently, new studies have determined the source of their internal directional device—trout *do* in fact have an internal compass of sorts. It lacks a needle and the designations for north, south, east, and west, but it functions well nonetheless.

Ironlike particles called magnetite have been found in the olfactory tissue in the head of Chinook salmon. These particles have nerve-pathway connections to the brain. They are large enough and arranged in such a manner to be sensitive to the geomagnetic field and function as a navigational device. Exactly where these particles come from and how they form is still not fully determined, but they appear early in the young fish and by the smolt stage—when migration to the ocean begins—the resulting formation is large enough for magnetic perception. It grows larger over time and the life of the fish.

Other theories propose that specialized cells in the retina of the trout's eye appear to have the capability to sense magnetic fields. Further research is needed before this can be stated with certainty.

The perception of the Earth's magnetic field is a tremendous advantage in navigation. Magnetoreception can be detected directly by perceiving the field or indirectly by sensing the weak electrical field created as the fish swims through the magnetic field. By sensing multiple magnetic elements such as field inclination angle and strength, directional and positional cues can be determined.

Inclination angle and field strength vary tremendously from site to site in a very constant manner around the globe, which endows each geographic region with a unique magnetic signature. Recent research suggests that salmon and migratory sea turtles imprint on their natal home waters and rely on that magnetic information later in life when they return to these sites to spawn.

New migratory models have been proposed that explain how animals can navigate to home waters from distant ocean locations. One such model suggests that the chemoreceptive cues do not extend far enough into the ocean at sufficient concentrations to be detected by returning salmon, in spite of the tremendous sensitivity of their olfactory system. Instead, the salmon initially rely on geomagnetic imprinting to guide them to the right general area, perhaps the site where their natal river discharges into the ocean. At that point the olfactory system, which senses stronger chemical signals, takes over and directs the later stage of migration, especially the freshwater stage. The salmon work upstream like a bird dog on scent, navigating the many branches and tributaries to reach their destination.

INTERNAL RECEPTORS

Our five classic senses—smell, taste, hearing, vision, and touch—are what immediately come to mind when we think of our sensory system. These senses convey to us information about the world around us. We are constantly bombarded with sound, visual images, smells, flavors, and other rich information. In a world of seemingly unending chaos, sometimes we go into sensory overload and just need some downtime on the river to decompress. Fly fishing provides a good respite from sensory overload.

But so much additional information is provided to us, both consciously and unconsciously, than we often realize. Internal sensory systems provide information about the status and function of our bodies. The hypothalamus, a region of the brain that interfaces with our hormonal system, helps to maintain homeostasis by keeping various parameters in a narrow range of acceptability. For people and other warm-blooded animals, the hypothalamus helps keep the body temperature within narrow limits. For fish, it senses changes in body temperature and initiates behavioral thermoregulatory changes. It also controls hunger and satiation and thirst and sleep cycles.

Other receptors detect changes in blood pressure and stimulate changes in heart rate to compensate for variation outside the norm. Blood sugar levels are constantly monitored, as are many other parameters, all oriented to maintaining homeostasis in the body. Homeostasis is the regulation of the internal environment of the body to keep a constant and stable condition. Covering everything from pH (acid-base balance) to blood pressure, receptors and control centers maintain parameters in a very narrow range of acceptable variation.

There are receptors (known as nociceptors) that detect damage to tissues so we can protect the injured area. They remind us to stay off of a sprained ankle. Stretch receptors indicate the degree of stretch in muscles and connective tissue, which aids in determining the position and attitude of our bodies (proprioception). Much of this internal sensory information is handled without our knowledge or conscious control.

Trout also rely on internal sensory information to maintain homeostasis in much the same manner. Some obvious differences exist, such as their method of regulating body temperature and pain perception, which was discussed previously.

COMMON SENSE

"When I was a boy of fourteen, my father was so ignorant I could hardly stand to have the old man around," Mark Twain once said. "But when I got to be twenty-one, I was astonished at how much he had learned in seven years." Common sense was something my parents waited years to see materialize in their second son. It still remains in me a virtue with occasional lapses. As a teenager, I went through a time when I thought I knew everything, but common sense and its inherent wisdom seems only to come with age. At least, that's my hope.

Common sense often takes a vacation when angling is involved. We try to convince ourselves that we can keep fishing when the approaching storm's rumbly voice shouts that we should quit and seek shelter. Just a few more casts, we tell ourselves. The fishing is always best right before a storm, right? Ever use that one? I once raised a rod in my hand and wondered why it hummed. Clearly a lapse.

Some anglers believe there is a sixth sense—the nuance through which they detect a subtle strike when nymph fishing. I have seen some very good anglers who just seem to know when a fish is even remotely interested in their flies. They always catch more fish. I believe this is an effective combination of focus, observation, preparedness, and luck. When I discuss this with my friend R. B. MacCallister, who is an extraordinary nymph fisherman, I always emphasize the luck part of it.

chapter nine

Making Sense

Our annual "guys trip" this year was to Jackson, Wyoming. For many years, the trip included just my son, Evan, and I, enjoying a father-son bonding experience amid the rivers and mountains. Hiking, rafting, rock climbing, and of course, fly fishing have always been the focal point of our trips. In the distant past, when my dad's health was better, three generations of men in our family joined together in the outdoors. Evan considers himself lucky to have memories of these adventures with his grandfather. On the past few trips, my daughter's boyfriend, Clay, was invited, which in our family is the same as the acceptance of a young male into a pride of lions. Or hyenas, depending on which euphemism seems appropriate at the time.

The planning for this trip began months earlier when we arranged the date by collaborating three different schedules: my son's summer break before law school, Clay's limited vacation schedule at his new job, and my time away from work, which is a lot more flexible. Sometimes it pays to be the "old lion"—you have more vacation time! And, after many years of marriage, your wife is happier to get rid of you than when you were younger. Once the dates were set for the trip, we arranged airline tickets, hotels, and guides for fishing, rock climbing, and whitewater rafting.

Since I don't live on a river, almost all my fishing trips involve advance planning. I can't just grab the rod and walk out the front door, which means that long-range planning for a trip like this one is necessary. Much of the early preparation is simple logistics—travel plans, tickets, rental cars, motel arrangements, and such. Closer to the departure date, it involves getting gear ready, making sure any needed repairs are done, and the gear bag is packed. This seems to hasten the approach of the trip, allowing it to begin before it actually begins. The planning stage becomes part of the trip, raising excitement and expectation ahead of the actual departure date.

But, that doesn't mean that I'm not spontaneous sometimes. I like short-notice trips and last-minute surprises, too. My wife and kids once woke me on Father's Day with breakfast in bed at 5 a.m. and a day trip to the Driftless Area of Wisconsin for fishing and a picnic. But larger trips, especially those involving air travel, are certainly best planned in advance.

As part of the planning, I also research the river we intend to visit. I like to know ahead of time about potential insect activity and the fishing conditions we will likely encounter, even if I have already fished these waters before. A good trip begins with good preparation at home. I check hatch charts for the river, which are often published by local fly shops and guide services. I also talk to local fly shops and guides I know in the area or on the river.

I try to answer several questions at this stage of the game. Am I going to be fishing with a guide from a boat or am I going off on my own to wade the river? I need to know so I know which rods to bring, as well as all of the other stuff that goes with it. If drifting from a boat, I'll probably be doing some nymph fishing, perhaps long drifts below a strike indicator. So I better bring my favorite rod for nymph fishing from a boat, which is different from the one I like when I am wading. I'm often limited by available space—those overhead bins don't seem as large as they used to be. And the airlines make you pay for extra luggage.

Another question that needs to be answered in advance relates to the particulars of the river. Is it wide—a caster's dream—or is it tight and narrow? This also influences which rods I bring. I don't want my 4-weight, 7½-foot bamboo rod on a Snake River drift boat trip.

I also need to know if a hatch is expected, and if so, which one. I like to know which insects I'll encounter so I'll be sure to bring the right fly boxes. If it's early spring, I probably won't need three boxes of terrestrials. Familiarity with the local insects also allows me to have the right size and color in the box. I'll often tie flies for a specific trip after researching local patterns based on insects likely to be on the river. For instance, are the local caddisflies green or tan? And what size are they?

One of the most important details often overlooked by many anglers is to take advantage of publicly available information about the current state of the river as to flow, water temperature, and water conditions. Since river conditions change abruptly, I check these sources frequently close to the departure date. A lot of angler-relevant information can be gleaned from various websites. This includes water temperature, flow or discharge (if it's a tailwater), water clarity, and turbidity. These are all useful bits of information. I load the fly boxes based on this information. I have even been known to burn the midnight oil tying flies I think will be needed based on changing water conditions—I just might not have enough of my favorite flies for green turbid water. Or my favorite high-water fly.

The United States Geological Survey (USGS) publishes current stream and river conditions as part of the National Streamflow Information Program, or NSIP (http://water.usgs.gov/nsip/). Rates of flow and water depth are available for nearly every river or stream, but the USGS also publishes water temperature and water clarity data for many streams. The data is usually very up-to-date and helpful for everything from wading and floating conditions to fly selection and color. The information also influences what gear I bring. If the flow is low, I might just bring my waders, but if the water is warm enough, I might wet-wade instead.

For tailwaters, other government agencies or regulatory authorities often publish useful and sometimes vital information. For instance, the Tennessee Valley Authority (TVA) has data, discharge history, and predictions available online for the rivers its dams discharge into. The U.S. Army Corps of Engineers (USACE) also publishes tailwater discharge information for many of the rivers it regulates. Plans for dam discharges will certainly impact my plans for fishing. I might not be able to wade many of my favorite spots if the water is too high. For many tailwaters I've fished often, I have favorite spots during high water and favorite holes for low water. Or, based on USACE or TVA predictions, I might even leave the drift boat at home if the flows are too low to float.

During any trip, I check these organizations' websites daily. The dams' cycles of discharge affect my daily fishing schedule. If you have ever fished below the dam on a tailwater, you know how fast things can change. I have seen anglers stranded on islands because they didn't react quickly enough to rising water levels. I almost lost a gear bag once that I thought was safely on shore because I didn't get to it fast enough to beat the rising water.

I'll even check the weather conditions for the river and area we plan to fish—not only the forecast but also the weather conditions from the prior week. The National Oceanic and Atmospheric Administration's National Weather Service website (http://www.nws.noaa.gov/climate/index.php) is particularly helpful for current, previous day, and month-to-date information. If the prior week has been really rainy, surface watershed can affect water clarity in the river and create color shifts. Knowing this ahead of time allows me to anticipate and prepare for such conditions.

Knowledge is power, which allows me to stack the deck to meet the malleable conditions encountered when fly fishing in rivers and streams. I'll have the right gear and the right flies in my fly boxes, even flies tied for specific conditions. Knowing the water conditions ensures I'll have the right flies, ones I'm sure the trout will see. The angler who is prepared to rise to the challenge of the situation he or she will face will have the best success.

SITUATIONAL ANGLING

Fly fishing is a challenging sport under the best conditions. Add a stiff wind, driving rain, or freezing cold, and it really tests your mettle. Fortunately we can compensate for inclement weather: we can tighten our loops as we cast into the wind, we can put on a $500 rain suit to shield us from rain, or we can add extra layers of equally expensive thermal clothing or fleece to stay warm when the temperature plummets.

Too often, however, we fail to adjust our angling strategies with the same alacrity we bring to our personal accouterments. We simply tie on our favorite fly, regardless of conditions, and cast it into our favorite fishing hole, no matter the character of the water or volume of flow. We do this because it worked before and we assume it should work again. But if we are going to catch fish consistently, under all conditions, we have to adapt our strategy to the present situation.

Our knowledge about the expected color shifts under differing conditions of water quality, clarity, and visibility makes the job of fly selection much easier, especially as it relates to color. When we know the visual capabilities of trout and the color shifts that occur in the water, we can put the two together to come up with a fishing strategy based on water clarity and visibility.

You might think that your favorite fishing hole on your favorite river is too shallow to undergo color shifts, but this is not the case. Most rivers are obviously not as deep as lakes, but many deep pools are deep enough for color shifts. Some of my favorite large-trout spots are dark pools that may be 10 feet deep or more. Recall also the magnitude of the green color shift when we took our color board to a depth of 20 feet in the quarry. There was a green color shift evident well before we had descended the full 20 feet.

Also keep in mind that color shifts occur in shallow water for objects seen at a distance (see figs. 14 and 15). For instance, when a trout looks forward from a feeding lie to a food particle approaching in the current, a color shift occurs, especially if the water is stained or turbid. The extent of the color shift is determined by the distance to the food particle and the degree of discoloration of the water. The greater the distance to the object and the more discolored the water, the larger the color shift. When an object first enters the trout's visual range, its colors will be less distinct, muted by the water's discoloration. Given that the effective visual range for a trout is often less than 10 feet, a lot of color shift can occur. The color shift will diminish those colors whose wavelengths are not well transmitted in the stained or turbid water while other colors will remain more vibrant and visible. As the object approaches the trout, the true colors will become more apparent. By the time the trout commits to or refuses the food particle or fly, the color shift is negligible, but the trout has often already committed or refused by then.

Water visibility is one of the first factors I inspect when I arrive at the stream. Visibility is determined by two factors: water clarity and the amount of available light. In other words, how much light is there to begin with and what happens to it in the water in terms of attenuation and color shifts? Water visibility influences not only my fly choice, but also how I'm going to fish that fly.

The amount of available light is readily evident by simply looking at the sky. I can certainly tell night from day, and I am able to further subdivide full sunshine from dark, overcast skies. In the extremes of broad daylight and dark night, the amount of available light determines the trout's retinal population of cones and rods, and therefore its search image. In between these extremes, the amount of available light influences how well trout see our flies. But since available light is also reduced in shady stretches of the river and in deeper pools, shouldn't we fish these spots differently than we do sunbaked riffles?

Determining the other aspect of visibility, water clarity, requires a closer inspection of the water and takes a few extra moments. Categorizing water clarity into three classifications—clear, stained, or turbid—simplifies the task.

WATER CLARITY AND COLOR CHOICE

I was twenty-nine the summer my parents bought their retirement cabin in Michigan's Upper Peninsula. I was dealing with student loans, a new job, a young wife, and plans for a family, so not much time was left for fishing or much of anything else for that matter. In spite of this, Jo and I managed a long weekend visit in August of that first year. Jo never had the opportunity to fish much growing up but always wanted to try. This lake was to be the birthplace of her fishing passion.

There are two things a man should never teach his wife: how to golf and how to fish. I'm sure there are probably others items on the list, but these two stand out in my mind. Fortunately, my dad took over the instructional responsibilities. Thus, Jo had the same teacher as I did, albeit separated by many years in between. Across the lake we went in a 12-foot boat with dad on the tiller of a 10-horsepower motor. The lake, filled with lily pads, deep weed beds, and bass and northern pike, was a great place to learn. It was a sunny day and the water was clear, so dad selected a bright spinnerbait with flashy silver blades. After a few practice casts, Jo was fairly proficient with the spinning rod. Dad patiently answered the many questions and untangled the backlashes that would have certainly led to a divorce, or at least an argument, had I been the one instructing her. After catching several fish that afternoon, she was hooked for life.

Fishing the lake the following spring, we found entirely different water conditions. Heavy rains reduced water clarity, adding a muddy turbidity. We used fluorescent chartreuse spinnerbaits with bright gold blades to attract attention in the murky water and managed to catch several nice sized pike.

In each case, our choice of color was predicated on water clarity. In each case, we made adjustments and caught fish.

Clear Water

Bass fishermen have long believed that lure color should be based on water clarity and lighting conditions. Clear water means high visibility for the fish. The light penetrates to a greater depth in the water and the fish can see farther and with greater clarity. In the trout's retina, the light-sensitive rods are in hiding, buried deep in the protective pigmented layer, but the cones are engaged and offer maximum acuity and color perception. Fish see best under these conditions; they have better perception of true colors and are more skeptical of our angling subterfuge. With the clear water affording opportunity for careful scrutiny, our imitation must be convincing enough to fool them.

Color shifts, especially for top-water or shallow presentations, are less evident in clear water. My dad's rule for fishing was to use light-colored plugs and spinnerbaits for bright days with high visibility. He used pale blue crankbaits with light underbellies and nickel spinners with white skirts. The lighter colors showed up better and caught more fish. Under these conditions, he wanted his presentation to appear as lifelike as possible. He usually avoided fluorescent and other unnatural colors.

The same theory applies to fly fishing; subtle and understated lifelike flies appear more natural in high-visibility water. Since clear water on a cloudless day produces the highest visibility, we need to adjust our angling strategy accordingly. The trout can see better, so colors that mimic the natural prey produce the best results. We don't need to "oversell" our presentation with glaring colors. Starkly contrasting color combinations will not usually be needed and are perhaps even detrimental, especially to older fish more wary in the ways of angling subterfuge.

The trout's retina is light-adapted during the day, meaning that the cones are still activated and the highly sensitive rods are hidden. When light is diminished, whether by dense clouds, deep water, or full shade, the trout's effective visual range for maximum acuity is diminished. The sharpness of their vision is lessened, even in clear water. Shady lies are often prime summer lies since trout find relief from the sun as well as concealment lurking in the dark, so it's always worth a cast to these areas. When casting along the shade-covered bank or sections of the river overcovered by deep shade, a more eye-catching presentation is required. Sharper contrast between colors is needed to grab the trout's attention. And since contrast is a strong component of the search image for trout, it needs to remain evident. If the lack of sufficient light lessens visibility, the contrast needs to be stronger.

The same holds true for deep presentations in pools, which are another prime summer lie, especially for large trout. Dad's favorite deep-water bass lure is a "fire tiger" pattern with fluorescent yellow and green bands with black spots or stripes on the top and sides. The theory behind the lure makes sense when one remembers the color shifts on the rainbow color board—these are the colors that remain most visible in the freshwater color shift, which is more profound in deeper water.

Fly choice for deeper presentations should follow similar guidelines. Denser colors such as black, dark red or brown, or deep green are preferred. Adding a two-toned combination with a lighter, contrasting color will catch more fish. The contrast needs to be sharp, even to the point of adding a fluorescent color. Subtle contrast between colors will be less noticeable and less effective. I like a black Woolly Bugger as much as the next guy, but next time you swing it through a deep pool, especially one overshadowed by shade, try one with a sharply contrasting accent color. You could even consider a fluorescent, bicolored fly. You just might be pleasantly surprised!

The same theory applies to fishing weighted nymphs into deep, dark holes. The most effective nymphs for deepwater runs or pools are tied with dark colors. Try adding a "hot spot" in the body of your favorite nymph—a bright-colored, neon, or fluorescent contrast color in the middle of the fly. The fly will work much better! You'll probably never see a natural stonefly or mayfly nymph with a bright fluorescent-orange thorax, but trout are so firmly keyed on contrast as part of their search image under these visual conditions that flies with contrasting hot spots catch more fish than those without.

The reason the contrast needs to be striking in deepwater nymphs is twofold. The normal, daytime occurrence of cone activation in the trout's retina means they are using the less-light-sensitive receptor. It's all or none for rods and cones; trout are using either one or the other. The exception is the period of transition—dawn and dusk—when, for a short time, both cones and rods are used, which may explain why trout often feed the heaviest at these times. During the day, regardless of transitory changes in available light, the cones are exclusively used. The retina doesn't automatically switch to night-vision rods in the middle of the day just because the trout move to a deep hole. Remember, trout can't simply dilate the pupil to adjust to changing light condition. A more complex control mechanism determines the cone-to-rod switch, including the cyclic influence of the pineal gland.

Added to that is the fact that the penetration of light in deeper water means there is less available light to detect—the second reason for using striking contrast. During the day, the trout's color-sensing cones are engaged, but their lower light sensitivity compared with rods will reduce visual acuity in conditions where less light is available. The combination of less available light and a receptor not ideally suited for low-light conditions means our presentation needs to pop just a little to get the trout's attention. Fluorescent or bright colors with a darker contrasting color work well. A sinking-tip line gets the fly to any trout holding in deeper water. A dark-bodied fly with a sharply contrasting color gets noticed, and catches more trout.

Have you noticed how many of the tungsten Czech-style nymphs have a fluorescent hot spot? I remember when I saw my first set, which I ordered online. Most of these flies, which are designed to drift in the lowest and often dimmest layer of the water column, have a strongly contrasted hot spot. The fluorescent color contrast is needed to catch the attention of trout lurking in deep pools and runs.

Stained Water

Stained water is a different story. The most commonly encountered stained water is a weak brown color that is a product of dissolved tannins, which are usually a feature of the watershed for that particular river. Tannins are dissolved in the water similar to the way sugar dissolves in water, and they occur in rivers that arise or receive flow from peat bogs or other marshy headwaters. Tannins are released through the organic decomposition of trees, leaves, or other terrestrial debris. Tannin-stained water is still transparent; it is similar to a glass of iced tea (minus the ice), as opposed to the cloudy or opaque nature of turbid water. In other words, you could easily read a newspaper through it. It is a bit like looking through rose-colored glasses; the discoloration affects visibility and produces profound color shifts.

Stained water also differs from turbid water in that the discoloration of stained water is more constant—a persistent characteristic of the river. Turbidity is often a temporary state, existing on any river under conditions that introduce more particulate matter into the river, such as spring runoff or heavy rains. Stained water tends to be stained regardless of flow or discharge but turbidity often increases from any condition that increases flow.

I cut my fly-fishing teeth in the tea-colored water of the Pere Marquette River in Michigan and I still consider it my home water even though I don't get to fish it near as often. Its water is tea-stained by natural tannins generated from its marshy headwaters. After joining Baldwin Creek, it flows through a fly-fishing only, catch-and-release stretch whose riffles and holes I have prowled many times. With fairly reliable hatches and consistent flows, it is an ideal training ground for a fledgling angler.

When the afternoon shadows lengthened and sunny days edged toward dusk, I loved to strip a gold-ribbed Muddler Minnow with a flashy, bright-yellow tail across sweepers and logjams hoping to catch a nice brown trout just waking up. The bright yellow provided contrast to the drab, brown deer hair head, and the color combination was highly visible in the water, which was the color of weak tea. These colors offered optimum visibility because of the yellow-brown color shift in tannin-stained waters.

Low-light conditions develop more rapidly on cloudy evenings, making contrast a priority earlier than on sunny days. On the Pere Marquette River, my favorite cloudy-evening choice is a wet fly called the Black Queen, which has a black floss body and silver tinsel rib that contrasts nicely with the light-gray-speckled duck flank feathers that compose the swept-back wings. It is a favorite fly of Bob Nicholson, who taught me to fish wet flies by swinging them under sweepers, in front of rocks, and across other likely lies. It is a great "prospecting fly"—a searching pattern that mimics a wide variety of prey species and covers a lot potential food choices for trout feeding opportunistically.

On the same river in the spring, I like a fly with flash of red. This imitates the alevins, which have a bit of red or orange color under their chins that is a remnant of the yolk sac. If water clarity is diminished by the turbidity of spring runoff and high water, I favor a fly with a fluorescent-colored throat (such as orange) for better visibility.

Turbid Water

Turbid water, often called "dingy water" by bass fishermen, is characterized by a cloudy discoloration, usually brown, green, or white. Depending on the degree of turbidity, the water varies from opaque to a semi-opaque when viewed from above. Under water, turbidity limits the visibility, both in visual range and acuity. Caused by solid particles of material mixed and suspended in the water, turbid water assumes the same color as the suspended particulate matter. The difference between stained water and dingy water is the size of the particles and the manner in which they are incorporated into the water. Smaller *dissolved* molecules such as tannins produce staining. Larger particles such as soil, organic debris, and microorganisms including algae and plankton are *suspended* in the water, producing turbidity. The distinction between dissolved and suspended material is important because the heavier particles causing turbidity have a faster sedimentary rate, meaning they settle to the bottom faster than dissolved particles. This leads to the eventual clearing of the turbid water. Stained water, with less precipitation of particles, is more likely to remain stained whereas turbid water will slowly clear.

If you arrive at the river and can't see the bottom in a foot of water, you can be fairly sure the water is turbid. Sometimes it's not as obvious, though. Turbidity varies by degrees; it's not an "all or nothing" deal. Learning to recognize the subtleties of water clarity takes a little time and observation, but is well worth the effort. Even minor turbidity affects what the trout see and how they adjust to the visual limitations, and this impacts their feeding behavior and ultimately our fly choice. The angler who recognizes and adjusts to turbid water will catch more fish.

Early in the season, muddy brown turbidity arises when there is a heavy sedimentary load from streambed erosion during high flows, surface runoff from heavy spring rains, or the thaw of ice and snow. It is a common water condition for late-winter and early-spring rivers. In summer and fall, muddy water often follows heavy rains because of excess surface runoff. If rain falls faster than the ability of the soil to absorb it, runoff will result and the material that ends up in the river causes turbid water.

Green discoloration arises from suspended organic organisms such as algae and plankton, which proliferate in the warm summer months. Sometimes this type of turbidity may appear brownish-green depending on the nature of the suspended vegetation. It is more common in lowland streams and rivers with a large biomass than in high mountain streams where the biomass is less. A warmwater creek flows placidly behind my house and by midsummer is a dirty green color. The warm, turbid water is unsuitable for trout but is a great place for catfish, bullheads, and creek chubs.

Milky-white turbidity is usually due to high mineral content in the water such as is found in mountain streams originating from glacial melt. The glacier's movement and its grinding against the rock layer underneath it mix inorganic minerals into the snowmelt runoff that is carried into streams. While hiking and fishing above the treeline in Alaska a few summers ago, I followed a narrow stream formed by the melt-off trickling from several points along the base of a large glacier. It was interesting to witness the birth of the stream from the combination of these small trickles, which served as the part of the headwaters for what would be a much larger river as it collected with other streams along its course.

As I watched the stream flow, the mineral-rich water looked like a dirty, weak skim milk that eventually fed into a small alpine lake. The cloudy water formed a billowing white tongue that extended well into the lake. The stream draining the lake from the other side was clearer since some of the mineral load had dropped out of the water by then.

The precipitation of suspended particles is a feature of turbid water. In time, most of the suspended material settles out from the water, which then clears. Soil particles, excavated from high water flows, drop out of the water as it slows, depositing layers of soft sedimentary material in alluvial regions (floodplains). Or minerals precipitate to the bottoms of mountain streams. Or in the case of algae discoloration, winter arrives and the cold weather halts algae proliferation. In most cases, turbidity is transitory, although for massive rivers like the Mississippi, it is more or less a constant feature.

Turbidity obscures visibility in the water, reducing not only the effective range of vision for fish, but also impairing the acuity of that vision. Depending on the nature of the suspended particles, turbidity also causes color shifts. Many species of fish can't live in the murky water of persistently turbid rivers. In fact, you won't find trout in rivers like the Mississippi. Not only is the water too warm and low in oxygen for them, but they also lack the adaptive features needed to live and feed successfully in such an environment. Remember that catfish, ideal inhabitants of warm, murky rivers, have special adaptations for chemoreception, including barbels and solitary superficial chemoreceptors scattered on the body to aid in food procurement, making up for the visual limitations of dingy water.

Brown Turbidity

Fly fishers frequently encounter turbid water conditions during excessive spring runoff or heavy rains, which produce a brownish discoloration. For streams and rivers, water turbidity and the volume of discharge usually go hand in hand. While fishing the Green Drake hatch on a British Columbia mountain stream one July afternoon, my daughter, Erin, and I got caught in a sudden storm. I was fishing while Erin was relaxing when the storm appeared. She made it back to the car, but I huddled beneath a rock outcropping while the storm, complete with dime-sized hail, raged for twenty minutes and then passed. When I walked back to the stream, its waters had risen dramatically and the water was brown from runoff and full of leaves, sticks, and other debris.

During an early April trip to Timber Coulee Creek in the Driftless Area of southwestern Wisconsin, the water was stained from recent rains and snowmelt. The flow was still high, but water levels had receded somewhat as evidenced by bent-over grass, now exposed along low-lying banks where it had recently been submerged by high water flow. A heavy sedimentary load added a turbid ocher color to the water. This is one of my favorite times of the year to fish. Maybe it is the reawakening of the river after the long winter's rest that I love. Or maybe it is just me, reawakened from my own angling dormancy and eager to get my feet wet again.

Upon the recommendation of local fly shop owner Mat Wagner, I bought two tannish-gray flies called MW Scuds whose color nearly matched the color of the water (see fig. 16). Each had a small fluorescent-pink bead tied into the forward half of the body that added a nice contrast to the drab color. The dense, earth-toned body showed up well in a brownish color shift, and the fluorescent contrast made it pop!

Scuds lack hold-fast mechanisms to remain attached to the substrate, and so they often appear in the drift during increased water flows. A scud imitation is a good fly for high-water conditions—trout see a lot of the naturals during these times. By midmorning of that April day, I wished that I had bought more than two MW Scuds. I lost one on a submerged log at the onset and the remaining fly was chewed to bits by the time I had lunch. After lunch, I finally abandoned the tattered scud. By this point most of the dubbing trailed like a shuck and the soft plastic shellback had been cut in pieces by trout teeth. I walked back to the log where I had lost the first fly and tried to retrieve it, but the water was too deep. Nothing else I had in my fly box worked as well.

I have since fished the MW Scud effectively in many other rivers that boast a robust scud population. The MW Scud has become my favorite late-winter and early spring fly, especially if the water is a bit muddy from the spring thaw. Its tan body, tied on a hook straighter than most scud patterns, mimics the more natural drifting and swimming position of a scud. Scuds don't curl up into a coiled ball when they float as was once thought. In fact, scuds are nicknamed "side swimmers" because of their tendency to roll onto their sides while swimming, stretching out their bodies to a nearly straight position. A tungsten "bomb bead" is tied into the middle of the MW Scud; this not only adds a bit of weight, but the pink fluorescent color of the bead adds sharp contrast to the body and imitates the brood pouch the female carries after mating. After mating, the female deposits her eggs into the orange-pink pouch and carries them beneath her body until the young are ready to hatch.

The first consideration when fishing heavy flows associated with spring runoff is to find the trout, since their customary feeding lies will be vacated. The heavy water flows also change feeding lanes, so trout relocate to areas, often along the margins of the river or behind obstructions, where they can find both food and relief from the stronger current. Trout will first seek safety and refuge from the maelstrom, holing up in these safe havens. Feeding may be suspended temporarily but usually resumes quickly as trout adjust to the conditions. Trout will hold tight in strong current. The stronger the current, the more trout are dedicated to structure that offers protection and the less willing they are to expose themselves to the exhaustive force of the current. In strong current, trout are less likely to chase food very far; such excursions are costly in terms of energy. Catching fish under these conditions involves presenting flies close to structure since that's where the fish will be. Edge seams, backwater eddies, and the water behind large obstructions are ideal areas to target.

If I encounter muddy water during other times in the season, say following a heavy midsummer thunderstorm, I might try a San Juan Worm. Dark-colored San Juan Worms with highly visible, sharply contrasting colors work well when high water flows erode riverbanks, excavating earthworms from the soil. The natural incidence of worms in the drift peaks during periods of heavy flows. The trout gobble them up greedily and will often fall for a San Juan Worm.

Crane fly imitations are also effective for the same reason; the erosive effect of heavy water rips them from their soil habitat, where they had burrowed into the riverbanks. You may have to add a few extra sinkers to reach the bottom in the swifter current.

Where you fish during high muddy flows is nearly as important as *what* you fish with. Because of the force required to turn a river around a bend, the outside banks in riverbends are sites of heavy erosion during strong flow, meaning worms are frequently dislodged. Be sure to drift the San Juan Worm to likely feeding lies in the initial straight stretch just downstream of the bend, where the worms are carried to waiting fish. Pay close attention to the drop-off behind the gravel or sandbar that often trails the inner bank of the riverbend, since this site is often a prime lie for trout, who receive food bits from the crosscurrent along the riverbed. The crosscurrent is created by centrifugal force, which causes water to spiral around a riverbend in a helical fashion much like the stripes on a barber pole. The helical current produces a crosscurrent along the streambed that sweeps food from the outside bank, from where erosion has dislodged it, toward the inner bank amid and after the bend. The helical current and resulting crosscurrent at the bottom persists in the initial section of the straightaway downstream of the bend. Trout, well aware of this conveyor belt of food, lie along the back edge of the drop-off and along the inner aspect of the deeper channel after the bend, feeding near the bottom.

Conversely, helical currents at riverbends also produce a crosscurrent at the water's surface traveling from the inner bank to the outer bank, sweeping food (and drift boats) toward the outer bank. Rounding a riverbend in a drift boat requires the oarsman to row away from the outer bank to keep the boat from hitting shore. Likewise, foam, jetsam, flotsam, and dead-floating insects after emergence collect along the outer bank in the

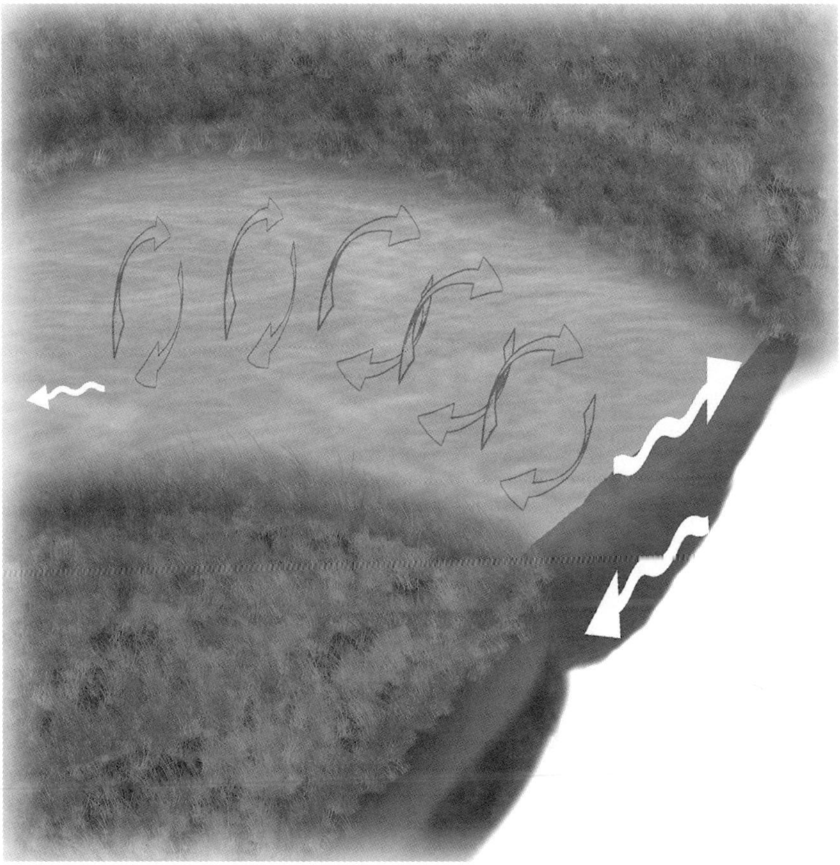

Helical currents develop when water rounds a bend in the river, spiraling through the curve like the stripes on a barber pole. The resulting crosscurrent at the bottom moves food from the outer bank to the inner bank.

tailout of riverbends, which makes this surface depositional zone an ideal site to cast a spinner or crippled emerger.

Don't overlook the possibility of catching trout on a dry fly in high, muddy water. I like to drift large terrestrials in surface depositional zones during high flows following heavy summer rains. Such areas are easy to locate; look for back eddies, soft-water edges, and any places where surface foam and debris collect. The outer bank of the river following the bend is an ideal area for this. Depending on the season, ants, beetles, and grasshoppers are often washed into the stream from rainfall or surface runoff and collect in depositional zones, becoming easy meals for trout. In early summer, try a beetle or ant; from midsummer to early fall, try a

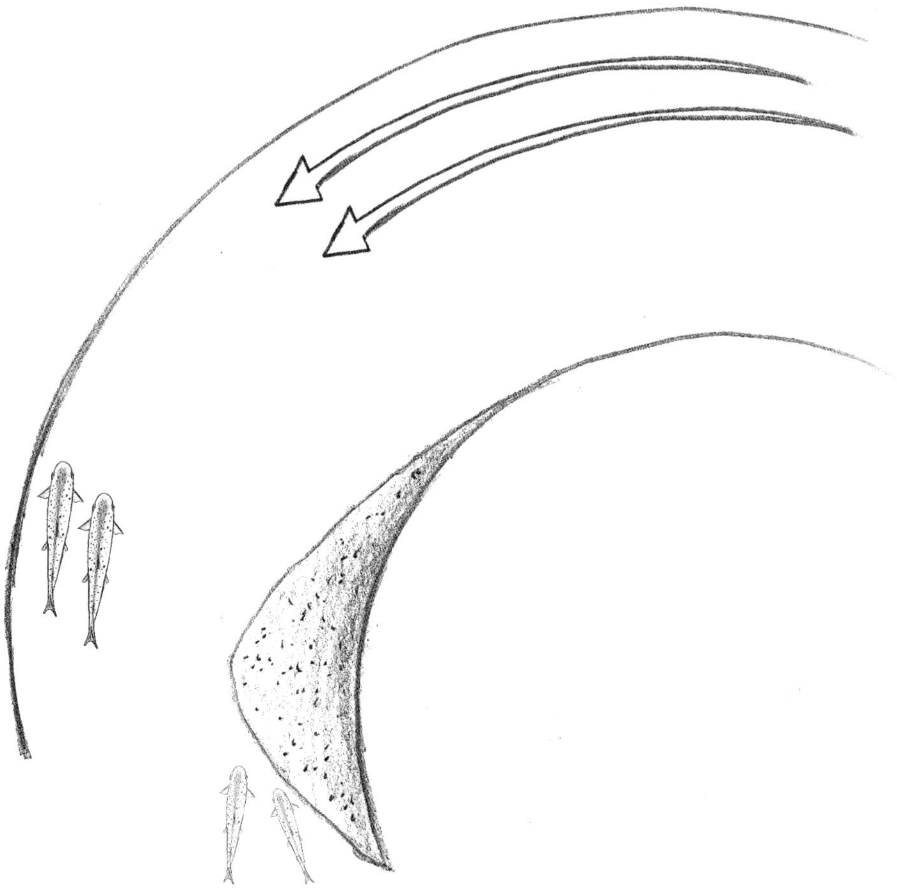

Trout, aware of the crosscurrent delivery of food, choose lies that offer the best feeding opportunities. Check out the back edge of the gravel bar that often develops along the inner bank just past the bend.

hopper pattern. Sometimes a subtle twitch of the fly can make it more noticeable amid the plethora of other debris.

Green Turbidity

Even though trout don't favor slow-moving, warm rivers where microalgae and plankton proliferate to massive populations, the summer proliferation of suspended vegetative organisms imparts turbidity to many trout streams, producing a green color shift and limiting underwater vision for trout. You can actually see bits of brown and green algae suspended in a river water sample collected in a clear container during the warm summer weather.

The same Timber Coulee Creek that was muddy in early spring showed a greenish turbidity later in the year. With a high biomass from the verdant valley that feeds it, it usually has green turbid water by midsummer. When Jo and I arrived for hopper season, the channels I had fished in April were choked with weed beds and dense vegetation and the water showed a marked green color shift.

Selecting the fly color most visible in turbid water is important and should be based on the color shift. Once again following the principles of bass fishermen, turbid or heavily stained water means that we should select denser colors for our main color choice, rather than light colors, especially white, since white tends to acquire the color of the water. A contrasting color makes the fly stand out in the turbid water but the contrast needs to be more dramatic, with fluorescent colors adding the necessary vividness. Blacks and dark earth tones show up well, but are more noticeable when coupled with a fluorescent color.

A Gunni Special would be an ideal fly choice in green-shifted, low-visibility water (see fig. 17). Ben Furimsky, the fly's designer, uses it as his go-to fly in green, discolored water. With a bushy, two-toned, black and fluorescent-green tail, the Gunni Special retains high visibility in turbid water. It has a nice profile and a contrasting color combination that ensures it will be noticed. A strip-and-pause technique adds lifelike movement to the tail and rubber legs, which combined with a beadhead nose causes the fly to pop and drop vertically in the water column to further attract the attention of trout. A sinking-tip line helps keep this fly in front of tight-holding trout.

Since many rivers have sufficient microalgae such as diatoms, and other plankton proliferation in the summer to create a green color shift, it is a handy fly to have in the box for fishing turbid summer water. It is also a good choice for stillwater ponds and lakes with a green color shift (see fig. 18).

For warmwater rivers where small- and largemouth bass are frequently found, the green color shift may be more profound. Fly selection based on the degree of color shift becomes more important. I've noticed that many of the smallmouth flies, particularly the Clouser Minnow color combinations favored by Bob Clouser, show up well in greenish turbid water.

Contrast Rules the Night

Because fish can't see color under the low-light conditions of night, the specific color choice for nighttime flies matters less. Contrast in color selection, however, is paramount. The color-sensing cones in the trout's retina are dormant and the light-sensitive, contrast-oriented rods are engaged. The search image for night-feeding trout relies heavily on size, silhouette, and footprint (for dry flies), but contrast is vital and still very recognizable to trout, even in near darkness. Pay attention to the different shades of the fly, as well. If needed, take a black-and-white photograph of the fly. It will give you a more accurate idea of the contrast and shading of the fly and offers a realistic representation of what the trout sees. Like the classic silver-screen movies, shades become more evident when color is absent.

If you like to swim streamers or drift mouse patterns after dark, remember to switch to a fly that emphasizes contrast as the light diminishes. Just before first light in the morning is also an ideal time for streamer fishing near logjams, undercut banks, and other home sites for large trout. Choose a strongly contrasted color pattern for your streamer and keep fishing it longer on overcast mornings that extend the low-light conditions well past dawn, and begin to fish it earlier on cloudy afternoons.

Contrast is also important for fishing spinnerfalls after dark, especially Hex spinners that are nearly exclusively fished after dark. Jamie Clous introduced a new fly design during a Hex trip a few summers ago. It was a size 8, drab, colorless dry fly with clear wings made from material slightly thicker than cellophane, but still flimsy. It had a sharply contrasting two-toned abdomen and long tail fibers.

With its flimsy wings vibrating through the air, the fly sounded like a rubber band-powered balsa airplane when it whizzed by your ear during the forward cast—but it landed on the water with a soft splat. Sometimes the wings would lie fully extended in a spent position, and sometimes one wing would be up or folded back, just like a natural.

That night, we made fun of the buzzing sound we heard from each other's boat, but toasted the success of the new fly afterward on the porch. The spent-wing design allowed the contrasting, two-toned abdomen to ride low on the water's surface, clearly visible to the trout, which was proven several times that night.

FURTHER STRATEGIES BASED ON WATER CLARITY

Water clarity and visibility should influence our choice of fly color, and we also need to adjust the way we fish accordingly, particularly the speed of our presentation or our retrieve speed for streamers. If the sky is bright and the water clear, I like to keep the flies moving quickly to offer the trout only a glimpse of the fly. This means selecting faster water for a dead-drift presentation or using a faster retrieve speed for streamers. To again borrow from our bass-fishing cousins, bass pro Kevin VanDam explains his clear-water strategy in an article for Strike King Lures: "When I'm retrieving a spinner bait in clear water, I'm cranking that reel from ¾ to as fast as I can possibly turn the handle on the reel."

Fishing clear water on a sunny day is probably the toughest fishing condition I can imagine; give me turbid water any day! Not only can trout see well under high-visibility conditions, but they are also very conscious about being seen by predators. Many normally occupied feeding lies are often vacant. For instance, trout avoid feeding lies in shallow water where they are exposed to other predators. Their innate wariness is on full alert because they sense their own vulnerability in the clear water.

I usually target deep runs where trout feel more secure from predation or turbulent stretches where the choppy water obscures their visibility. The air entrained in water from turbulence, which gives whitewater its opacity, offers a natural camouflage to trout holding in feeding lies below. Many anglers often overlook fast-moving water as a potential feeding lie because they feel trout will not hold in such strong current. But friction at the bottom of the river slows the current in the lower water layer to the point where the bottom 6 inches of a 4-foot-deep run is moving at one-quarter the speed of the water in the center of the vertical water column, where the speed is greatest. Trout take advantage of the slower current at the bottom and rely on it to deliver food to their positions, while at the same time benefiting from the concealment provided by fast runs.

The turbulent water that offers trout obscurity in their feeding lies also limits their visual capacity to inspect our flies as the current whisks them by. The brisk current speed allows only a glimpse of the fly, which hopefully triggers a reactionary strike. Be sure to add enough weight to get the fly to the bottom and use short, upstream casts to ensure it drops through the water column to the waiting trout.

It's important to get the flies close to the trout since they will not venture far to chase a fly if it exposes them to a higher risk in the clear water. When fishing in high-visibility conditions, target your casts close to structure, whether it is the shoreline or the bottom. Wary trout, conscious of their vulnerability, will dart out from hidden lies to snap a morsel from the current and then just as quickly return to the safety of their lie. Evan, Clay, and I faced clear water and high-visibility conditions when we fished the Gros Ventre River during our trip to Wyoming. We hiked several miles from the gravel parking lot to the skinny-water upper stretches, where the river was barely wider than my 9-foot rod. When the morning shadows still overstretched the river, trout occupied nearly every expected feeding lie even though the water was very clear. They felt safe and confident lurking in the shadows. Although there was no insect hatch, cutthroat trout rose to stimulators and small foam terrestrials. Catching fish was fairly easy, inaccurate casts were forgiven by eager trout, and overall, the fishing was less demanding and technical.

As the morning waned, however, trout gradually became harder to catch. The interval between caught fish increased incrementally and almost imperceptively at first until we stood in the midday sunshine and realized that none of us had caught a fish for more than forty-five minutes. What had changed, we wondered? No insect hatch had accounted for our earlier fishing success, so the lack of one could not then be blamed. Each of us had changed flies multiple times; thus, many different flies were offered and refused by the once-willing trout. It quickly dawned on us that the visibility had changed between the morning and afternoon. The slanting shadows of morning were gone and the midday sun blazed directly overhead, causing trout to be conscious of their vulnerability. Many previously occupied lies were deserted.

Once we realized this, we adjusted by factoring the angle of the sun into our fishing tactics. For one thing, we became more conscious of where our shadows fell on the river, both in where we stood as well as our angle of approach to the river. We were careful not to let our shadows scare the trout away. It's not only the trout you scare away that is frightened—the next trout or two up or down the river are agitated and alerted to your presence. Fear is contagious among trout and is easily communicated from one trout to another. When you send one trout fleeing for cover, all other trout in proximity are warned and on high alert. They're more conscious of security than interested in feeding.

We also tried to predict how the trout had reacted to the changing conditions, which included where we should expect to find fish. We began to target specific areas beneath undercut banks in swift water and in sections of the river where shadows still covered the water. When the river was running perpendicular to the sun, in other words when the river aligned in an east-west direction, the southern bank offered shade to that edge of the river, especially if the bank was steep or high. It was better yet if overhanging vegetation or grass was also present. We started catching fish again once we adjusted our tactics and our choices of targeted lies. The trout reacted to the high-visibility conditions by seeking more protected and concealed lies along shady banks. Our casts had to be on target to their lies in order to draw their attention. They would not risk a long excursion after a wayward fly—it had to be right on their lie.

The type of water I avoid in high-visibility conditions is flat, slack water where the trout can inspect any offering at their leisure and spot anglers from far away. Trout are inherently wary in the clear water anyway and usually don't let you get very close without spooking. Through the unbroken surface of the water, they can clearly see anglers near the lower edge of Snell's window.

Conversely, in the low-visibility conditions of turbid water, many bass fishermen use a slower retrieve, leaving the lure in the strike zone a bit longer to give the fish time to respond. Years ago, when fishing on Wisconsin's Lake Geneva, we used a slow-roll retrieve with crankbaits that wobbled and rattled to create water displacement and noise whenever the visibility was reduced. By midsummer, the water would acquire a mild greenish turbidity and we caught a lot of smallmouth with a slow retrieve on warm evenings.

Don't be afraid of dingy water when fly fishing; I much prefer it to clear water. A change of tactics is once again in order. In turbid water, I generally slow the presentation or retrieve. Animation is important.

Since trout feel more secure in their relative obscurity in the turbid water, they feed with more confidence. In fact, turbid water often offers a good chance to catch a trophy trout. In the low-light conditions of turbid water, large trout often begin foraging earlier in the afternoon and extend their feeding later into the morning. Identify the home sites of large trout, such as logjams, rock piles, deep pools, and undercut banks. Also look for the first bit of cover upstream from their home site, which is often the first place they visit as they begin their forays.

When seeking large trout, bear in mind that their feeding strategy is to intercept smaller fish moving to and from feeding lies and shelter lies. Since both feeding and shelter lies offer protection from predation, fish are most vulnerable in transition as they move back and forth. Predatory trout don't normally try to root out smaller fish from their shelter lies and rarely will a large trout attack a smaller fish while it occupies a feeding lie, since doing so would involve a chase through strong current once the fish is displaced from the lie. Instead, the big trout often lurk along soft-water edges or cruise gravel bars and flats to intercept smaller fish moving between feeding stations and shelter when they are in the open and exposed.

This has everything a large trout could hope for in a home site: deep water, steady but mild current, a logjam, and a boulder bottom and bank. This is a great place to look for your trophy. JO RANDALL

A run that ends in a pool is a great place to find large trout, but most anglers focus only on the pool. As daylight dwindles, the big boys move upstream from the pool and cruise along the edges of the run to intercept fish moving from their feeding lies beneath the swift current to the safety of their shelter lies. Learning to identify the intercept routes favored by large trout will aid your quest for trophy fish.

Water clarity and visibility change drastically on tailwaters relative to water flow. While I was fishing on the White River last August, a sudden flux in water discharge from Bull Shoals Dam created a surge of turbid water carrying leaves, sticks, vegetation, and clumps of didymo (or "rock snot") dislodged by the high flow. The previously clear water immediately became a turbid maelstrom clouded by swirling bits of material. In response to the change in water discharge, the fish changed their feeding strategy; this, in turn, required a change in fishing strategy in order to continue catching them. White River guide Chad Johnson, who has a natural instinct for understanding and catching large trout, pointed out brown trout on the gravel bars trailing the inside curve of a riverbend. These fish had moved from deep runs in the center of the river. Attracted by new feeding opportunities, the browns fed not only on the organisms that had been dislodged by the strong flows, but also on the smaller fish that had been displaced from their feeding lies as they moved to safe shelter. Chad suggested switching flies from the hoppers we had been using to something the browns would see better in the cloudy water. We chose a San Juan Worm with a highly visible hot spot of fluorescent pink, but a highly visible streamer fished off the back edge of the gravel bar would probably have worked just as well.

For high flows of turbid water, I like to have plenty of streamers on hand in dark, dense colors with added fluorescent contrast. I often use soft plastic nose cones in turbid water since sound and water displacement are essential in prey location when visibility is impaired. Noisy streamers with plastic nose cones create a large disturbance in the water that attracts a trout's attention. A rattle device incorporated into the body of the streamer also works well. Fish are alerted to the presence of a prey species through their long range sense of hearing and can approximate their quarry long before the sense of sight comes into play.

The larger, eye-catching presentation of large streamers can be further enhanced with animation, another aspect of the search image that becomes more important in reduced visibility. Twitching and pausing with a slow retrieve can be effective, especially when imitating a sculpin, which, lacking a swim bladder for neutral buoyancy, sinks between swimming efforts. In turbid water, the presentation can be slower. You don't need fast movements and rapid line strips.

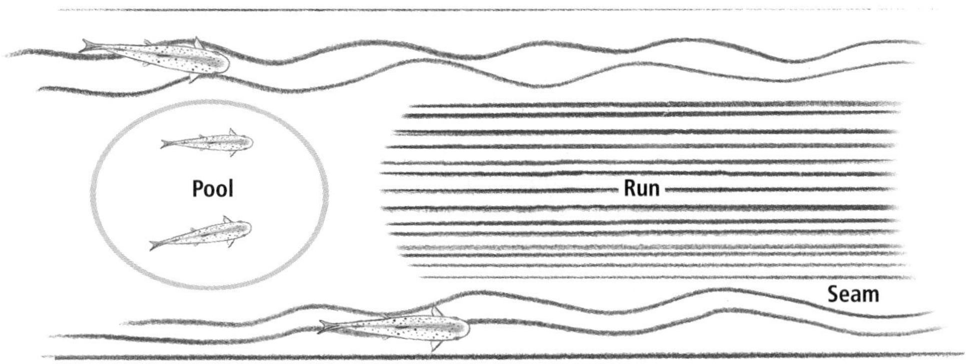

Pools offer ideal home sites for large trout, but don't overlook the soft-water seams along the edges of fast runs often just upstream of pools. Large trout often cruise these edges hoping to intercept smaller fish traveling between feeding lies in the brisk water and shelter lies along the river margins.

THE SEARCH IMAGE IN FLY DESIGN

How can we use search image to catch more trout, remembering that the search image changes under different conditions? One way is to design and construct more convincing flies, ones that fool more trout. Not too long ago, popular opinion held that our flies had to be exact duplicates of the original organisms, even if it meant they were hard-plastic replicas made of rosins and glue. These flies looked good in photographs and appealed to anglers, but not so much to the trout because they often acted stiff and lifeless in the water.

Trout are visual predators, yet their search image involves not only the visual appearance of the prey, but also how the natural organism acts in the water. The actual search image trout use for prey encounters is less like a photograph of the organism in question and more like a video of it in action. A photograph only shows one aspect of the organism's character—its outward appearance—while a video of the same organism shows not only its appearance, but also the way it interacts with its environment. In other words, the way it rests on or moves through the water and how it interacts with current. If you have ever dropped a beetle, hopper, or ant into the water, you are aware of the exaggerated, flailing attempts of a land-based insect swimming to safety. An insect breaking through its nymphal shell or through the surface film also involves movement. Even a newly emerged mayfly unfolding and drying its wings on the water's surface moves as it does so; wings unfurl and stretch out and legs move as they rest on the surface, causing the dimpled footprint to sparkle in the sun.

It turns out that our angling forefathers were pretty insightful in their use of natural components in the construction of flies. Hackle fibers and natural dubbing materials often add lifelike subtlety of movement as the fly encounters microcurrents in the water flow. Palmered hackle on the body of a fly imitates these miniscule movements, as do the rubber legs on hoppers and other flies.

Remember, our flies don't have to be exact copies of the original. As an example, simply hold an Elk Hair Caddis next to the Western Sedge it imitates. It is a little like an impressionist painting compared to a photograph. A Renoir or a Monet is definitely not an exact duplicate of the original subject, but it bears enough resemblance to be easily recognizable, and has an allure that enhances its attractiveness. Think of our flies as impressionist works of art matching enough criteria of the original to pass inspection but with an element of uniqueness that is an attractant rather than a deterrent.

We also need to bear in mind that the search image changes under different conditions and that we must construct flies that are designed to meet those conditions. We should have flies for night fishing, flies for bright clear water, and flies for different conditions of turbidity. That way, we'll always be ready to meet the conditions we find on the river.

Certain additional aspects of the trout's search image have come to light through recent underwater photography and videos. Take, for example, the importance of painted eyes on streamers such as the Clouser Minnow. I remember the nearly iridescent appearance of the trout eyes as captured on an underwater video by Ozzie Ozefovich; the eyes literally glowed, drawing my immediate attention like a neon sign. I agree with Ozzie when he states that the prominent appearance of the prey fish's eyes underwater may explain the success of flies like the Clouser Minnow. Perhaps, to take it one step further, we should consider the use of "tiger

Note the attention-grabbing eyes of these trout parr; they seem to pop from the photo, even those of the parr in the background. The large, nearly luminescent eyes are a feature of the search image for predatory trout. Note the sharp contrast created by the black pupil.

eyes" in the place of painted eyes. (A tiger eye is a type of gemstone that displays natural *chatoyancy*—a type of luminescence that adds the impression of movement.) It would certainly raise the cost of the streamer, but the visual effect may well imitate the eye movements of trout and also add vibrancy and depth. New dumbbell eyes, called dazl or prismatic eyes, are now available that add the same illusion.

The importance of UV reflecting materials in the construction of flies is under much scrutiny and debate. Current research certainly raises doubt as to the importance of UV light to the vision of large trout. But, although large trout have diminished UV sensitivity compared to the younger (pre-smolt) stages, dubbing and other UV material still have qualities that are attractive to fish.

Natural iridescence may explain the success of UV dubbing material. The term *iridescence* refers to items that seem to change hues relative to the viewing angle, creating a shimmering effect that can be attention-grabbing. Think of soap bubbles, blown by kids from a loop dipped into soapy water. The surface shimmers in the sunlight, reflecting different colors in the filmy surface. Even though large trout lack the pronounced UV light detection that has been ascribed to them in the past, trout may still be attracted to these products due to their natural iridescence. They add a sense of movement even when there is none, simply by the changes in the way the light illuminates them. Peacock herl and the feathers from the heads of drake mallards are natural products common in fly construction that have the same iridescent property. Look at the head of a drake mallard from different angles; sometimes it appears green, sometimes blue, and at times even black. These materials have been successfully used in flies for a long time.

I have had the opportunity to examine many different "UV" materials, including feathers, hair, and dubbing treated with UV-enhancing dyes. Many of these materials have not been properly analyzed for UV reflectance to substantiate claims of UV capability, and even if they had been analyzed, we know that UV light only plays a nominal ecological role in trout feeding anyway. But many of the products I examined have other visual properties that may attract fish, such as color enhancement, similar to the eye popping characteristics of fluorescent colors. It may be that these products catch fish, not based on their UV light characteristics, but on other visual properties.

Further analysis and scientific evaluation of the many products that claim UV enhancement is clearly needed. I think we'll find that their success, previously ascribed to UV enhancement, may be due to other properties of the material.

THE SEARCH IMAGE IN FISHING STRATEGY

It can't be overstated that the most important prerequisite for matching the search image for trout, especially when the prey species is an insect, is to match the correct stage of the life cycle. You can't possibly match the search image with a dry fly on the surface if the trout are eating emergers just below the film. The visual characteristics of the dry fly are much different from those of an emerger, including footprint on the water and depth in the film.

Sometimes identifying the riseform offers clues as to the stage of the insect that the trout are eating, but there are as many different riseforms as there are authors to identify them. Sometimes you have to collect samples in a seine net to determine the specific food source. There are times, however, when collecting samples just isn't possible.

If I am uncertain whether the trout are taking an insect just before emergence or just after as the insect waits to lift from the water's surface, I sometimes use a dry fly trailing an emerger. Recently I have come to appreciate the value of a Klinkhamer, which is an emerger that rides just below the surface film on a downward-curved hook suspended from a parachute collar near the hook eye. Designed in the 1980s by Dutch angler Hans van Klinken, it was originally conceived to imitate an emerging caddis. It is now tied in many different colors and useful for nearly any insect species that hangs in the surface film.

I also use it in combination with a small nymph or beadhead fly in a technique that has been appropriately and rather humorously labeled "klink and dink." An orange-bodied soft-hackle fly, sparsely collared with partridge hackle and trailed behind a Klinkhamer, can also be deadly during a caddis emergence. I allow it to swing at the end of a dead drift to make full use of the soft-hackle fly.

Trailing a wet fly or soft hackle during an insect hatch is called "fishing below the hatch," and is particularly effective during most caddis hatches. When you see the splashy rises of small fish at the surface and are tempted to tie on an Elk Hair Caddis, instead give this technique a try. The larger fish are often feeding below the hatch, making this an opportunity to catch bigger fish. I often trail a LaFontaine-style sparkle emerger behind an X-wing caddis; both can be fished on the swing after a dead-drift period.

The shape of the hook is the key to the Klinkhamer's effectiveness; it allows the body of the fly to hang below the film like an insect trying to break through the surface.
DARIN SAKAS

This combination may more effectively match the search image of trout that are seeing pharate pupae (the caddis, recently freed from its pupal case in the act of emergence at the water's surface as the winged adult) darting through the water column to the surface; it also appeals to those fish actually feeding on the surface.

Matching size in the search image is important. Make sure your fly is the same size as the natural prey species the trout are eating. Size is one of the most consistent aspects of the search image, regardless of whether you fish during daylight or at night. The next time you collect insects with a seine net or pass a standard bug net through a cloud of insects hovering over the water, notice the uniformity in size of the insects in the bottom of your net; there is very little variance in size, provided they are all of the same species and stage. Our flies need to be the same size as the natural insects the trout are seeing in the stream.

Remember the seasonal variation in insect size when fishing in the winter and adjust your fly size accordingly. Most species overwinter in an immature stage, during which the insect is smaller than during the summer stages closer to emergence. As an immature insect molts through various *instars* or substages on the way to winged maturity, it grows larger in size. Drift samples collected in the winter will yield smaller insects, with an absence of pharate pupae and the larger, more mature nymphs that are characteristic of summer samples. The obvious exceptions are midges, which cycle through the winter in most climates, and the BWOs, which often have a winter generation.

Our winter flies should also lack highly developed wing pads, as well. The earlier stages of the nymphs, which typify the overwintering stage, have not yet developed the wing cases they will have closer to emergence. Summer flies should be tied with highly developed wing pads.

At times, however, I deviate from the size of the search image, especially if my fly must compete for the trout's attention with a plethora of natural insects. I might select a fly that is one hook size larger than the natural, rather than a perfect match. In a heavy hatch, sometimes you have to stand out from the crowd, sort of like being the biggest bull in the herd. The key is attracting attention and getting noticed. When there is a ton of bugs on the water or rising to the surface, sometimes being more noticeable is the difference between catching fish and not catching fish.

SEARCHING FLIES

A searching fly is one used to "prospect" for trout when no obvious feeding pattern is evident. By definition, searching flies are those we depend on to catch trout when we can't figure out what they are feeding on or if, in fact, they are feeding at all. We wouldn't use them to rising fish during an emergence, which is a time when trout would be feeding selectively with a narrow search image—one we had better figure out if we are going to catch them. Instead, search patterns are for the times when you stand on the bank scratching your head in dismay after the logical choices have failed.

Many flies have been proposed as ideal searching flies, such as Madame X, hare's ear nymphs, and the Parachute Adams. We each have our own favorite that seems to work for us. All may work under different conditions, but versatility should govern our decision. A searching fly should resemble many different prey species.

When trout are feeding as prey generalists, or opportunistically, they accept a wider range of potential prey meals than when one prey species receives their exclusive predatory focus. This feeding pattern often emerges when there is a lack of one predominant species in overall prey availability. The search image trout use when feeding opportunistically is less firmly established and broader, lacking the repetitive prey encounters from a single prey source that are essential to closely define a narrow search image. Thus, a searching fly that can pass for multiple prey species is more productive than a searching fly that fits a narrow search image of only one prey type. A good searching fly can pass for a number of different prey species.

Since the trout search image is based on food availability, which changes from one season to another, the predominant search image also changes seasonally, thus my searching pattern preference also changes from one season to the next. For example, trout shift their predatory focus from aquatic to terrestrial insects as the season progresses. In fact, the predominant search image evolves drastically throughout the year, from early spring to late spring and from late spring to midsummer. In early spring, I like scuds and smaller nymphs that represent the smaller mayflies that have overwintered in the streambed and that will later molt through successively larger and more mature stages on their way to emergence. In the absence of an emergence of BWOs or other early-season insects, most of the trout feeding at this time occurs below the surface and our searching patterns should prospect in the richest vein, which is the bottom portion of the vertical water column.

By late spring or early summer, the river is teeming with insects, which are larger and more active than before because they are close to emergence. They dart along the streambed and are more common in the drift. Again, our searching fly should be a subsurface presentation since trout, in the absence of a hatch, will have a subsurface search image. Wet flies and soft hackles are effective searching flies in this condition. I favor some of the old-school wet flies like the Picket Pin and Queen of Waters since they imitate many potential prey species. This might also be a good time to try a hare's ear nymph.

By midsummer, the aquatic insects have passed their peak and trout are "looking up" for terrestrials, which predominate in the drift. This is not to say that a late-summer caddis hatch or BWO emergence won't offer an exciting fishing opportunity, just that the main feeding focus of trout shifts to terrestrial insects appearing more consistently in the drift.

For that time of year, I like a different searching fly. Chernobyl ants, foam hoppers, beetles, and ants make ideal searching fly choices, but I especially like Turck's Tarantula. It floats well enough to use a dropper, adding another opportunity to hook some fish, and it looks like several potential prey species. It can also be fished with animation by twitching it on the swing. Its versatility makes it a good searching pattern from midsummer through fall and it works well for most rivers.

I try to avoid fishing indiscriminately; it just doesn't make sense and certainly isn't productive. I am the kind of person who likes to have a definite plan. If a feeding pattern is evident, I try to capitalize on it whether it is an emergence or other event. If I can't figure out the trout's feeding pattern, at least my searching pattern and fishing strategy is based in logic and should give me the best chance to catch the most fish. My best effort is demanded by this most worthy adversary.

A WORTHY ADVERSARY

Trout spend part of their lives as prey and part as predator. Because of this, mature trout have the behavioral characteristics of both prey and predator. They have the typical wariness of prey species and the hunting skills of a predator. They are on constant alert for potential threats and potential meals. They are willing and skeptical at the same time, making them a worthy adversary against whom we pit our wits and skills.

Trout's senses are uniquely developed to serve them in their dual role, with adaptations that have evolved to suit both lifestyles. Their hearing is an early warning system for potential threats and also a means of long-range food identification. Their vision is adapted in the lateral visual field for threat identification and in the forward visual field for prey location and tracking. Even the focal distance for each task is tuned to its specific needs. To survive in the demanding world of rivers and streams, trout had to develop the best characteristics of both prey and predator.

So, in the study of trout senses, we have to be aware of both roles the senses play in trout behavior. Sound has the ability to repel and attract trout, and it's our goal to emphasize one without accentuating the other. We have to be careful of the sounds we make to avoid triggering their early warning threat detection, but we want to incorporate the benefits of natural, prey-mimicking sound into our flies and fishing techniques. We want to eliminate the negative impact of sound that sends trout fleeing for cover, yet at the same time use sound to our benefit so that we can entice more trout to bite. Our approach to the river, our entrance to the stream, our movements about our boats, and our casts should be planned accordingly to minimize sound, but the enticing sounds that prey make need to be used to our fullest benefit.

The same goes for trout's sense of sight and chemoreception. If we disregard their visual warning alert system, most trout will flee long before we have a chance to tempt them. If we are careless of noxious scents in the water or on our flies, we won't catch many of those left around to tempt. Once again, we need to enhance the positives and minimize the negatives. We want to avoid scaring "trout the prey" and attract "trout the predator."

I hope we never master the art of catching trout. I don't think I really have to worry though. Granted, I'd like to consistently improve, but it is the fact that I get beat by them on a regular basis that keeps me coming back.

bibliography

Ahlbert, I. B. "Organization of the Cone Cells in the Retinae of Salmon (*Salmo salar*) and Trout (*Salmo trutta trutta*) in Relation to Their Feeding Habits." *Acta Zoologica* 57 (1976): 13–35.

Allan J. D. "Determinants of Diet of Brook Trout (*Salvelinus fontinalis*) in a Mountain Stream." *Canadian Journal of Fisheries and Aquatic Sciences* 38 (1981): 184–192.

———. "The Size Composition of Invertebrate Drift in a Rocky Mountain Stream." *Oikos* 43 (1984): 68–76.

Allan J. D., A. S. Flecker, and N. L. McClintock. "Prey Size Selection by Carnivorous Stoneflies." *Limnology and Oceanography* 32, no. 4 (1987): 864–872.

Allison, W. T., S. G. Dann, J. V. Helvik, C. Bradley, H. D. Moyer, and C. W. Hawryshyn. "Ontogeny of Ultraviolet-Sensitive Cones in the Retina of Rainbow Trout (*Oncorhynchus mykiss*)." *Journal of Comparative Neurology* 461, no. 3 (2003): 294–306.

Allison, W. T., S. G. Dann, K. M. Veldhoen, and C. W. Hawryshyn. "Degeneration and Regeneration of Ultraviolet Cone Photoreceptors during Development in Rainbow Trout (*Oncorhynchus mykiss*)." *Journal of Comparative Neurology* 499, no. 5 (2006): 702–715.

Amano, M., S. Moriyama, M. Ligo, S. Kitamura, N. Amiya, K. Yamamori, K. Ukena, and K. Tsursui. "Novel Fish Hypothalamic Neuropeptides Stimulate the Release of Gonadotrophins and Growth Hormone from the Pituitary of Sockeye Salmon." *Journal of Endocrinology* 188 (2006): 417–423.

Appelt, C. W., and P. W. Sorensen. "Freshwater Fish Release Urinary Pheromones in a Pulsatile Manner." In *Advances in Chemical Signals in Vertebrates*, edited by R. E. Johnston, D. Müller-Schwarze, and P. W. Sorensen, 247–256. New York: Plenum Press, 1999.

Avery, J. A., et al. "Ultraviolet Sensitive Receptors in a Freshwater Fish." *Journal of Physiology* 334 (1983): 23.

Baker, K., and R. C. Smith. "Bio-Optical Classification and Model of Natural Waters." *Limnology and Oceanography* 27 (1982): 500–509.

Baldwin, D. H., J. F. Sandahl, J. S. Labenia, and N. L. Scholz. "Sublethal Effects of Copper on Coho Salmon: Impacts on Nonoverlapping Receptor Pathways in the Peripheral Olfactory Nervous System." *Environmental Toxicology and Chemistry* 22, no. 10 (2003): 2266–2274.

Bandoh, H., I. Kida, and H. Ueda. "Olfactory Responses to Natal Stream Water in Sockeye Salmon." by BOLD fMRI. PLoS ONE 6, no. 1 (2011): e16051. doi:10.1371/journal.pone.0016051

Barbier, C., and J. A. C. Humphrey. "Drag Force Acting on a Neuromast in the Fish Lateral Line Trunk Canal. I. Numerical Modelling of External-Internal Flow Coupling." *Journal of the Royal Society Interface* 6, no. 36 (2009): 627–640.

Bergman, R. *Trout*. New York: Alfred A. Knopf, 1938.

Bird, N. C., and L. P. Hernandez. "Building an Evolutionary Innovation: Differential Growth in the Modified Vertebral Elements of the Zebrafish Weberian Apparatus." *Zoology* 112, no. 2 (2009): 97–112.

Bjerselius, R., W. Li, J. H. Teeter, J. G. Seelye, P. J. Maniak, G. C. Grant, C. N. Polkinghorne, and P. W. Sorensen. "Direct Behavioral Evidence That Unique Bile Acids Released by Larval Sea Lamprey Function as a Migratory Pheromone." *Canadian Journal of Fisheries and Aquatic Sciences* 57 (2000): 557–569.

Bleckmann, H. *The Behavior of Teleost Fishes*. London: Chapman and Hall, 1993: 201–214.

———. "Prey Identification and Localization in Surface-Feeding Fish and Fishing Spiders." *Sensory Biology of Aquatic Animals* New York: Springer-Verlag, 1988: 619–641.

Bone, Q., and R. H. Moore. *Biology of Fishes*. 3rd ed. New York: Taylor and Francis, 2008.

Bonica, J. J. "The Need for Taxonomy." *Pain* 6, no. 3 (1979): 247–248. Adopted in 2011 by the International Association for the Study of Pain.

Boulcott, P., and V. Braithwaite. "Ultraviolet Light and Visual Behaviour in the Three-Spined Stickleback, *Gasterosteus aculeatus*." *Physiological and Biochemical Zoology* 78 (2005): 736–743.

Bowmaker, J. K., and Y. W. Kunz. "Ultraviolet Receptors, Tetrachromatic Colour Vision and Retinal Mosaics in the Brown Trout (*Salmo trutta*): Age-Dependent Changes." *Vision Research* 27 (1987): 2101–2108.

Bracis, C. "A Model of the Ocean Migration of Pacific Salmon." Masters thesis, University of Washington, 2010.

Brooks, R. E. "Ultrastructure of the Physostomaous Swimbladder of the Rainbow Trout (*Salmo gairdneri*)." *Zeitschrift fur Zellforschung und Mikroskopische Anatomie* 106, no. 4 (1970): 473–483.

Browman, H. I., et al. "Ultraviolet Photoreception Contributes to Prey Search Behaviour in Two Species of Zooplanktivorous Fishes." *Journal of Experiment Biology* 186 (1994): 187–198.

Brown, G. E., C. K. Elvidge, M. C. Ferrari, and D. P. Chivers. "Understanding the Importance of Episodic Acidification on Fish Predator-Prey Interactions: Does Weak Acidification Impair Predator Recognition?" *Science of the Total Environment* 439 (2012): 62–66.

Brown, G. E., and R. J. Smith. "Acquired Predator Recognition in Juvenile Rainbow Trout (*Oncorhynchus mykiss*): Conditioning Hatchery-Reared Fish to Recognize Chemical Cues of a Predator." *Canadian Journal of Fisheries and Aquatic Sciences* 55 (1998): 611–627.

Brown, J. A., C. J. Gray, G. Hattersley, and J. Robinson. "Prostaglandins in the Kidney, Urinary Bladder and Gills of the Rainbow Trout and European Eel Adapted to Fresh Water and Seawater." *General and Comparative Endocrinology* 84, no. 2 (1991): 328–335.

Cardwell, J. R., P. W. Sorensen, G. J. VanDerKraak, and N. R. Liley. "Effect of Dominance Status on Sex Hormone Levels in Laboratory and Wild-Spawning Male Trout." *General and Comparative Endocrinology* 101, no. 3 (1996): 333–341.

Carlsson, J., J. E. Carlsson, K. H. Olsen, N. M. Hansen, T. Eriksson, and J. Nilsson. "Kin-Biased Distribution in Brown Trout: An Effect of Redd Location or Kin Recognition?" *Heredity* 92, no. 2 (2004): 53–60.

Cheng, C. L., and I. Novales. Flamarique. "Chromatic Organization of Cone Photoreceptors in the Retina of Rainbow Trout: Single Cones Irreversibly Switch from UV (SWS1) to Blue (SWS2) Light-Sensitive Opsin during Natal Development." *The Journal of Experimental Biology* 210 (2007): 4123–4135.

———. "Opsin Expression: New Mechanism for Modulating Colour Vision." *Nature* 428 (2004): 279.

———. "Photoreceptor Distribution in the Retina of Adult Pacific Salmon: Corner Cones Exhibit Blue Opsin." *Visual Neuroscience* 24 (2007): 269–276.

Cheng, C. L., K. J. Gan, and I. Novales. Flamarique. "Thyroid Hormone Induces a Time-Dependent Opsin Switch in the Retina of Salmonid Fishes." *Investigative Ophthalmology & Visual Science* 50, no. 6 (2009): 3024–3032.

Collin, S. P., and H. B. Collin. "The Foveal Photoreceptor Mosaic in the Pipefish, *Corythoichthyes paztoni* (Syngnathidae, Teleostei)." *Histology and Histopathology* 14 (1999): 369–382.

Collin, S. P., and J. C. Partridge. "Fish Vision: Retinal Specializations in the Eyes of Deep-Sea Teleosts." Supplement A, *Journal of Fish Biology* 49 (1996): 157–174.

Cooke, S. J., J. F. Schreer, D. H. Wahl, and D. P. Philipp. "Physiological Impacts of Catch-And-Release Angling Practices on Largemouth and Smallmouth Bass." *American Fisheries Society. Symposium* 31 (2002): 489–512.

Coombs, S., P. Gorner, and H. Munz, eds. *The Mechanosensory Lateral Line: Neurobiology and Evolution*. New York: Springer, 1989.

Crawshaw, L. I., and H. T. Hammel. "Behavioral Thermoregulation in Two Species of Antarctic Fish." *Life Sciences* 17, no. 1 (1971): 1009–1020.

Curry, R. F. *The New Scientific Angling: Trout and Ultraviolet Vision*. Wilton, NH: Buckram Publishing, 2009.

Dann, S. G. "Opsin and Retinal Genomics in Salmonid Fishes: Implications for Phylogeny and Retinal Development." PhD dissertation, Department of Biology, Saint Xavier University, 1997.

Danylchuk, A. J., A. J. Adams, S. J. Cooke, and C. D. Suski. "An Evaluation of the Injury and Short-Term Survival of Bonefish (*Albula* Spp.) As Influenced by a Mechanical Fish-Handling Device Used by Recreational Anglers." *Fisheries Research* 93, nos. 1–2 (2008): 248–252.

Deutschlander, M. E., D. K. Greaves, T. J. Haimberger, and C. W. Hawryshyn. "Functional Mapping of Ultraviolet Photosensitivity during Metamorphic Transitions in a Salmonid Fish, *Oncorhynchus mykiss*." *Journal of Experimental Biology* 204 (2001): 2401–2413.

Diogo, R. "Origin, Evolution and Homologies of the Weberian Apparatus: A New Insight." *International Journal of Morphology* 27, no. 2 (2009): 333–354.

Dittman, A. H., and T. P. Quinn. "Homing in Pacific Salmon: Mechanisms and Ecological Basis." *Journal of Experimental Biology* 199 (1996): 83–91.

Douglas, R. H., and M. B. A. Djamgoz. *The Visual System of Fish*. New York: Chapman and Hall, 1990.

Dunlop, R., and P. Laming. "Mechanoreceptive and Nociceptive Responses in the Central Nervous System of Goldfish (*Carassius auratus*) and Trout (*Oncorhynchus mykiss*)." *The Journal of Pain* 6, no. 9 (September 2005): 561–8.

Essington, T. E., and P. W. Sorensen. "Overlapping Sensitivities of Brook Trout and Brown Trout to Putative Hormonal Pheromones." *Journal of Fish Biology* 48 (1996): 1027–1029.

Essington, T. E., P. W. Sorensen, and D. G. Paron. "Redd Superimposition in Stream Resident Brook Trout (*Salvelinus fontinalis*) and Brown Trout (*Salmo trutta*) Cannot be Explained by Habitat Alone." *Canadian Journal of Fisheries and Aquatic Sciences* 55 (1998): 2310–2316.

Evans, D. H., and J. B. Clairborne, eds. *The Physiology of Fishes*. 3rd ed. Boca Raton, FL: CRC Press, 2006.

Ferguson, R. A., and B. L. Tufts. "Physiological Effects of Brief Air Exposure in Exhaustively Exercised Rainbow Trout (*Oncorhynchus mykiss*): Implications for 'Catch and Release' Fisheries." *Canadian Journal of Fisheries and Aquatic Sciences* 49, no. 6 (1992): 1157–1162.

Fernald, R. D. "Aquatic Adaptations in Fish Eyes." In *Sensory Biology of Aquatic Animals*, edited by J. Atema, R. R. Fay, A. N. Popper, and W. N. Tavolga, 435–466. Berlin, Germany: Springer-Verlag, 1988.

———. "Review Teleost Vision: Seeing while Growing." Supplement, *Journal of Experimental Zoology* 5 (1990): 167–80.

Finger, T. E. *Evolution of Taste and Solitary Chemoreceptor Cell Systems. Brain, Behavior and Evolution* 50, no. 4 (1997): 234–243.

Formicki, K., and T. Perkowski. "The Effect of Magnetic Field on the Gas Exchange in Rainbow Trout *Oncorhynchus mykiss* Embryos (Salmonidae)." *Italian Journal of Zoology* 65 (1998): 475–477.

Formicki, K., and A. Winnicki. "Reactions of Fish Embryos and Larvae to Constant Magnetic Fields." *Italian Journal of Zoology* 65 (1998): 479–482.

Fraser, D. J., P. Duchesne, and L. Bernatchez. "Migratory Char Schools Exhibit Population and Kin Associations beyond Juvenile Stages." *Molecular Ecology* 14, no. 10 (2005): 3133–3146.

Frost, W. E., and M. E. Brown. *Trout*. London: Collins, 1967.

Gan, K. J., and I. Novales. Flamarique. "Thyroid Hormone Accelerates Opsin Expression during Early Photoreceptor Differentiation and Induces Opsin Switching in Differentiated TR- Expressing Cones of the Salmonid Retina." *Developmental Dynamics* 239 (2010): 2700–2713.

Genfron, R. P. "Searching for Cryptic Prey: Evidence for Optimal Search Rates and the Formation of Search Images in Quail." *Animal Behavior* 34, no. 3 (1986): 898–912.

Gil, J. M., and J. M. Pleguezuelos. "Prey and Prey-Size Selection by the Short-Toed Eagle (*Circaetus gallicus*) during the Breeding Season in Granada (South-eastern Spain)." *Journal of Zoology* 255, 131–137.

Gingrich, A. J., S. J. Cooke, K. C. Hanson, M. R. Donaldson, C. T. Hasler, C. D. Suski, and R. Arlinghaus. "Evaluation of the Interactive Effects of Air Exposure Duration and Water Temperature on the Condition and Survival of Angled and Released fish." *Fisheries Research* 86 (2007): 169–178.

Goddard, J. *John Goddard's Trout Fishing Techniques: Practical Fly-Fishing Solutions from an International Master*. Guilford, CT: The Lyons Press, 2003.

Goetz, C. F. "Ovarian and Plasma Prostaglandin E and F Levels in Brook Trout (*Salvelinus fontinalis*) During Pituitary-Induced Ovulation." *Biology of Reproduction* 27, no. 5 (1982): 1216–1221.

Gonzalez-Bellido, P. T., H. Peng, J. Yang, A. P. Georgopoulos, and R. M. Olberg. "Eight Pairs of Descending Visual Neurons in the Dragonfly Give Wing Motor Centers Accurate Population Vector of Prey Direction." *Proceedings of the National Academy of Sciences of the United States of America* 110, no. 2 (January 8, 2013): 696–701.

Grande, T., and M. de Pinna. "The Evolution of the Weberian Apparatus: a Phylogenetic Perspective." In *Mesozoic Fishes 3: Systematics, Paleoevironments and Biodiversity*, edited by G. Arratia and A. Tintori, 429–448. Munich, Germany: Verlag, 2004.

Grant, G. C., B. Vondracek, and P. W. Sorensen. "Spawning Interactions Between Sympatric Brown and Brook Trout May Contribute to Species Replacement." *Transactions of the American Fisheries Society* 131 (2002): 569–576.

Groot, C., and L. Margolis, eds. *Pacific Salmon Life Histories*. Vancouver: University of British Columbia Press, 1991.

Grover-Johnson, N., and A. I. Farbman. "Fine Structure of Taste Buds in the Barbel of the Catfish, *Ictalurus punctatus*." *Cell and Tissue Research* 169, no. 3 (1976): 395–403.

Grubb, T. C. *In the Mind of Trout*. Madison: University of Wisconsin Press, 2003.

Gupta, B. B. P., and Y. Premabati. "Fish Pineal: Structure, Function and Regulation." *Treatise on Pineal Gland and Melatonin* (2002): 77–102.

Haight, C., K. McNamara, K. McQueeney, and Y. Courtney. "Comparing Measured Fluorocarbon Leader Breaking Strength with Manufacturer Claims." Optics Letters, 37; 1400-1402. Cornell University Library, 2012.

Hairston, N. G., Jr., K.T. Li, and S. S. Easter Jr. "Fish Vision and the Detection of Planktivorous Prey." *Science* 218 (1982): 1240–1242.

Halvorsen, M. B., D. G. Zeddies, W. T. Ellison, D. R. Chicoine, and A. N. Popper. "Effects of Mid Frequency Active Sonar on Hearing Fish." *Journal of the Acoustical Society of America* 131, no. 1 (2012): 599–607.

Hanson, L. R., P. W. Sorensen, and Y. Cohen. "Sex Pheromones and Amino Acids Evoke Distinctly Different Patterns of Electrical Activity in the Goldfish Olfactory Bulb." *Annals of the New York Academy of Sciences*, ed. Murphy, C. New York (1998): 521–524.

Hara, T. J. "The Diversity of Chemical Stimulation in Fish Location and Gustation." *Reviews in Fish Biology and Fisheries* 4 (1994): 1–35.

———. "Olfaction and Gustation in Fish: An Overview." *Acta Physiologica Scandinavica* 152, no. 2 (1994): 207–217.

Harosi, F. I., and Y. Hashimoto. "Ultraviolet Visual Pigment in a Vertebrate: a Tretrachromatic Cone System in the Dace." *Science* 222 (1983): 1021–1023.

Hasler, A. D., and A. T. Scholz. *Olfactory Imprinting and Homing Salmon*. Berlin, Germany: Springer-Verlag, 1983.

Hasler, A. D., and W. J. Wisby. "Discrimination of Stream Odors by Fishes and Relation to Parent Stream Behavior." *American Naturalist* 85 (1951): 223–238. Hawkins, A. D., and A. D. F. Johnstone. "The Hearing of the Atlantic Salmon, *Salmo salar*." *Journal of Fish Biology* 13, no. 6: 655–673.

Hawkins, L. A., A. E. Magurran, and J. D. Armstrong. "Ontogenetic Learning of Predator Recognition in Hatchery-Reared Atlantic Salmon, *Salmo salar*." *Animal Behaviour* 75: 1663–1671.

Hawryshyn, C. W. "Review Ultraviolet Polarization Vision in Fishes: Possible Mechanisms for Coding E-Vector." *Philosophical Transactions of the Royal Society B: Biological Sciences* 355, no. 1401 (2000): 1187–90.

Hawryshyn, C. W., et al. "Regeneration of Ultraviolet-Sensitive Cones in the Retinal Cone Mosaic of Thyroxin-Challenged Post-Juvenile Rainbow Trout (*Oncorhynchus mykiss*)." *Journal of Experimental Biology* 206 (2003): 2665–2673.

Helfman, G., B. B. Collette, D. E. Facey, and B. W. Bowen. *The Diversity of Fishes: Biology, Evolution and Ecology*. West Sussex, UK: John Wiley and Sons, 2007.

Horváth, G., and D. Varju. *Polarized Light in Animal Vision*. Berlin, Germany: Springer-Verlag, 2004.

Huntingford, F., M. Jobling, and S. Hadri. *Aquaculture and Behavior*. West Sussex, UK: John Wiley and Sons, 2012: 44.

Ishii, Y., and M. Shimada. "The Effect of Learning and Search Images on Predator-Prey Interactions." *Population Ecology* 52, no. 1 (2010): 27–35.

Johnsen, S., N. J. Marshall, and E. A. Widder. "Polarization Sensitivity as a Contrast Enhancer in Pelagic Predators: Lessons from In Situ Polarization Imaging of Transparent Zooplankton." *Philosophical Transactions of the Royal Society B: Biological Sciences* 366, no. 1565 (2011): 655–70.

Joselevitch, C., and M. Kamermans. "Review Retinal Parallel Pathways: Seeing with Our Inner Fish." *Vision Research* 49, no. 9 (2009): 943–59.

Kageyama, C. J. *What Fish See: Understanding Optics and Color Shifts for Designing Lures and Flies*. Portland, OR: Frank Amato Publications, 1999.

Karlsen, H. K. "Infrasound Sensitivity in the Plaice (*Pleuronectes platessa*)." *Journal of Experimental Biology* 171 (1992): 173–187.

Kezuka, H., M. Ligo, K. Furukawa, K. Aida, and I. Hanyu. "Effects of Photoperiod, Pinealectomy and Ophthalmectomy on Circulating Melatonin Rhythms in the Goldfish, *Carassius auratus*." *Zoological Science* 9 (1992): 1047–1053.

Kim, J. W., G. E. Brown, N. N. Dolinsek, A. O. Leduc, and J. W. Grant. "Combined Effects of Chemical and Visual Information in Eliciting Antipredator Behavior in Juvenile Atlantic Salmon, *Salmo salar*." *Journal of Fish Biology* 74, no. 6 (2009): 1280–1290.

Knono, H., P. Reid, and A. C. Kamil. "The Effect of Background Cuing on Prey Detection." *Animal Behavior* 56, no. 4 (1998): 963–972.

Kreysing, M., R. Pusch, D. Haverkate, et al. "Photonic Crystal Light Collectors in Fish Retina Improve Vision in Turbid Water." *Science* 336, no. 6089 (2012): 1700–1703.

Kroese, A. B., and N. A. Schellart. "Velocity- and Acceleration-Sensitive Units in the Trunk Lateral Line of the Trout." *Journal of Neurophysiology* 68, no. 6 (1992): 2212–2221.

Kulczykowska, E. "Diel Changes in Plasma Arginine Vasotocin, Isotocin, and Melatonin in Rainbow Trout (*Oncorhynchus mykiss*)." *Fish Physiology and Biochemistry* 21 (1999): 141–146.

Kyle, A. L., P. W. Sorensen, N. E. Stacey, and J. G. Dulka. "Medial Olfactory Tract Pathways Controlling Sexual Reflexes and Behaviour in Teleosts." In "The Terminal Nerve (*Nervus terminalis*): Structure, Function and Evolution," edited by L. S. Demski and M. Schwanzel-Fukuda. *Annals of the New York Academy of Science* 519 (1987): 97–107.

Ladich, F., and A. H. Bass. "Sonic/Vocal Motor Pathways in Catfishes: Comparisons with Other Teleosts." *Brain, Behavior and Evolution* 51, no. 6 (1998): 315–330.

Leech, D. M., and S. Johnsen. "Ultraviolet Vision and Foraging in Juvenile Bluegill (*Lepomis macrochirus*)." *Canadian Journal of Fisheries and Aquatic Sciences* 63 (2006): 2183–2190.

Leech, D. M, J. B. Wiebke, S. L. Cooke, C. E. Williamson, and L. Torres. "UV-Enhanced Fish Predation and the Differential Migration of Zooplankton in Response to UV Radiation and Fish." *Limnology and Oceanography* 54 (2009): 1152–1161.

Liao, J. C. "The Role of the Lateral Line and Vision on Body Kinematics and Hydrodynamic Preference of Rainbow Trout in Turbulent Flow." *Journal of Experimental Biology* 209 (2006): 4077–4090.

Loew, E. R., et al. "A Chromatic Action Spectrum for Planktonic Predation by Juvenile Yellow Perch." *Canadian Journal of Zoology* 71 (1993): 384–386.

Lohmann, K. J. "Q & A: Animal Behavior: Magnetic-Field Perception." *Nature* 464 (2010): 1140–1142.

Lohmann, K. J., N. F. Putman, and C. M. F. Lohman. "Geomagnetic Imprinting: A Unifying Hypothesis of Long-Distance Natal Homing in Salmon and Sea Turtles." *Proceedings of the National Academy of Sciences* 105 (2008): 19096–19101.

Maitra, S. K., M. Seth, and A. Chattoraj. "Photoperiod, Pineal Photoreceptors and Melatonin as the Signal of Photoperiod in the Regulation of

Reproduction in Fish." *Journal of Endocrinology and Reproduction* 10, no. 2 (2006): 73–87.

Mann, S., N. H. C. Sparks, M. M. Walker, and J. L. Kirchvink. "Ultrastructure, Morphology and Organization of Biogenic Magnetite from Sockeye Salmon, *Oncorhynchus nerka*: Implications for Magneoreception." *Journal of Experimental Biology* 140 (November 1988): 35–49.

Marinaro, V. C. *In the Ring of the Rise*. Guilford, CT: Globe Pequot Press, 1976.

Mettam, J. J., C. R. McCrohan, and L. U. Sneddon. "Characterisation of Chemosensory Trigeminal Receptors in the Rainbow Trout, *Oncorhynchus mykiss*: Responses to Chemical Irritants and Carbon Dioxide." *Journal of Experimental Biology* 215, no. 4 (2012): 685–693.

Meyer, P., P. Salzer, M. C. Grieshaber, and A. Meyer. "Contribution to Comparative Ophthalmo-Morphology: The Eye of the Brown Trout." *Klinische Monatsblatter fur Augenheikunde* 226, no. 4 (2009): 337–340.

Michel, W. C. "Chemoreception." In *The Physiology of Fishes*, 3rd ed., edited by D. H. Evans and J. B. Claiborne. Boca Raton, FL: CRC Press, 2006.

Migaud, H., A. Davie, C. C. Martinez-Chavez, and S. Al-Khamees. "Evidence for Differential Photic Regulation of Pineal Melatonin Synthesis in Teleosts." *Journal of Pineal Research* 43, no. 4 (2007): 327–335.

Mirza, R. S., and D. P. Chivers. "Predator-Recognition Training Enhances Survival of Brook Trout: Evidence from Laboratory and Field Enclosure Studies." *Canadian Journal of Zoology* 78 (2000): 2198–2208.

Modarressie, R., and T. C. M. Bakker. "A Limited Role for Ultraviolet Radiation when Three-Spine Sticklebacks (*Gasterosteus aculeatus*) Prey upon Daphnia." *Canadian Journal of Fisheries and Aquatic Sciences* 64 (2007): 1573–1580.

Morrissey, J. F., and J. L. Sumich. *Introduction to the Biology of Marine Life*. Sudbury, MA: Jones and Bartlett Learning, 2012.

National Aeronautics and Space Administration (NASA). "Maven Mission to Investigate How Sun Steals Martian Atmosphere." October 5, 2010. http://www.nasa.gov/mission_pages/maven/news/confirmation.html

Nordtug, T., and O. K. Berg. "Optical Properties of the Pineal Window of Atlantic Salmon (*Salmo salar L.*)." *Fish Physiology and Biochemistry* 8, no. 6 (1990): 541–546.

Novales Flamarique, I. "The Ontogeny of Ultraviolet Sensitivity, Cone Disappearance and Regeneration in the Sockeye Salmon, *Oncorhynchus nerka*." *Journal of Experimental Biology* 203 (2000): 1161–1172.

———. "Opsin Switch Reveals Function of the Ultraviolet Cone in Fish Foraging." *Proceedings of the Royal Society B: Biological Sciences* 280, no. 1752 (2012): 1–8.

———. "Unconvincing Evidence for Polarization Sensitivity in Rainbow Trout." Letter to the editor, *Journal of Neuroscience* 33, no. 17 (2013): 7428–7438.

Novales Flamarique, I. and H. I. Browman. "Foraging and Prey-Search Behavior of Small Juvenile Trout (*Oncorhynchus mykiss*) under Polarized Light." *Journal of Experimental Biology* 204 (2001): 2415–2422.

Novales Flamarique, I. and C. W. Hawryshyn. "Retinal Development and Visual Sensitivity of Young Pacific Sockeye Salmon (*Oncorhynchus nerka*)." *Journal of Experimental Biology* 199 (1996): 869–882.

Ojala, J. V. "Invertebrate Phenology and Prey Selection of Three Sympatric Species of Salmonids: Implications for Individual Fish Growth." Master's thesis, University of Massachusetts–Amherst, 2008.

Olsen, K. H., T. Jarvi, and A. C. Lof. "Aggressiveness and Kinship in Brown Trout (*Salmo trutta*) Parr." *Behavioral Ecology* 7, no. 4 (1996): 445–450.

Ozefovich, W. *The Underwater World of Trout: Trout Vision and Refraction*. South River, NJ: Underwater Oz Productions, 2009.

Partridge, B. L., and T. J. Pitcher. "The Sensory Basis of Fish Schools: Relative Roles of Lateral Line and Vision." *Journal of Comparative Physiology* 135 (1980): 315–325.

Pignatelli, V., S. E. Temple T. H. Chiou, N. W. Roberts, S. P. Collin, and N. J. Marshall. "Behavioural Relevance of Polarization Sensitivity as a Target-Detection Mechanism in Cephalopods and Fishes." *Philosophical Transactions of the Royal Society B: Biological Sciences* 366, no. 1565: 734–41. Pohlmann, K., F. W. Grasso, and T. Breithaupt. "Tracking Wakes: The Nocturnal Predatory Strategy of Piscivorous Catfish." *Proceedings of the National Academy of Sciences of the United States of America* 98 (2001): 7371–7374.

Popper, A. N., and R. R. Fay. "Sound Detection and Processing by Fish: Critical Review and Major Research Questions." *Brain, Behavior and Evolution* 41 (1993): 14–38.

Proper, D. C. *What the Trout Said: About the Design of Trout Flies and Other Mysteries*. New York: Alfred A. Knopf, 1989.

Prosser, C. L., ed. *Comparative Animal Physiology: Environmental and Metabolic Animal Physiology*. 4th ed. Hoboken, NJ: Wiley, 1991.

Przybilla, A., S. Kunze, A. Rudert, H. Bleckmann, and C. Brucker. "Entraining in Trout: A Behavioral and Hydrodynamic Analysis." *Journal of Experimental Biology* 213 (2010): 2976–2986.

Putman, N. F., and K. J. Lohmann. "Compatibility of Magnetic Imprinting and Secular Variation." *Current Biology* 18 (2008): R596–R597.

Quinn, T. P., and E. L. Brannon. "The Use of Celestial and Magnetic Cues by Orienting Sockeye Salmon Smolts." *Journal of Comparative Physiology* 147 (1982): 547–552.

Quinn, T. P., and T. J. Hara. "Sibling Recognition and Olfactory Sensitivity in Juvenile Coho Salmon (*Oncorhynchus kisutch*)." *Canadian Journal of Zoology* 64, no. 4 (1986): 921–925.

Radford, C. A., J. C. Montgomery, P. Caiger, and D. M. Higgs. "Pressure and Particle Motion Detection Thresholds in Fish: A Reexamination of Salient Auditory Clues in Teleosts." *Journal of Experimental Biology* 215 (2012): 3429–3435.

Rahman, H., G. Jeserich, and I. Zeutzius. "Ontogeny of Visual Acuity of Rainbow Trout under Normal Condition and Light Deprivation." *Behavior* 68 (1979): 315–322.

Ramsay-Kunz, Y. *Developmental Biology of Teleost Fishes* (Fish and Fisheries Series). Dordrecht, Netherlands: Springer, 2004.

Ramsden, S. D., L. Anderson, M. Mussi, M. Kamermans, and C. W. Hawryshyn. "Retinal Processing and Opponent Mechanisms Mediating Ultraviolet Polarization Sensitivity in Rainbow Trout (*Oncorhynchus mykiss*)." *Journal of Experimental Biology* 211, no. 9 (2008): 1376–1385.

Reynolds, W. W., and M. E. Casterlin. "Thermoregulatory Behavior of Brown Trout, *Salmo trutta*." *Hydrobiologia* 63, no. 1 (1979): 79–80.

Rick, I. P., and T. C. M. Bakker. "UV Wavelengths Make Female Three-Spined Sticklebacks (*Gastrosteus aculeatus*) More Attractive for Males." *Behavioural Ecology and Sociobiology* 62 (2008): 439–445.

Rick, I. P., et al. "Males Do Not See Only in Red: UV Wavelengths and Male Territorial Aggression in the Three-Spined Stickleback (*Gasterosteus aculeatus*)." *Naturwissenschaften* 95 (2008): 631–638.

Ristovska, M., B. Karaman, W. Verraes, and D. Adriaens. "Development of the Cranial Lateral-Line System and Canal-Related Bones in Salmo Letnica Kar. (Teleostei: Salmonidae)." *Proceedings of the Congress of the Balkan Water Observation and Information System for Decision Support* (2004): 1–7.

Rocco, V., J. P. Barriga, H. Zagarese, and M. Lozada. "How Much Does Ultraviolet Radiation Contribute to the Feeding Performance of Rainbow Trout, *Oncorhynchus mykiss*, Juveniles under Natural Illumination?" *Environmental Biology of Fishes* 63, no. 2 (2002): 223–228.

Rose, J. D., R. Arlinghaus, S. J. Cooke, B. K. Diggles, W. Sawynok, E. D. Stevens, and C. D. Wynne. "Can Fish Really Feel Pain?" *Fish and Fisheries* (2012). doi: 10.1111/ faf.12010.

Sabbah, S., M. F. Habib-Nayanyl, Z. Dargaei, F. E. Hauser, M. Kamermans, and C. W. Hawryshyn. "Retinal Region of Polarization Sensitivity Switches During Ontogeny of Rainbow Trout." *Journal of Neuroscience* 33, no. 17 (2013): 7428–7438.

Shropshire, R. F. "The Eye of Trout." *Archives of Ophthalmology* 10, no. 4 (1933): 498–507.

Siregar, Y. I. "Morphology and Growth of Lateral Line Organs of the Rainbow Trout (*Oncorhynchus mykiss*). *Acta Zoologica* 75, no. 3 (1994): 213–218.

Sorensen, P. W. "Hormones, Pheromones, and Chemoreception." In *Fish Chemoreception*, edited by T. J. Hara, 199–228. London: Chapman and Hall, 1992.

Sorensen, P. W., and J. Caprio. "Chemoreception in Fish." In *The Physiology of Fishes*, 2nd ed., edited by R. E. Evans, 375–406. Boca Raton, FL: CRC Press, 1998.

Sorensen, P. W., J. R. Cardwell, T. Essington, and D. E. Weigel. "Reproductive Interactions between Brook and Brown Trout in a Small Minnesota Stream." *Canadian Journal of Fisheries and Aquatic Sciences* 52 (1995): 1958–1965.

Sorensen, P. W., T. J. Hara, N. E. Stacey, and F. W. Goetz. "F Prostaglandins Function As Potent Olfactory Stimulants That Comprise the Postovulatory Female Sex Pheromone in Goldfish." *Biology of Reproduction* 39, no. 5 (1998): 1039–1050.

Stacey, N. E., P. W. Sorensen, J. G. Dulka, J. R. Cardwell, and A. S. Irvine. "Fish Sex Pheromones: Current Status and Potential Applications." *Bulletin of the Institute of Zoology, Academia Sinica* Series Monograph 16: 189–227.

Suliman, T. and I. Novales Flamarique. "Visual Pigments and Opsin Expression in the Juveniles of Three Species of Fish (Rainbow Trout, Zebrafish, and Killifish) Following Prolonged Exposure to Thyroid

Hormone or Retinoic Acid." The Journal of Comparative Neurology 522 (2014): 98–117.

Sullivan, C. M. "Temperature Reception and Responses in Fish." *Journal of the Fisheries Research Board of Canada* 11, no. 2 (1954): 153–170.

Swisher, D. and C. Richards. 1972. Selective trout. Guilford, CT: Lyons Press.

Tinbergen, L. "The Natural Control of Insects in Pine Woods: I. Factors Influencing the Intensity of Predation by Songbirds." *Archives Néerlandaises de Zoologie* 13 (1960): 265–343.

Van Dam, K. "My Five Favorite October Patterns." *Strike King Journal*, entry 125-1.

Van Leeuwena, E., and V. A. A. Jansen. "Evolutionary Consequences of a Search Image." *Theoretical Population Biology* 77 (2010): 4955.

Vra ar, M. S., and M. Miji . "Ambient Noise in Large Rivers (L)." *Journal of the Acoustical Society of America* 130, no. 4 (2011): 1787–91.

Wagner, H. J. "The Connectivity of Cones and Cone Horizontal Cells in a Mosaic-Type Teleost Retina." *Cell and Tissue Research* 175, no. 1 (1976): 85–100.

Walker, M. M., T. P. Quinn, J. L. Kirschvink, and C. Groot. "Production of Single-Domain Magnetite Throughout Life by Sockeye Salmon, *Oncorhynchus nerka*." *Journal of Experimental Biology* 140 (1988): 51–63.

Ware, D. M. "Predation by Rainbow Trout (*Salmo gairdneri*): The Effect of Experience." *Journal of the Fisheries Research Board of Canada* 28, no. 12 (1971): 1847–1852.

Weigel, D. E., and P. W. Sorensen. "The Influence of Habitat Characteristics on the Longitudinal Distribution of Brook, Brown, and Rainbow Trout in a Small Midwestern Stream." *Journal of Freshwater Ecology* 16, no. 4 (2001): 599– 613.

Windsor, S. P., S. E. Norris, S. M. Cameron, G. D. Mallinson, and J. C. Montgomery. "The Flow Fields Involved in Hydrodynamic Imaging by Blind Mexican Cave Fish (*Astyanax fasciatus*). Part I: Open Water and Heading toward a Wall." *Journal of Experimental Biology* 213 (2010): 3819–3831.

Whitea, A. J., J. F. Scheera, and S. J. Cooke. "Behavioral and Physiological Responses of the Congeneric Largemouth (*Micropterus salmoides*) and Smallmouth Bass (*M. dolomieu*) to Various Exercise and Air Exposure Durations." *Fisheries Research* 89 (2008): 9–16.

Wisenden, B. D. "Olfactory Assessment of Predatory Risk." *Philosophical Transactions of the Royal Society* 355 (2000): 1205–1208.

Wisenden, B. D., and K. Barbour. "Antipredator Responses to Skin Extract of Redbelly Dace by Free-Ranging Populations of Redbelly Dace and Flathead Minnows." *Environmental Biology of Fishes* 72 (2005): 227–233.

Wisenden, B. D., and D. P. Chivers. "The Role of Public Chemical Information in Antipredator Behavior." In *Communication in Fishes*, edited by F. Ladich, S. P. Collins, P. Moller, and B. G. Kapoor, 259–278. Science Publishers, 2006.

Wisenden, B. D., D. P. Chivers, and R. J. F. Smith. "Damselfly Larvae Learn to Recognize Predators from Chemical Cues in the Predator's Diet." *Animal Behavior* 52 (1996): 315–320.

———. "Early Warning in the Predation Sequence: A Disturbance Pheromone in Iowa Darters (*Etheostoma exile*). *Journal of Chemical Ecology* 21: 1469–1480.

Wisenden, B. D., J. Karst, J. Miller, S. Miller, and L. Fuselier. "Anti-Predator Behavior in Response to Conspecific Chemical Alarm Cues in an Esociform Fish, *Umbra limi* (Kirtland 1840)." *Environmental Biology of Fishes* 82, no. 1 (2008): 85–92.

Wisenden, B. D., J. Klitzke, R. Nelson, D. Friedl, and P. Jacobson. "Predator-Recognition Training of Hatchery-Reared Walleye and a Field Test of a Training Method Using Yellow Perch." *Canadian Journal of Fisheries and Aquatic Sciences* 63 (2004): 2144–2150.

Wisenden, B. D., J. Pogatshnik, D. Gibson, L. Bonacci, A. Schumacher, and A. Willett. "Sound the Alarm: Learned Association of Predation Risk with Novel Auditory Stimuli by Flathead Minnows (*Pimephales promelas*) and Glowlight Tetras (*Hemigrammus erythrozonus*) After Single Simultaneous Pairings with Conspecific Chemical Alarms Cues." *Environmental Biology of Fishes* 81 (2006): 141–147.

Wisenden, B. D. and T. A. Thiel. "Field Verification of Predator Attraction to Minnow Alarm Substance." *Journal of Chemical Ecology* 28: 433–438.

Yamamoto, Y., and H. Uedal. "Physiological Study on Imprinting and Homing-Related Olfactory Functions in Salmon." North Pacific Anadromous Fish Commission Technical Report No. 7: 113–114.

Yambe, H., S. Kitamaura, M. Kamio, M. Yamada, S. Matsunaga, N. Fusetani, and F. Yamazaki. "L-Kynurenine, an Amino Acid Identified as a

Sex Pheromone in the Urine of Ovulated Female Masu Salmon." *Proceedings of the National Academy of Sciences of the United States of America* 103, no. 42 (2006): 15370–15374.

Yoshizawa, M., and W. R. Jeffery. "Shadow Response in the Blind Cavefish, Astyanax, Reveals Conservation of a Functional Pineal Eye." *Journal of Experimental Biology* 211 (2008): 292–299.

index

Page numbers in italics indicates illustrations.